Listening to Japan

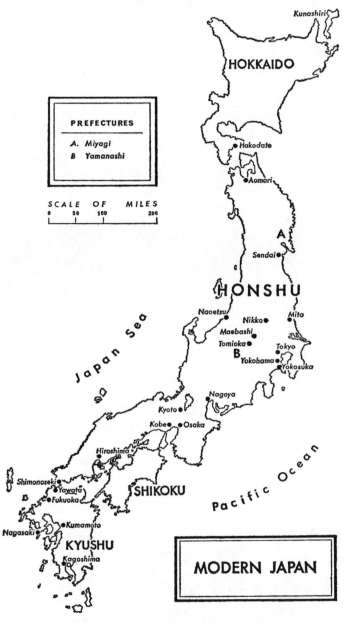

MODERN JAPAN

LISTENING TO JAPAN

A Japanese Anthology

EDITED BY Jackson H. Bailey

PRAEGER PUBLISHERS
New York · Washington · London

To the many Japanese friends whose assistance made this book possible.

PRAEGER PUBLISHERS
111 Fourth Avenue, New York, N.Y. 10003, U.S.A.
5, Cromwell Place, London SW7 2JL, England

Published in the United States of America in 1973
by Praeger Publishers, Inc.

"Cycle of the Months," copyright © 1971 by Harold P. Wright
"Early in Spring," copyright © 1970 by *TransPacific*
"Stones," copyright © 1970 by *TransPacific*
"White Cloud," copyright © 1972 by Harold P. Wright

This is one of the volumes assisted by the Asian Literature Program of
the Asia Society, New York City, N.Y., with a grant from the National
Endowment for the Humanities. One of the purposes of the Asian Literature Program is to bring before the American public divergent ideas of
individual authors, but neither the Asia Society nor the National Endowment is responsible for obtaining permission to publish the selec-
tions included in this volume, or for the views expressed therein.

Library of Congress Cataloguing in Publication Data

Bailey, Jackson H   comp.
    Listening to Japan.
      1. Japan—History—1945-   —Addresses, essays, lectures. 2. Japan
—Civilization—1945-   —Addresses, essays, lectures.   I. Title.
DS889.B25   915.2′03′4   70-168336

Printed in the United States of America

Contents

v

27687

Part Four: The World Scene

Acknowledgments

Many of the contributions to this volume were commissioned by the editor; others have been previously published in Japanese or in English.

Hidetoshi Katō's "Soybean Curd and Brine" was first presented in Kyoto at a 1969 briefing for American visitors to Japan and was then revised for inclusion in this book. His second essay, "Changing Images Among Youth in Modern Japan," appears here for the first time in English. It was published in *Jiyū*, Vol. 8, No. 6 (June, 1966), under the title "Seinen-Zō no Tankyū."

The essays by Teiji Itoh, Jōji Mori, Toshinao Yoneyama, Mitsuru Uchida, and Yasuo Sakakibara, the short story by Shintarō Ishihara, and five poems—"Hands" by Shuntarō Tanikawa; three others by Tsutomu Fukuda, "The Big Shadow," "My Watch," and "Sunlight"; and "Hammer Throw" by Shirō Murano—have not been published before.

Shuntarō Tanikawa's "Cycle of the Months" was originally published in *Sumac*, Vol. IV, No. 1 (Fall, 1971); Kiyoshi Akiyama's "Early in Spring" appeared in *TransPacific*, Vol. I, No. 4 (1970); and Kyōzō Takagi's "Stones" appeared in *TransPacific*, Vol. I, No. 5 (1970). "White Cloud" by Shinkichi Takahashi originally appeared in *Chelsea* 30/31 (June, 1972).

The poems by Shuntarō Tanikawa and Shinkichi Takahashi are taken from a forthcoming anthology of modern Japanese poetry that is being edited and translated by Harold P. Wright with assistance from the Asian Literature Program of the Asian Society. "Early in Spring" is taken from *White Blossom,* a forthcoming collection of Kiyoshi Akiyama's poems that is being edited and translated by Atsuhiro Sawai for publication by *TransPacific*.

Two essays were first published in the *Journal of Social and Political Ideas in Japan*: Tsutomu Ōno, "Student Protest in Japan: What It Means to Society" (Vol. V, Nos. 2 and 3, December, 1967), and Yōnosuke Nagai, "Japan's Foreign Policy Objectives in a Nuclear Milieu" (Vol. V, No. 1, April, 1967). Both essays have been abridged for publication in this book. A third essay, "Systems of Power Balance and the Preservation of Peace," by Hiroharu Seki, was translated by the Center for Japanese Social and Political Studies in Tokyo for this book. It has also been abridged.

Two other essays originally appeared in *The Japan Interpreter*: Makoto Oda, "Making Democracy Our Own" (Vol. VI, No. 3, Summer, 1970), and Sōichi Ōya, "The 1970's: Japan Enters the 'Losers' Return Match' " (Vol. VII, No. 1, Winter, 1971).

Note: In Japanese usage and in scholarly practice, the Japanese surname precedes the given name. On the other hand, most English-language newspapers and general-interest magazines print Japanese names in Western order, where the given name precedes the family name. This book follows the latter practice because it is more familiar to the general reader.

Introduction

The re-emergence of Japan as a world power was a major international development of the 1960's. If the reasons for it are to be understood, it is important to know something of the culture and people of this island nation.

The intent of this book is to bring out aspects of Japanese life that are often not observed by the outsider. The societies of the West and Japan are increasingly concerned with the same problems—education, mass communication, affluence, international status and rivalries, to name a few—and I have searched for essays that deal with these universal topics. In some cases, the subject of an essay has made headlines (for example, student strikes and the Mutual Security Treaty between Japan and the United States), but its treatment for the Western reader has been superficial or misleading. The material offered here, I hope, will be a corrective. In other cases, the topic is new and suggests the need to re-think old, subconscious assumptions or to view some facet of life from an entirely new perspective (for example, the nature of a curved line or the creative impulse in literary expression).

Another purpose of this book is to present a representative collection about the subjects that concern the Japanese today when they talk among themselves as if no one were listening. The Japanese assume that their debates go unheeded outside of Japan because of the difficulty many foreigners have in learning to read their language. Thus, many of the essays here were written for a Japanese audience and recommend themselves as representing a "real" Japan. Other essays were written especially for this book. I must confess to the belief that some aspects of a culture are more apparent to the observer than to the participant. That is to say, the inner workings of social groups, aesthetic responses, and core concepts in a culture often are so unconsciously operative that the participant must be alerted to them and asked to explain them to outsiders before they become significant for him.

Each of the authors here has a special competence that enables him to speak with authority, but few of them are well known even in Japan. This has been a matter of deliberate choice. For decades, there has been a tendency for a small coterie of bilingual Japanese to be the interpreters of Japan to the West. They have been men and women of remarkable ability, but they constitute a relatively closed group beyond which another Japan has moved with all too little direct relationship with what they are doing and saying. The authors in this book do not typify the man in the street, but the topics they deal with are of general concern— either conscious or unconscious—to their fellow Japanese.

Culture—Ideas—Values

A knowledge of wars, politics, and mass movements provides a sadly incomplete understanding of a people. Such larger issues are faced in the later sections of the book, but first there must be some effort to comprehend individuals and their ways of life. What new and different ways of expression can be discovered in their everyday thought and action? What does it mean to be a Japanese? What are the wellsprings of emotion and aesthetic response? The first two sections of the book are devoted to such questions.

Soybeans are a staple in the Japanese diet, and *tōfu* (a soft, bland curd made from the soybean that is used as a part of so many dishes from soup to sukiyaki) provides a symbol and an evocative image of an essential quality in Japanese culture. Because of *tōfu*'s very blandness, the foreigner passes it by; it is so much a part of the daily routine that Japanese would not normally think to single it out. Yet the more one considers what Professor Kato has to say in his short essay on "Soybean Curd and Brine," the more apt the analogy seems.

The Japanese are not preoccupied with the past. They find

room for it to live on in the present and future. Students of architecture who visit Japan have found this fact easy to grasp, con-
fronted as they are with visual, material evidence. The link between art and everyday life in Japan is nowhere better illustrated
than in architecture. Visitors to Japan's 1964 Olympic sites were
seized with admiration at the monumental lines and movement
of Kenzō Tange's work. The quiet simplicity of the ceremonial
teahouse and garden can be equally gripping.

Photographic essays on ancient and modern Japan abound, but
most are found, on close inspection, to be little more than "pretty
picture books." An exception—and a pioneer work—is *The Roots
of Japanese Architecture,* for which Teiji Itoh wrote the essay
material. In the selection in this book, he has taken very simple
expressions of Japanese aesthetic sense and examined them as
cultural phenomena.

A cultural heritage is often most clearly reflected in literature,
but literature, too, can envelop the reader in the immediate to
the exclusion of the larger context; or else, the reader's concern
with forms and comparisons may distract him from the cultural
import of what he reads. This has frequently been the case when
Westerners have considered Japanese literature. In "The Liberation of Japanese Ghosts," Professor Mori counteracts this tendency
by proposing an interesting new interpretation in his presentation
of the "ghostly" principle.

Japanese concern with the contemporary is nowhere more obvious than in the attention paid to Vietnam. The torment of
Vietnam for Americans has been exceeded only by that of the
Vietnamese themselves. The Japanese, from the beginning, have
suffered, mostly vicariously, with both sides. A friend of mine
once said, comparing the approach of American and Japanese
newspapermen to reporting on Vietnam, "Americans tend to be
analytical and 'objective,' talking about strategy, firepower, and
casualties, while Japanese are prone to emphasize the human interest and emotive elements." Nowhere in his short story does
Shintarō Ishihara expiicitly identify the locale of the action or
the participants other than the Japanese, yet there can be no
question as to where and who they are. Where but Vietnam?
This fact adds to the eerie and poignant quality of the story.
This is not political polemic; it is a probing of the nature and

condition of modern man victimized by his modernity and re-discovering his primordial self.

Concern with the present and memories of the past are often most effectively expressed and linked by poetry. The traditional poetry of Japan is widely translated, quoted, and even imitated. More recently there have been some excellent anthologies of twentieth-century poetry in translation. No attempt is made here to be either inclusive or even representative of contemporary life. The poems included are not necessarily Japanese, except that Japanese wrote them; they are universal in appeal.

The essays in the first section of the book focus on the people of Japan, singly and en masse, wrestling and cavorting with ghosts; expressing fear, hate, sorrow, ambition; working together; searching for meaning in human existence; expressing it beautifully, simply. However, even if a clearer image of the individual Japanese emerges, the picture is not complete. Japan must be viewed as a nation and as a people, internally and externally, if one is to understand what it is and where it is going. On this level, controversy is rife.

Society—Politics—Economics

In the years from 1945 to 1955, while Western attention was focused on Europe and the cold war, Japan completed the leap into modernity and constructed a mass-producing, mass-consuming society. In the late 1940's, demographers projecting Japan's future population growth in relation to its estimated resources concluded that there was no hope of prosperity. Yet by 1955 population growth had been arrested; by 1960 Japan was virtually self-sufficient in food production; by 1965 it was the second largest producer of automobiles and had the world's fastest train; and in 1970 it stood third in gross national product among the countries of the world. Some now predict that in 1980 Japan will catch up with the United States in per capita production. But is this progress real? What does it mean? How did it come about? Like others elsewhere, the Japanese are searching, rather self-consciously, for answers to these questions.

The inner workings of a society are often better understood when subjected to the careful analysis of a trained social scientist who has lived and studied in more than one culture. In this regard, Professor Yoneyama's essay "Basic Notions in Japanese Social Relations" breaks new ground. While he uses technical terms, they do not amount to jargon for its own sake. The Japanese terms he employs often have no single English equivalent.

Daily speech and action reveal much to the astute observer, but most of us are so unaware of our "cultural baggage" that we do not understand how our everyday relationships are ordered or why. Professor Yoneyama has given careful thought to such questions—but he has done much more. He has challenged the usual Western view that Japanese society is rooted in familism and reflects the traditional "universal" values of premodern societies everywhere.* In place of this view, he proposes that Japanese society can best be understood as groupings of people organized in *nakama,* or "in-groups," which provide a context for social functioning that is neither hierarchical nor tied primarily to kinship or geographically defined groupings. In developing and expanding this idea, he draws on his own research and experience, presenting concrete examples and developing themes related to his central theory. Most important is his discussion of the causes of Japan's success in modernization. If Professor Yoneyama is correct, the roots for this success lie deep in Japan's traditional culture.

Perhaps most difficult for the thoughtful observer of the Japanese scene to grasp is the emotional content of the ideological debates that continually swirl across the intellectual skies. As relative newcomers to a full-fledged democratic process, the Japanese have been analytical of the experience, perhaps to a fault. Certainly they have been critical of their own democratic institutions and practices, sometimes in doctrinaire left-wing terms, sometimes in the harsh traditional perspective that views imported democracy as destructive of the traditional "Japanese way of life." During most of the 1950's, the hold in postwar Japan of a rather doctrinaire Marxism was remarkably pervasive. The insularity of the Japanese intellectual, withdrawn to his ivory tower, heightened the impression for some of an almost monolithic dominance of the country's intellectual life by one line of thought.

* This view is associated with the pioneering work of Ruth Benedict, the distinguished cultural anthropologist and author of the classic study of Japanese society and culture, *The Chrysanthemum and the Sword.*

By the late 1950's, however, a group of able political scientists had appeared to challenge the Marxian orthodoxy. Since then, these men and other younger scholars have produced a series of constructive and provocative essays that go to the core of the political experience of man in modern mass society. The refreshing openness of Japanese intellectual life over the past decade is a tribute to their work. Two essays in this book illustrate this development.

Professor Uchida, a well-trained, widely experienced, and astute political scientist draws upon his own and others' social science research to assess Japanese democracy in practice. He views the situation with alarm but not despair. He pointed out, in a lecture at Earlham College, that by 1975 a totally new generation of leaders will be in control in Japan, men with none of the stigmata of prewar militarism that beset Kishi, Satō, and others of the dominant leadership. The new men will be postwar graduates, committed to and experienced in the new way of life. This process was already in evidence in 1972 with the selection of Kakuei Tanaka as Prime Minister. Tanaka is a man of the postwar period.

In the realm of thought, Mr. Oda's examination of contemporary mass society in China, Japan, the Soviet Union, and the United States casts a fresh and very different light on the meaning of democracy. The term "state democracy," which is so important in his analysis, adds a significant new dimension to any consideration of democracy and mass political experience. Moreover, he represents an important bridge between intellectual pursuits and political activism, a rarity in Japan. In fact, this quality marks him as one of the three or four most important people to emerge in Japan in the 1960's. The breadth of perspective that he brings to his task is suggested by his quotation from Pericles' funeral oration as well as by his comments on contemporary developments in China and the Soviet Union.

Important as politics may be, to understand Japan one must pay careful attention to the economic scene. Some outside observers have even characterized the Japanese as an "economic animal," in contrast to Aristotle's reference to man as a "political animal." What has given stability to the volatile dynamism of Japan's forward rush? Scholars and journalists have vied to produce the answer, sensing that it lies in the mix called modernization.

The problem of modernization—its causes, nature, and processes—occupies the attention of all who are interested in understanding today's world. Japan as a case study in modernization has special significance, but the interpretation of the Japanese experience is a matter of dispute, partly because of a lack of clarity in distinguishing between modernization and Westernization. Professor Sakakibara cuts through these complexities with a straightforward, sophisticated assessment of the state of Japanese economic life at the beginning of the 1970's and then projects the trends he believes will determine the course of events in the economic sphere over the next few years.

Youth—Ideals—Education

However much debate there is about the nature and process of modernization in Japan and elsewhere, there is no doubt that men's perceptions of life and values today differ sharply from those of two generations ago. Here, Professor Katō, a distinguished sociologist, reflects upon the interplay between the economic and social realities of Japan's modernization and its popular standards and ideals. How does popular fiction reflect (and does it also mold) youth's values and expectations? He illuminates the cultural dimensions of Japan's modern transformation.

Youth has been one of the most sensitive barometers of social change in the twentieth century. Perhaps more has been written in the Western press about student movements in Japan than about any other aspect of Japanese life. Much of this writing has been superficial, because the reporter knew so little about the inner workings of the groups he observed. The nature of student protest also receives much attention from Japanese writers, and some of their analysis has special relevance to other areas of the world, as student movements in various countries seek to respond to similar social problems and the older generation tries to understand the causes of their protest. A decade ago, student protest in Japan was essentially political and its organization had a modicum of cohesion. Today, its causes and objectives are more diverse, but students are also concerned about educational issues that are directly related to their lives. The data in Professor Ōno's chapter reveal a profound sense of dissatisfaction among Japanese students with the quality of education and of life itself.

The World Scene

The world context within which Japan operates is crucial to its continued existence, and Japanese writers are keenly aware of this. Their views of the world and of Japan's potential role in it are colored by their assumptions about the nature of that world.

Mr. Ōya's essay—meant, of course, for a Japanese audience—is of special interest for the treatment he gives to the return of Okinawa to Japan, which came about in 1972. Few Japanese have even recognized the implications of reversion for internal Japanese life. Will Japanese accept Okinawans as full citizens and Okinawa as an integral part of the nation, sharing in the affluence and development that has come to the main islands? The problem is usually viewed almost exclusively in its strategic and international aspects. Mr. Ōya has identified and clarified the issue impressively.

Mr. Ōya's nomination of Daisaku Ikeda, the head of the Sōka Gakkai, the militant Buddhist sect, as a potential leader in the 1970's suggests the importance of this group and its political party, the Kōmeitō. The movement is many-faceted, bringing personal religious experience and commitment to the lives of millions, effectively mobilizing time, energy, and money for massive social and religious projects, and even threatening to change the whole political mix with its remarkable growth in political power. Sōka Gakkai was controversial from its inception,* but a storm of protest blew up in January, 1970, at the disclosure that it had sought to prevent the publication of a book that was starkly critical of the movement and, when this failed, to block its distribution and sale. The political fallout from these disclosures was severe. It remains to be seen whether the meteoric rise of the Sōka Gakkai in the 1960's will continue through the

* Its people spent much of World War II in prison as enemies of the state; its conversion techniques of psychological pressure are a constant source of debate.

1970's. The movement continues to be strong, but its growth seems to be leveling off.

Mr. Ōya's discussion of Japan's "national charisma" and the role of the Emperor system is fascinating. Equally illuminating is his analysis of the leadership potential of three contemporary figures in Japanese politics. Ten years ago, none of them would have been mentioned in a serious discussion of politics. Even now, Ōya's speculation seems far-fetched. His crystal ball may well be cloudy, and he is cautious and equivocal. Yet he offers a new way to view Japan and its role in the 1970's.

The second half of 1971 and 1972 witnessed the destruction of the precarious web of assumptions and relationships in East Asia based on the myth that the Chinese Nationalists on Taiwan represented China. President Nixon's visit to Peking in February, 1972, touched sensitive political and economic nerves in Japan. Two essays deal with the forces behind these changes in East Asian politics and international relations and discuss their implications for the future. Although they were written in the 1960's, the issues raised and the policies proposed continue to be in the mainstream of political and strategic thinking in Japan.

Professor Nagai and Professor Seki differ in their assumptions, with Professor Nagai taking the more traditional position that the balance of power is still the primary characteristic of international relations today. His advocacy of a step-up in Japan's defense capabilities was strongly criticized in Japan, yet his pungent and concrete proposals suggest how far the temper of thought among certain Japanese writers had moved in a few years. The hold of doctrinaire ideology, whether of the right or the left, has been successfully challenged. The debate over rearmament and the balance of power still rages.

In recent years, as Japan's power and status have grown, Japanese scholars and commentators have given increasing attention to the world scene and their country's relationship to it. A number of Japanese writers, among them Professor Seki, are producing stimulating analyses that merit much wider attention. Here, he takes a new look at world power relationships and their uses. He probes the question of Sino-American relations from a new angle and places them in a fresh global context. His criticism of the balance-of-power approach to international affairs is an important challenge to this time-honored way of viewing the world. Professor Seki represents a growing group of thinkers in Japan who are critical of the contemporary scene but are not doctrinaire in their approach.

What role should Japan play in the 1970's: Should it maintain the Japanese-American partnership that Ambassador Reischauer worked so hard to establish in the early 1960's? For the United States, is Japan an economic rival to be opposed with tariffs and import quotas? Is it a pawn in the chess game of East Asian power politics? Or is it the leader of Asia, and if so, in what direction will it lead? Perhaps there will be a mixture of these roles as Japan redefines its identity as both an Asian and a world power.

My hope is that there will be far more interchange with Japan in the future than there has been in the past. We have barely begun to explore the creative potential in greater cultural interaction with Japan—in music, art, drama, literature, and still other fields. In political, economic, and social exchanges, far more could be done, though there have been some pioneering efforts in the fields of urban problems and environmental control.

Events move swiftly, and the nations of the world are drawn ever closer. Throughout the postwar period, the Japanese were viewed as upstart imitators at best. That period has ended, and the rest of the world must make its peace with this new and driving force, as Japan must with the world. Time and distance seem much shorter than they did a decade ago. The 1970's offer the possibility for more constructive international relationships than we have ever had. The task of achieving them will be difficult; it is not impossible.

JACKSON H. BAILEY

Richmond, Ind.
January, 1973

PART ONE

Culture—Ideas—Values

1

Soybean Curd and Brine

Hidetoshi Katō

In his essay entitled "What Is Japanese Culture?" Kōnan Naitō, one of the most unusual historians of modern Japan, said that the process of the formation of Japanese culture resembles the process of producing soybean cake. The initial ingredient in making soybean cake is clear soybean soup. When brine is added to it, the soup is transformed into soft soybean cake. Naitō's metaphor suggests that the original Japanese way of life was clear soup and that the brine added to it was Chinese civilization.

Historically, this metaphor seems to be not only valid but pregnant with implications for many aspects of Japanese culture. Take, for example, the Japanese written language. Japan did not have its own written language until the Chinese system of writing was imported in the sixth century A.D. Chinese characters, needless to say, are iconographic signs with their own grammatical system. However, when imported, some of the iconographic signs were simplified and came to be used as phonetic symbols to express a completely different grammatical system. The native oral Japanese language was the soup, Chinese characters were the brine, and the phonetic sign system (the *kana* syllabary) was the end product, the soybean cake, a part of Japanese culture.

The same is true for many other Japanese cultural items, or "things Japanese." Japanese Buddhism can be viewed in a simi-

3

lar way. It was introduced to Japan from India via China in the sixth century A.D., and classic Japanese Buddhism was the "pure" form of Chinese Buddhism of that time. Then another soybean cake was produced, in the sense that Buddhism fused with native Japanese religious thought. The native religion, which had emerged as Shinto, is essentially pantheistic: The spirit of the dead was regarded as a god, or *kami*. Buddhism in Japan entered a fundamental compromise with this Shinto orientation, with the result that ancestor worship became the vital characteristic of Japanese Buddhist sects. The distance between original Buddhism and Japanese Buddhism is far greater than the distance between Roman Catholic Christianity and Protestant Christianity.

The concept of brine, however, can be discussed in more general terms. Not only Chinese culture but also all other foreign ingredients acted as brine. In the early seventeenth century, European civilization began to influence Japanese culture. For instance, tempura,* one of the most representative Japanese dishes, was one of the "soybean cakes" invented as the result of Japanese contact with the Portuguese. Fried cooking is said to have been unknown to the Japanese people until "French-fried" seafoods were introduced by the Westerners in the seventeenth century. However, French-fried seafoods in Portuguese style were modified and transformed into tempura, whose taste and method of preparation is completely different from the original Portuguese form.

Let me give another example. The Westerners brought many things from Europe to Japan. In the seventeenth century, sailors were substantial cultural messengers. They had their recreations, such as gambling with cards. As Japanese sailors met their Western counterparts, they were immediately attracted by these games and brought cards back to Japan. However, they found that the symbols on the cards (kings, queens, hearts, spades, and the like) were not appropriate or did not appeal to them, and, as a result, Japanese cards appeared with such symbols as cherry blossoms, the moon, or Japanese bush warblers. Even today, Japanese cards are called *karuta,* a word that originally came from the Portuguese word *carta*. Here again, we have soybean cake produced from the interaction of the soybean soup and brine.

* Seafood and vegetables dipped in batter and deep-fat fried.—ED.

It is not correct to say that tempura, *karuta,* and other items are culturally "authentically" Japanese in the sense of being exclusively and uniquely produced by the Japanese. As a matter of fact, there is practically nothing "authentic" in Japanese culture. The "authenticity" of Japanese culture has been, in my opinion, the *ability* to precipitate soybean cakes from the clear soup through the addition of brine.

In other words, the essence of the Japanese way of life and way of thinking should be sought in the "process" of modification and transformation, which is sometimes interpreted as the process of imitation. Indeed, because of the extraordinary high rate of industrialization in the past hundred years, the precipitation of soybean cake in modern times has not really taken place as yet. But, in due course, the time may come when we produce something like a "Coca Cola ceremony," just as we produced the tea ceremony in the fifteenth century.

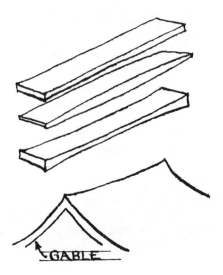

GABLE

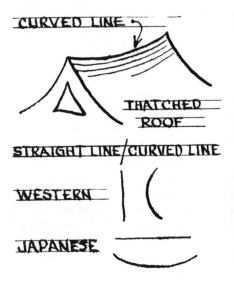

CURVED LINE

THATCHED ROOF

STRAIGHT LINE / CURVED LINE

WESTERN

JAPANESE

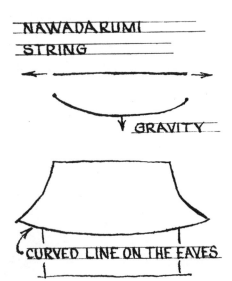

NAWADARUMI

STRING

GRAVITY

CURVED LINE ON THE EAVES

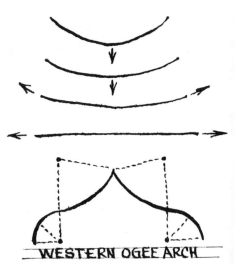

WESTERN OGEE ARCH

2

Tradition in Japan's Formative Culture

Teiji Itoh

The Flexible Batten

Westerners may experience a vague feeling of disquiet when they look at the curved lines of buildings and art objects in Japan. The Japanese may experience a similar feeling of strangeness looking at Western curved lines. This is because Eastern and Western curved lines are different in nature. To understand this, let us first consider how the traditional Japanese drew or created curved lines.

It is often said that Westerners use a straight edge to draw a straight line and use either a compass or a French curve for a curved line. This has also been true of the Japanese for the past hundred years, but before that they employed entirely different methods for both straight and curved lines. For example, a master carpenter used such tools as a *tawami-jaku* or a *shinai-jōgi* in designing a building. *Tawami-jaku,* a tool for creating curved lines, literally means a "flexible ruler," but since it does not have graduated markings, it is not used for measurement. When the need for a curved line arose, a master carpenter did not purchase a *tawami-jaku* but made it with an ordinary long, thin batten. Cedar or cypress is preferred for the batten simply because they are easily obtained in Japan; actually, anything flexible will do. The batten's length or thickness varied according to the needs of

Translated by Shōichi Oguro.

7

each case. For example, some battens were of equal thickness from end to end; others were somewhat thicker at the center than at either end; some had ends thicker than the center, and so forth. A master carpenter used the battens for determining the curved lines of a concave roof. It should be pointed out that the batten started out as a straight line but became a curved line when force was applied on both ends. The shape of the curve varied according to the degree of force applied and the length or thickness of the batten. If a carpenter did not like the curved line created, he could plane the batten to produce a new one. He would go through this procedure until he found a curved line that satisfied him. Almost all the curved lines of the roofs of old Shinto shrines and Buddhist temples in Japan were created in this way.

You have probably seen at one time or another a painting of bent bamboo trees covered with snow—an art subject much loved by the Japanese. The curved line created by the bent bamboo derives from the principle discussed above. The curve of the ridge beams of thatched roofs often found in Shimane Prefecture in the western part of Japan is achieved by warping bamboo. From this, we may conclude at least two things: One is that the original form of the curved line in Japan's formative culture is derived from nature; the other is that, to the Japanese, the curved line is merely a variation of the straight line, not a totally different form.

Another traditional method used for drawing a curved line was the *nawadarumi* (literally, "loosened rope") for which the craftsman used a long string or rope. A carpenter often used a long silk string attached to an ink marker called a *sumitsubo*. However, for all practical purposes the quality and length of the string were free and arbitrary. A string itself does not have a particular form, but if you pull it on both ends it becomes a straight line; and if you lessen the pull, there appears a curved line whose shape is determined by gravity and by the quality, thickness, and length of the string. Thus, we see that in this method, too, the shape of a curved line is decided by some degree of force, as in the *tawami-jaku* method described above. This technique may be said to be a Japanese invention. Some curved lines of stone walls of Japanese castles are thought to have been created in this way. This method was also used for determining the curves of the eaves of town houses; the lines of the eaves generally seem to be horizontal, but in fact they form loose curves. Just as long straight lines often present an illusion of curvature, these curved lines were used to present an illusion of straightness. In this case, a straight line is considered a special variation of a curved line; it is the shape of a string in the state of extreme tension. Thus, once again, the straight and the curved lines are thought to be merely different aspects of a single form.

In the West, there is a four-centered arch called an ogee arch. The Japanese have an arch of similar shape called a *katō*, which is often used in the design for windows in Buddhist temples. Though the two are similar in shape, the method for forming the lines is entirely different. That is to say, the ogee arch could be drawn with a compass, but a compass is never used in making the *katō*. According to old documents, the *katō* was drawn by the *tawami-jaku* method in imitation of the shape of the tips of apricot leaves.

Although the Japanese recognize the visual difference between straight and curved lines, they have long regarded the two as seemingly contrasting forms that can be traced back to one source. If Westerners can be said to see the two lines in a relationship something like that of man and woman, then they are something like twins to the Japanese. In this one can perhaps perceive the existence of one of the special characteristics of Japan's formative culture. It is, of course, possible to deal with that culture by means of the Western concept of contrast, but if one proceeds in that manner, one is always in danger of overlooking those subtleties that are unique to Japan.

Pivoting Space

Modern man, both Japanese and Western, usually divides space into two parts, interior and exterior, with all space classifiable as either one or the other. This classification seems workable even for traditional Japanese houses and gardens. Of course, if we define the inner side of the outer wall of a building as an interior space and the outer side as an exterior space, the space is certainly divided into two. However, in so doing, we may overlook some important characteristics of Japanese buildings.

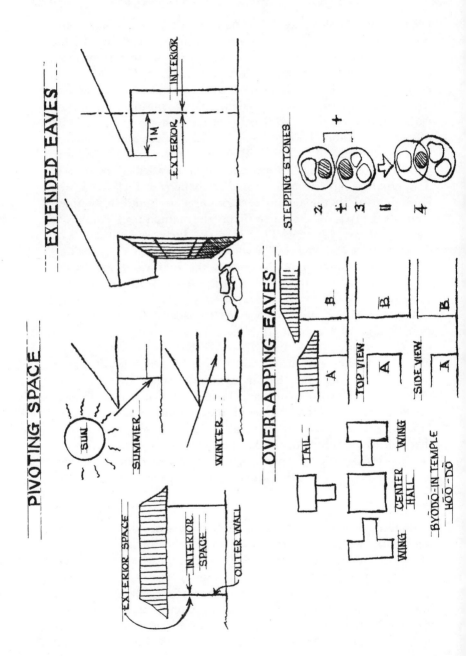

PIVOTING SPACE

SUN

SUMMER

WINTER

EXTERIOR SPACE

INTERIOR SPACE

OUTER WALL

EXTENDED EAVES

INTERIOR

EXTERIOR

1M

STEPPING STONES

2 + 3 = 4

OVERLAPPING EAVES

A   B

TOP VIEW

A   B

SIDE VIEW

A   B

TAIL

WING   CENTER HALL   WING

BYŌDŌ-IN TEMPLE
HŌŌ-DŌ

As you probably know, the eaves of Japanese houses are extended—usually 3 feet, and sometimes as much as 7 feet, in depth. Why do we have such deep eaves? Certainly one of the reasons is the climate of the monsoon area. If, in places of the same latitude as Japan (31° to 45° N.), houses are built facing due south with eaves of a certain depth, then the strong summer sunshine can be prevented from entering a room and, at the same time, the warm afternoon sunshine can be admitted in winter. In the days when there was no air conditioning equipment, this was a clever, effective, and economical method of controlling interior living conditions. Another reason for the deeply extended eaves is that Japan has a great deal of rainfall; the eaves preserve the exterior walls of a house from rain damage and make it possible to open the windows even on rainy days. During the summer rainy season, it would become terribly muggy indoors if one kept all the windows closed, and one could not enjoy the sight of the rain falling outside, which to the Japanese would be more terrible than anything else.

Extended eaves play another important role. In Japanese, the space under the eaves is called *noki-shita* or *noki-uchi,** words grammatically classified as nouns. (As far as I know, there are no nouns of corresponding meaning in European languages.) In other words, the Japanese regard this space as independent, belonging neither to the interior nor to the exterior. However, at one time, Japanese carpenters insisted that the *noki-shita* (their term) was interior space. A veranda was often built there, with no partitions to divide it from the outside world. One can feel the air directly there, and in terms of temperature and humidity the *noki-shita* might be taken for exterior space. However, the veranda was not exposed to the rain, and it was often used as the extension of a room or corridor. Furthermore, in most Japanese houses, sliding doors were all that separated room from veranda, and so there was relatively free access between them. It was even possible to remove the doors altogether and—in a sense—extend the room to the patio's outer edge. Consequently, it was not altogether unnatural for carpenters to consider the space beneath the eaves "interior" space.

---

* Literally translated, respectively, as "beneath the eaves" or "within the eaves."—ED.

Japanese gardeners, on the other hand, held this space to be a part of *their* domain, and for this reason they used their own word, *noki-uchi,* to describe it. Even when there are no plants under the eaves, there is still the soil—surely an extension of the garden itself. In traditional residences, stepping stones (an essential feature of the Japanese garden) are often arranged there, and there may even be some shrubbery. Nevertheless, there are important differences between the *noki-uchi* and the garden space. In the former, there is no rainfall and, at best, only meager sunlight. In consequence, it is not an especially good place for growing things. The *noki-shita* is and is not a part of the interior space; in the same way, it is and is not a part of the exterior space. In other words, the *noki-shita* has special features in common with both interior and exterior, and may be called a "gray space." Thus, the following provisions are found in modern Japanese building codes and regulations: one meter (3.28 ft.) in from the edge of the eave is classified as exterior space; the space from that point inward is classified as interior and is included in the architectural floor area. For example, if an eave extends 4 feet out, the "legal" floor area will be extended an extra .72 feet and will then be subject to a commensurate tax.

In this way, the *noki-shita* was a kind of connecting space between the interior and exterior. This characteristic was utilized in many traditional structures in order visually to connect two or more buildings that were physically distinct. A typical example is the Hoō-dō (Phoenix Hall) at the Byōdō-in Temple in Kyoto, which is modeled on the image of a bird extending its wings. The Phoenix Hall actually consists of four parts—a central hall, two wings, and a tail, though most people think of it as just one building. The illusion is created simply by the overlapping of the eaves.

The *noki-shita* was also the place where nature and architecture came together. The noblemen of the Heian Period (794–1184) and of the Kamakura Period (1185–1332) sat on the veranda under the eaves admiring the moon, listening to chirping insects in the garden, playing the *biwa,** and composing poems.

This means that, whether considered as linking an interior space with an exterior space, a garden with a building, or a natu-

* A musical instrument roughly comparable to a mandolin.—ED.

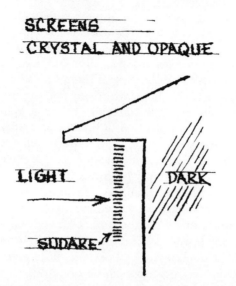

ral area with a man-made one, the *noki-shita* may be thought of as a "pivoting" space, and this basic "linking" approach is not at all limited to architecture. In a sense, it might even be called the birthplace of an important element in Japanese literature. In Japanese literature, there are the *kake-kotoba* ("pivot words"), words that convey twofold meanings, one sense of which is connected with the phrase preceding it, and the other with the phrase following. The same concept is also found in certain arrangements of stepping stones. A good example is called the "two plus three" arrangement, in which, as the name implies, a group of two stones is combined with another of three stones. However, not five but only four stones are used. The second stone of the first group is the first stone of the second group. It is, in this sense, the "pivotal" stone.

Screens, Crystal and Opaque

Each room in a traditional Japanese house is enclosed by *shōji* (sliding partitions), *fusuma* (sliding doors), and thin walls. The *shōji* and the *fusuma* are more important in composing the space than the walls. These sliding panels are not equipped with locks.

With respect to the two purposes that locks in general serve, demarcation and protection, traditional Japanese rooms are less than ideal. In Western houses, each room is named according to its function (bedroom, living room, dining room), while in Japanese residences the rooms are most often referred to by the number of *tatami* mats.* Moreover, one room functions in a complex manner: For instance, the same room is often used as a living room and a bedroom. It is natural, of course, that this feature should characterize the home of a poor man, but it was, in fact, also true of the residences of the highest noblemen. No matter how much importance the noblemen might have attached to their "privacy," it was simply unthinkable to seal off a room from its surroundings, both natural and architectural.

In Japan, bamboo screens called *sudare* or *ren* are often used in homes, restaurants, and special rooms for the tea ceremony. They serve two purposes: regulating the brightness in a room and permitting an occupant to peer out while remaining unseen. In this way, ancient emperors, whose presence was thought to be too awesome for viewing under ordinary circumstances, could keep track of their retainers' activities in the next room.

The *sudare* also became the source of a new kind of beauty. It not only divided space but became the medium through which the separated spaces were linked. Its beauty is often called *kakurenbai* ("plum blossoms viewed through a *sudare*"), although ponds, bamboo, clouds, and, of course, people were also viewed that way. A woman gazed at through one of these screens often took on greater beauty than she possessed in the plain light of day. This was the essence of *kakurenbai*. The *sudare* provided a frame or filter for the objects viewed, and, within or through it, objects became part of a special world of muted reality.

The image viewed through a *sudare* or any sort of transparent partition was called *sukikage* (literally, "transparent shadow"), a word that often appeared in classical literature. For example, in Lady Murasaki's *The Tale of Genji*,† lovers often converse

* Mats are of standard size, normally 6 feet by 3 feet, and thus constitute a convenient way of indicating the size of a room. The mats are about 3 inches thick, of woven straw, protected with a durable straw cover which can be reversed or changed as wear may require, making it possible to use the mats for years.—ED.

† The eleventh-century literary classic recognized as the world's first novel.

with each other through a partition (e.g., the young nobleman named Shikibu no Jō). These meetings (which were in fact quite commonplace in old Japan) were feasible because it was in the nature of partitions not to insulate but to mute and—in this sense—intensify.

There are, of course, examples in Japan of houses with walls and locking doors. During the feudal era, some townsmen kept fireproofed storehouses, and some samurai slept in fireproof bedrooms, though neither was very common.

Shōji screens, which consist of wooden frames and paper panels, first came into use around the twelfth century and, despite their imperfections, are still used today. They are loved by the Japanese for two reasons: They soften the sunlight and still permit one to sense the space on the other side. The sun shines off the garden pond and casts its light along with the shadows of trees, birds, and flowers upon the panel. The shadows move in the wind. A cloud moves across the sun—the *shōji* grows blank; the cloud passes—and the *sukikage* returns. It is a picture that is always moving, always changing. In this way it both divides and connects, just like the *sudare*.

The *fusuma* is constructed out of several layers of heavy paper and is completely opaque. Nevertheless, sounds pass through it easily and thus it, too, is a kind of link with the world on the other side. Just how the *fusuma* has traditionally worked on the Japanese imagination is perhaps best demonstrated in the following haiku:

> On a single panel of *fusuma*
> The Kōrin painting—
> As if crying out from its grasses
> The voice of an insect in the garden*

Kōrin was a seventeenth-century artist known for his *fusuma* paintings.

It becomes clear from these examples that Japanese partitions are not designed so much to protect or delineate as they are to connect and intensify. Of course, the trend in modern Japan has been toward the thick walls and glass partitions of the West, and the result has been a kind of heterogeneous blend of the two

* Translated by the author.

traditions. But in the eyes of the "modern" Japanese, this cultural mix, far from being strange, is an end devoutly to be desired.

Aesthetic Imperfection

In the West, victory or defeat is often decided by the toss of a coin. The coin comes up either heads or tails, and there is no such thing as a draw; there is always a conclusive outcome. But this is not so in the case of Japanese *janken,* a hand-signal game. In *janken,* there are three possible hand signs representing, respectively, scissors, paper, and rock. Scissors defeat paper, but are in turn defeated by rock, which can be wrapped in paper. If both players put out scissors it is a standoff. Since it is possible to have a draw, the final outcome may require several turns; obviously, *janken* is a far less efficient way to come to a decision than tossing a coin. It first came to be used by Japanese children late in the seventeenth century. Its most interesting feature is the systematic use of three different symbols in deciding victory or defeat. This, it seems to me, indicates that Japanese culture of the time did not include the Western concept of contrast or opposition.

The Japanese have never denied the efficacy of traditional culture, and they have never regarded new culture as almighty. This attitude seems to have been normative in the development of Japanese culture. For example, in the eighth century, the *wa-yō* style developed as a type of Buddhist architecture. Some five centuries later, two new styles, the *tenjiku-yō* and the *kara-yō,* came into prominence, but not, as might have been expected, at the total expense of the earlier style. There are, in Japan, almost no instances where new cultural values emerge through the complete destruction of existing ones, and the end result throughout Japanese history has been a kind of coexistence between persisting traditions and new ideas.

At any rate, the number three represents a special phase of Japanese cultural patterns. From that number come many methods of harmonizing, classifying, and systematizing. For instance, the Japanese music called *gagaku* is composed in three parts—*jo* (opening), *ha* (transition), and *kyū* (finale); there are three different kinds of tea ceremony—the *shin* (formal), *gyō* (ordinary), *sō* (informal); and in both stone and flower arranging, *ten* (heaven), *chi* (earth), and *jin* (man) are the three fundamental elements. For example, stone arrangements are often found in Japanese gardens. Most stones are used in their natural state, not sculptured. A major reason is that, according to Buddhist doctrine, all things in nature are—in their natural state—realizations of the Buddha and are best not tampered with. When the Japanese did anything to the rocks, it was only to accentuate some natural feature. Further, since no two stones are precisely the same in color, shape, or texture, it is not possible to create harmony through a symmetrical arrangement of two stones. Therefore, a technique was devised for producing harmony by using three stones of different size and shape, and they came to be called *ten, chi,* and *jin,* the names for what the ancients regarded as the three basic elements of the universe.

The same principles of harmony were applied directly to the art of flower arranging. There, the three elements are sometimes also called *ten, chi,* and *jin.* Other terms are also used, depending on the particular schools.

Not every arrangement of every kind has only three elements, of course. Arrangements of other odd numbers of elements are quite common, and there are even instances where even numbers are used (four being the least objectionable). However, no matter how many elements there are, they are always handled in such a way as to create a harmony of three. For example, four elements are arranged as 2-1-1; with five, the arrangement might be 2-2-1 or 3-1-1.

This aesthetic principle is basic to the Japanese idea of beauty, which is never something that has been brought to completion. It resides rather in a dynamic equilibrium that remains unbroken even with the addition of new elements. That is why the Japanese call it the "beauty of imperfection."

The Imaginary Stroke

Until the latter part of the nineteenth century, the Japanese had no concept of architectural space, and there was, accordingly, no term for it in the language. In the Meiji era (1868–1912) the

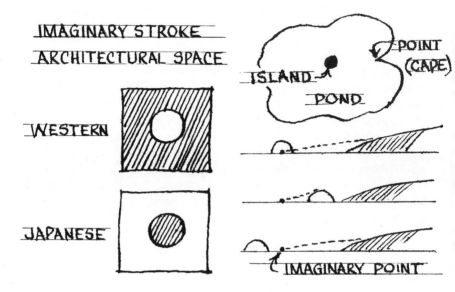

word space was introduced as a technical term and then translated into a Japanese word, *kūkan,* whose original meaning was something like "imaginary void." The Japanese already had some concept of space, although it had remained, until then, unexpressed. Space was always "imaginary." In other words, if Western architectural space can be represented by a defined solid white area on a black surface, then Japanese architectural space is symbolized by an area of black dots on a white background. The former has concrete physical boundaries, while the borders of the latter are but vaguely defined. In Japanese architecture, it is the roof, not the outer walls, that defines space.

The plan used by Japanese carpenters in construction included neither elevations nor sections. Although a special measuring rod (*kenzao*) was used, the plan remained basically two-dimensional. Its most important element was the pillar or post arrangement represented by dots, which, in fact, symbolized the entire building structure. Just by looking at these dots, a master carpenter was able to visualize the finished whole. The intervals between dots constituted "space" in Japan—if not visible as "space," at least in "imagination" something that can be clearly perceived.

This kind of spatial concept has had a long history in Japan. According to ancient Shinto belief, certain rocks and trees were considered symbols of the gods, and sacred festoons were hung upon them to mark their holiness. The people of the time further considered the area around these symbols to be a kind of "purified space," and, although its boundaries might not be clearly visible, there were few who dared venture near it. There were, in fact, many instances where the boundaries were marked off with a sacred rope, but in either case "purified space" was something defined in human terms, and its boundary lines can be thought of as "lines" of human activity. The Japanese word *kaiwai* is often translated as vicinity, but strictly speaking it means space delineated by human activity. In other words, the *kaiwai* of, let us say, Asakusa,* is determined by the grouping of activity lines of all the people gathered there. Consequently, the boundary lines are different at different times and are, in fact, never all that clear. But that is just the nature of Japanese space.

A similar idea can be found in Japanese garden architecture. Let us suppose that in a certain garden a small peninsula has been built out into a pond. It is the usual practice, in Japanese gardens, for a man-made island to be placed at some point just beyond the projection's tip. Traditional Japanese garden designers often said that one should build this island at the point in the water upon which the eye most naturally fell from a vantage point on the end of the peninsula. Of course, this point was not marked by anything, and so the island's location would vary according to who the viewer was. But the objective was to create an aesthetic balance in which island and peninsula were neither too close together nor too far apart.

The same sort of concept is present even in the art of calligraphy. Letters can be defined as the trace that emerges when the tip of the brush moves across the paper. It is this trace that remains visible afterward, but the movement of the brush through the air that links stroke to stroke disappears when the act of writ-

* A large downtown Tokyo amusement district.—ED.

ing is completed. This motion is called *kūkaku* ("imaginary stroke") in Japanese. Because it leaves no imprint on the page, it may perhaps be insignificant. Nevertheless, calligraphy masters have insisted that it is of tremendous importance in creating beautiful characters. As anyone who has studied calligraphy knows, it is not possible to write a decent character unless one has mastered the "imaginary stroke."

In this way, one was always required, in Japanese formative culture, to perceive what was not visible—the imaginary point, the imaginary stroke, and the imaginary space. In other words, the visible is taken to be merely an outward projection of that which cannot be seen.

3

The Liberation of Japanese Ghosts

Jōji Mori

Japan: Land of Ghosts

This short essay needs a prologue; and though it is about how the contemporary Japanese mind is reflected in writers' works, the prologue must provide a glimpse of the spiritual life of those ancient Japanese who lived on the four islands lying in a curved bow along the eastern edge of the Asian mainland. They were at once a realistic and a dreamy people; they did not believe in any supernatural or transcendental existence. They believed that things were as they saw them. Their minds were much too preoccupied with the beauty of nature to ponder over the possibility of some invisible hand behind it. Yet they were so realistic about their daily lives that they had to be fantastically imaginative about death. They believed there should be no sharp boundary between life and death. Death was just another possible form of life, one that continued in the natural surroundings they knew. The departed souls of those who were dear to them were not separated from them by any insurmountable walls. They had just hidden themselves, say, in the woods behind the garden. When a man felt like communicating with his departed mother, he had only to prepare a mirror or a round piece of well-polished stone,[1] and she would be only too glad to turn up, though unseen, to talk. They created no images for their gods, and they had no gods in the proper sense of the word. Their gods, called *kami*[2] (or *ujigami*), were no more than their ancestors who had left their routine abodes and had retired into the natural environment, where they were leading about the same kind of life as they had led when they were alive. So everyone was a god-to-be. These "godless" people were psychologically prepared to accept the Zen idea that "everyone is Buddha." More correctly, in their case, everyone was to become a spirit, for there was no idea among them of a supernatural life in heaven. The dead would just roam about in the woods, or along the river, eternally condemned to remain on this earth. But men did not seem to suffer from the idea. The only necessary condition for communication with dead souls was purity, and purity had less the connotation of "purity of heart" than of actual physical cleanliness, of freedom from any sort of pollution or contamination. These people

[1] *Kōtai Jingu Gishiki Chō* (*The Notebooks for the Rituals of the Imperial Shrine*), presumed to have been written in the ninth century, mentions objects of worship in forty-nine branch shrines of the Imperial Shrine. They are twenty-seven stones, five mirrors, one cup of water. Sixteen shrines have nothing in their sanctuary. (Cf. Yoshirō Tamura, *Introduction to the History of Japanese Buddhism* [1969], p. 26.)

[2] The Japanese word for deity. But as there was no clear demarcation between deities and ancestors, the term could also mean ancestor. Each family, each clan, each community ruled by the clan (*uji*) had its own *kami* (referred to as *ujigami* or tutelary deity). These numberless *kami* were incorporated into a hierarchical system just as the people were organized into a hierarchy of wealth and power. Thus, *kami* of the Yamato clan eventually came to dominate over the *kami* of all other clans. (Incidentally, by the end of the sixth century, when the Yamato dynasty had accepted Buddhism, it was only natural for the *kami* of other minor clans to accept coexistence with the new persuasion.) One of the oldest studies about the word *kami* is found in *Shindai Kūketsu* (1367) by Imbe-no-Masamichi, a Shinto theologian. In later years, Norinaga Motoori discussed the word in the third volume of the *Kojikiden* (*The Study of the Record of Ancient Matters*, 1798). Motoori explains that people designate as *kami* any object of awe and power however benign or evil. Some scholars speculate that *kami* is a shortened form of *kagami* (mirror), but the etymology is not certain. Other scholars divide the word into *ka* and *mi*, so it may mean *kanata no mi* (literally, "body corporate beyond"). *Kami* were also designated by other names, *chi, mi, tama,* and *mono,* as in *ikazu-chi, wadatsu-mi, mi-tama* and *mono-noke*. These synonyms of *kami* also stress that *kami* is a part of nature. So *ujigami* represented both one's ancestor's spirit and the spirit of nature around one's village.

loved white and space in which nothing had been written. They so loved clean water that they devised the celebrated Japanese bath. They even took pains to rebuild their Shinto shrines, called *yashiro*,* every twenty-five years to keep clean the place in which their *kami* came to rest.

The character some 1,500 years ago of the inhabitants of the four islands now called Japan gives us some clues about one of the mysteries of modern Japanese writing. Mysteries? Yes, indeed. If we look at Tanizaki, Kawabata, Mishima, to mention only three representative names, they are eerily antimodern, if by "modern" we mean something scientific, free from any form of superstition, listening solely to the voice of reason. We shall have no convincing explanation, I fear, for the work of such men, if we have recourse to theories of modernization and progress, though this is still popular in some academic quarters. Did Kawabata write *House of the Sleeping Beauties (Nemureru Bijō)* either because he had been "modernized" enough to conceive of someone like Lolita, or because he was inclined toward free sex or wished to uphold sex as a means of resistance to a system that was still undemocratic? Nonsense! An attempt to find some comparable quality in these contemporary Japanese writers and modern Western writers like Samuel Beckett, Arthur Miller, Saul Bellow, and others may be interesting, but it is not convincing, because the former authors are unmistakably Japanese, not in their nationality but in their works. Their works are a strange and unwittingly honest mirror of the Japanese mind.

On the literary scene, a strange paradox persists: As social institutions, systems of government, and the law are "modernized" or "democratized," the antimodern "ghost impulse" becomes more and more pervasive in the works of our best authors. Many of the masterpieces by modern Japanese writers are masked varieties of ghost tales. One suspects there is even something atavistic about them. However, ghosts have always been an important part of the Japanese literary tradition. The young mistress of Hikaru Genji, the hero of *The Tale of Genji*, was killed by a ghost while the prince was making love with her in one of his

---

* *Yashiro* means the house that contains a *yorishiro*, the object used to give *kami* something to alight on, just as a bird alights on a twig. The Grand Shrine at Ise, most important of the Shinto shrines, is being rebuilt in 1972–73.

villas. Ghosts in *nō* theater play more than minor roles. Of course, in the works of present-day authors, there are no such obtrusive apparitions that directly challenge the credulity of science-oriented modern people. Still, these stories are, as any alert and uninhibited reader will sense, eerie; we would not be surprised to come across a passage in which a ghost, phantom, or specter suddenly appears. It seems to me that modern Japanese writers are indeed ready to sit and chat with departed souls, whether those of the ancients or those who died in World War II.

Japanese literature has always been haunted by its familiar ghosts, but I have called the present literary phenomenon "atavistic" because there can be no doubt that modern Japan started from what we may call the age of reason, the Meiji Period (1868–1912), when claims of reason, given a philosophical basis by the fruits of the Enlightenment of eighteenth-century Europe, were more attentively listened to than in any preceding period. The political novels of the early Meiji years by Ryūkei Yano, Sanjin Tōkai, Tecchō Suehirō, and others were naïve expressions of an optimistic faith in the effectiveness of reason. Ironically, however, even this faith needed a somewhat irrational social framework to support it in the Emperor system.* Indeed, the pursuit of reason in the Meiji Period was only made feasible by the delicate yet relatively stable balance of two forces, old and new. The old was the Neo-Confucianism of the "frozen" feudal system of the Edo period (1600–1867) fortified by the theory of Chu Hsi† and the asceticism of *bushidō*.‡ The new was what Japanese were learning, or thought they were learning, from Western civilization: science, technology, and a mode of idealism deriving from the Greco-Hebraic tradition, often with an admixture of American aspirations for freedom and transcendentalism. In literature also, this balance of old and new provides helpful insights. Writers were feeling and thinking anew; they believed that their

* The political structure of Meiji Japan was based on a definition of the role of the Emperor as all-powerful, drawing on both modern German and early Japanese experience. In fact, decisions were made by his advisers, but they were always issued in the name of the Emperor.—ED.

† Chu Hsi (1130–1200) was the great synthesizer of a new and lasting systematic philosophy in twelfth-century China.—ED.

‡ Literally "the way of the warrior," an ethical code developed for the samurai in the Tokugawa Period. The nature, role, and meaning of *bushidō* in Japanese life are much debated among scholars.—ED.

work must be wholly different from the writings of the Edo Period in both theme and style. They seemed to know what to reject and what to accept. Nevertheless, they were not so separated from their fathers as they liked to think they were. Like their fathers, they believed that conflicts between the old and the new, however severe they might look, were not dangerous, if only the individual conscientiously pursued the way of learning through hard and ascetic self-discipline. This had also been the most honored way of preparing oneself for life in the Edo Period. A motto once popular among Meiji intellectuals, *"wakon, yōsai"* (in spirit, Japanese; in technique, Western), well illustrates this belief.

With the death of the Emperor Meiji in 1912, something was lost from the Japanese mind. The Meiji Period is now remembered as a golden age to which there is no hope of return. Japanese are now much too sophisticated to believe in the reign of the Emperor as a social mediator, a great patron of reason as well as of art. They have again found themselves with the inevitable ancient ghosts that have never forsaken them, even if their sole concern has been a very modern one, like the realization of a democratic society where no exploitation of man by man exists—the theme often stated by liberal intellectuals.* This was even more the case following World War II, when the American Occupation introduced democracy as an authorized social principle. It is as if the social system, which up to that point had absorbed the energy of the Japanese ghosts and had held them in check through, among other things, the institution of the invisible *ie,*† could no longer contain them because it had become democratized. It is as if a more rational social system, having lost any official rationale for countenancing ghosts, had left the burden of their care to writers. And indeed, Japanese ghosts have rarely been allowed such free play on the pages of literature as they have today.

Technically speaking, there are reasons for the use of an anach-

---

* Makoto Oda, Shunsuke Tsurumi, and Yūzuru Katagiri are only a few names among the many such intellectuals. Incidentally, those who believe they are acting only by the voice of reason would flatly deny my point. But I am not dealing with the "conscious" level that often veils the unconscious one.

† A Japanese word for family. Before World War II, it meant a group of families with a common paternal ancestor. Family solidarity and honor were stressed.—ED.

ronistic term such as ghost. Historically, the word "beauty" (*bi* in Japanese) or words designating delicate nuances within the category of beauty,* have often been used to explain the nature of Japanese literature. But to my mind, the concept of "beauty" cannot adequately convey something that has been so far concealed. Moreover, the idea of beauty as the sole artistic value cannot but be irrelevant to the works of such modern writers as Kenzaburō Ōe and Kimifusa Abe, and the same is generally true of words that specify various aspects of beauty, though they are valuable in suggesting the characteristics of our ghosts.

Instead of beauty, I find the concept of ghost much more helpful. The ghost quality in Japanese writers and literature can be examined from the point of view of at least three important disciplines: archetypal study (including ethnology and folklore), social psychology, and aesthetics. The archetypal study of ghosts needs no explanation. As for psychology, the mental state of a ghost is alienation. He is an uncooperative soul, separated from his fellows, unable to have a true love on earth, lacking the hope of inhabiting paradise after death. He is even alienated from the reader. This is why the reader of these modern Japanese "ghost" tales feels what Nancy Wilson Ross has called a "freedom from emotional identification with any character, [which] does not, however, lessen the book's power."[3] Thus, modern Japanese stories may be looked upon as fables of man's alienation in modern industrialized society. But how can one consider ghosts from the point of view of aesthetics? Because of his alienation, a ghost harbors a strange aspiration to become a beautiful thing; seeing beautiful things is not enough, as Mishima knew. A beautiful thing and an ugly thing may be regarded as different aspects of one existence, the first benign and the second sinister.[4] If we approach literature from the points of view of the idea of beauty, or the voice of the oppressed, or a means of protest, we shall find ourselves obliged unfairly to neglect either most of the modern problems of man's alienation in society or the traditional values

---

* Such as *miyabi, mono no aware, yūgen, sabi, wabi,* and others.

[3] *The Temple of the Golden Pavilion* (New York: Alfred A. Knopf, 1959), p. xi.

[4] The concepts of "benign" and "sinister" were first introduced in Kenneth Burke, *Philosophy of Literary Form: Studies in Symbolic Action,* 2d ed. (New York: Random House, 1957).

of Japanese culture. Thus, the use of the term ghost does not require the reader to believe, however momentarily, that ghosts exist in reality. The term is presented instead as a tool of analysis to deal simultaneously with three factors in literature, the archetypal, the aesthetic, and the sociopsychological.

If we accept the idea that modern Japanese literature is haunted—archetypally, aesthetically, and psychologically—by ghosts as defined here, then we may regard that literature also as an attempt to liberate these ghosts. It is in some sense an attempt to encompass and control the alienation of modern man or to probe its causes and examine its nature.

Technically speaking, again, the idea of the liberation of Japanese ghosts can help explain the development of modern Japanese literature. When I speak of the liberation of Japanese ghosts, I am not referring to composite dramas where the characters have positions and roles as citizens, responsible or not, in modern society and grow or are stultified mainly as a result of their interaction with other characters. Instead, I have in mind literary works that merely extend the hero's or the author's inner world, works in which there is no clear distinction between that world and the ethos of the work as art. The lack of such a distinction may suggest romantic poetry written in prose, but this is not the case. In works of the liberation of ghosts, there is no platonic love of intellectual beauty nor of a sublime idea, however vague. In that such a work shows no hunger for anything transcendental, it is realistic, down to earth. But curiously enough, it is anything but realistic; it even makes one feel an eerie "other" existence and sends a shiver up one's spine. This paradox of down-to-earth realism and unearthly fantasy parallels the paradox of Japanese life more than fifteen centuries ago, when people were realistic about daily life but saw no reason for drawing a sharp line between life and death.

Taishō and Shōwa: Paradise Lost

Taishō (1912–25) was an embarrassingly new age; many people lost their psychological balance. Even writers who had regarded themselves as "new men" somehow realized that they could no longer be what they had been; the meanings of belief and hope were undermined. It is interesting to see the shift from a lighter to a darker mood in the works of writers who had been representative of the Meiji Period. Sōseki Natsume's *Sorekara* (*And Then*), written in 1909, describes a youth, Daisuke, who, obedient to the voice of nature, marries a friend's wife despite the opposition of his social group. He could believe that he was right and society was wrong, that people would someday become "enlightened" and congratulate him. Until then, he and his love, Michiyo, would endure the cold, unsympathetic eye of society.

> There was a confidence in him that he had taken the right path. He felt satisfaction with himself for that. Michiyo understood his satisfaction. Everything and everyone except her—his father, brother, society, every human being was his enemy. They were thinking of burning them to death, enveloping them in a white-glowing fire. Daisuke looked upon it as a sort of wish fulfillment to have Michiyo and himself burned in a sheet of flame, saying nothing, embracing each other.[5]

But in *Mon* (*The Gate*, 1910), a novel that is rightly regarded as a sequel to *Sorekara*, the protagonist, Sōsuke, is worried over matters that he can never resolve. A yet later novel, *Kokoro* (*The Heart*), written in 1914, two years after the Emperor's death, is a very symbolic work suggesting that the balance of forces, old and new, has finally been completely upset. It ends with a letter of confession left to the hero by his respected teacher, who kills himself when he hears of General Nogi's *harakiri* after the Emperor's death. The letter says: "Now, the Meiji [Period] has ended. Why should it be necessary that such a man as I, most influenced by the spirit of Meiji, survive it?" In his youth, the teacher, like most young men, had considered himself a champion of the new age; he saw a straight road before him from which he need swerve for no man. He behaved like a "new" man, and if some act of his had unpleasant social repercussions, he believed, like Daisuke, that it was society that was dishonest and wrong. Now, however, he found that he was no better than those he had despised for their hypocrisy; like the heroes of the earlier novels, he had stolen the girl his best friend loved and caused his despairing friend to commit suicide. Could he say that his friend

[5] *Sorekara*, Chapter XVII. Translated by Jōji Mori.

was just a bad loser? No! that was rationalization under the pretext of "modern love." He had known that his friend was deeply
in love with the girl and had a noble heart and ascetic character
in the Confucian tradition, according to which carnal love was
a great hindrance to man's spiritual growth. Because the hero
wanted the girl's love and feared that his friend would win her,
he had advised his friend against physical love and had shamed
him out of thinking of the girl as his. He was thus aware that he
was driving his friend into the wilderness where passions and the
voices urging chastity would engage in endless war; but he so desired her for himself that he thought, let the devil take his friend.
For the rest of his life, his heaviest burden was that he knew what
he had done and what kind of man he was. This knowledge was
a prison that held him back from meaningful activity.

> When it becomes unbearable for me to stay in this prison, impossible
> as it is for me to break out of it, I come to this one conclusion: that
> considering my character I have no exit but suicide to escape. You
> may wonder and ask wide-eyed: why? But that mysterious, fearful
> power that grips my heart, while holding me back from any kind of
> activity, keeps always open for me the exit of death.[6]

Another important figure in Meiji literature, Ōgai Mori, a
somewhat pessimistic writer from the start, became more so later.
His *Maihime* (*The Girl Dancer*, 1890) is the story of a promising
young man who abandons the German girl he loves, who is pregnant with his child. He does so under pressure from his superior,
Count Amataka, and the Meiji government. The book contains
some of the most beautiful Japanese ever written, but the conclusion, in which the hero chooses his post rather than love, drew
much criticism. Yet would it not have become just another popular magazine story if the hero had snubbed the count to sing a
love duet in a shabby cottage? As the author responded to one
such literary criticism, *Maihime* is not a tragedy of situation but
a tragedy of weak character that the hero could not overcome.
For Mori, who had a very high post in the government bureaucracy and the army, it was a severe self-criticism; one might even
say it was not the German girl who was the dancer, but he, dancing for his post. His novel may, however, have been more than

6 *Kokoro,* Chapter LV. Translated by Jōji Mori.

that: a criticism of the system, but within the limits of the balance of forces mentioned earlier. The author accepts and prizes two things at the same time: love and the Emperor Meiji. If it is impossible to accommodate one's private and public ideals, the fault must lie somewhere in between. Is there something wrong with the bureaucratic system itself; does it still need change? Or does the fault lie with Kenkichi Aizawa, who takes such pains to persuade the hero to give up the girl so that he may remain in the count's favor? Or is the problem, perhaps, within the author? Still, the world is not all darkness; with constant effort, it must be possible to find a path that connects the two ideals; peace under the reign of the great Emperor and the bliss of individual love. The last passage in the story says: "Oh, how well I know that one only rarely comes across such a good friend as Kenkichi Aizawa! But to this day, I must confess, a bit of rancor against him remains here in my bosom like an indelible stain."

Gan (*The Wild Goose*), written by Mori between 1911 and 1913, the years of transition from the Meiji to the Taishō era, is more a tragedy of situation than one of character and therefore has a more pessimistic tone. The hero, Okada, a medical student at Tokyo Imperial University, meets Ōtama, the young mistress of an old loan shark, Suezō, who has retired from the post of janitor at the university. One day, Okada happens to pass by the house where Suezō keeps his mistress. A snake has just caught one of the caged birds that Suezō keeps, and Okada kills the snake. This incident awakens the woman in Ōtama, and her struggle to get away from Suezō begins. The only daughter of an old man who sells sweets, she has a past: She had been seduced by a married policeman. Having thus become *"kizumono"* ("chipped china," that is, a woman who has lost her honor), she decided to be useful in the only way she could be. By becoming the mistress of Suezō, who loved her, she could earn money to help her poor father. She does not know Suezō's trade at first, but several insults enlighten her about her position in the eyes of the world. Okada lives in a world beyond her reach, but he and Ōtama come to a nodding acquaintance in the course of his neighborhood strolls. As Suezō's affection for her grows, Ōtama cools toward him and her yearning for Okada intensifies. One day, when Suezō has gone to the nearby prefecture of Chiba, she decides to invite

Okada in, but he is about to leave for Europe to become an assistant to a German professor of medicine. The story is similar to that of the earlier *Maihime,* but a symbolic scene near the end of *Gan* suggests that the two novels have somewhat different meanings. In this scene, the hero, while strolling one evening with a few friends, picks up a stone and throws it idly at a wild goose on a pond. He does not expect to hit it, but the stone kills the goose. This symbolism suggests that Ōtama was the wild goose Okada has unintentionally killed. Then it dawns upon the reader that the snake Okada killed for her was Suezō, the loan shark, and that the little bird in the cage was Ōtama. Although Okada had first saved her life, he had then unwittingly killed her. Was the stone with which he killed her the symbol of the modernization of Japan? Was the Western civilization that Japanese intellectuals were so earnestly learning killing the good, traditional Japan? Thus, in *Gan,* there is no problem of weak character as in *Maihime.* The problem is an insoluble one. In a sinister way, *Gan* suggests that human efforts will inevitably be thwarted.

After the death of Emperor Meiji, Mori began writing historical fiction, though his later works were much too close to historical fact to be called fiction. In these works, he tried to penetrate the historical fate that hung like a pall over vain, human acts and passions. *Abe Ichizoku (The Abes,* 1913), his first historical novel, deals with the tragic end of the Abe clan. On his deathbed, Lord Tadatoshi Hosokawa grants *junshi,* the privilege of killing oneself after the death of one's master, to eighteen of his vassals but does not give permission to Yaichiemon Abe, the head of the Abe clan of his vassals, because he dislikes him. Although the custom of *junshi* may sound cruel to us today, samurai regarded it as a privilege granted only to the favorites of the lord. After *junshi,* those favorites would continue to serve their lords in the land of death, a place not so very different from the human world. Yaichiemon's omission means that he has fallen from the lord's grace and has brought shame to his house. It is a great blow. Not only is he forbidden the honor of *junshi,* which would have demonstrated his loyalty and status as one of the master's favorites, but he also becomes the object of general ridicule. People spread the rumor that Yaichiemon had not killed himself because he feared death. Deeply chagrined and hoping to restore the honor of his house, he assembles his sons and before committing *harakiri* tells them: "Now, my sons, look well how the man who has been blamed for being a coward cuts his belly. Be good brothers after my death and never have a quarrel!" But a stain once on a name does not easily wash away. The eldest son and heir, Gonbei, is not allowed to succeed to his father's fief; instead, it is divided among the brothers, thus demoting the Abe clan. At the first anniversary service for their dead lord, Gonbei, while offering incense before the master's mortuary tablet, cuts off his topknot (the symbol of samurai status) and places it in front of the tablet, indicating thereby his renunciation of his class. This protest, which expresses his sorrow and his feeling that the name of the house of Abe has been unfairly sullied, is interpreted as a flamboyantly insolent act. It incurs the displeasure of the young lord, who feels he has been personally challenged by his vassal. The lord immediately orders Gonbei hanged, the most dishonorable means of execution for a samurai. Suffering from the disgrace of their father and brother and remembering their vow to their father of fraternal loyalty, the other brothers get together at Gonbei's house and, after deliberation, decide to make their final resistance there. After killing their wives and children, they receive their pursuers and die.

It would be shallow to think of *Abe Ichizoku* as just a barbarous story. We are conducting no less barbarous acts in the name of holy wars, freedom, democracy, Communism, and so on. It is a story of human passion most poignantly presented. Passions and obsessions are signs of humanity, although being human may sometimes mean that we are dangerous animals, not only to others but also to ourselves. The purpose of Mori's historical fiction was to study the relationship between the system set up by human dreams, which had become encrusted with tradition, and human passions. When the two conflict, the walls of the system crack, and the Japanese ghosts confined within them are released. We hear them moan with the pain they never felt while they were frozen and packed inside. The appearance of works like those of Mori gives evidence of the breakdown of the balance that had existed between reason and passion in the Meiji Period.

Literary trends after the Meiji Period can be divided roughly into two streams. One group of authors in the Taishō and Shōwa

(1926–present) periods, now unable to believe in the intellectual enterprise by which Meiji writers had hoped to harmonize reason and passion throughout all levels of society, limited their concerns to becoming complete artists or solitary moralists. Expelled from paradise, they no longer felt qualified to deal with such large themes as the nation, society, and world peace. The enemy they had to control was not outside of them, but within them. What could they do, lacking even the ability to achieve their own humble goals?

The other group turned to socialism and termed everything in the Meiji era a fraud. The supporters of this approach still wished to be the sons of reason, a commitment made even firmer by their concern with theoretical matters. They used such magazines as *Tanemakuhito* (*The Seed-scatterer*), *Bungeisensen* (*The Literary Front*), and *Senki* (*The Banner*) as forts from which to fire destructive fusilades at the image of the good, old Japanese tradition and to awaken workers to the miseries of their exploitation.

Between 1921 and about 1933, the socialist movement in literature completed the cycle of rise, flowering, and decline. Its decline was due partly to governmental repression and partly to the defection of key people from the movement. As in most countries, the movement has left few monumental works and almost none by radical authors.* But despite its meager fruit, the movement attracted writers of no small talent and left lasting impressions on their minds.

The socialist movement in literature, though it was in a sense the Japanese counterpart of proletarian literature in Europe and America, may be defined as the attempt of "angels looking homeward"—men who had been exiled from the spiritual paradise of the Meiji era—to become the reincarnation of the samurai mind, a state in which there would be no disheartening imbalance between reason and passion, and, even better, between the will of the government and the dream of the proletariat. Yet even the imagined walls of the new revolutionary system, fortified by the Marxist theory of class strife, could not long contain Japanese

---

* The few memorable pieces all come from authors who were anything but belligerent fighters: Yuriko Miyamoto, Fumiko Hayashi, Yaeko Nogami, and Shigeharu Nakano. Note that three of these four writers were women.

ghosts. The moans of the repressed people described by these writers often mingled with those of the aboriginal ghosts.

The first group of writers, however, was more important as a productive force than the second. Most of the writers in the first stream seemed to have forsaken the samurai mind forever, if we mean by the phrase an ambition for social leadership. Their ambition, if they still had one, was to be either an artist or a moralist. They felt they could no longer find a large, comprehensive frame of reference in which they might coordinate their thoughts and passions as the preceding generation had done. There was no way left, it seemed to them, but to delve into their inner life and the world that surrounded it. In this exploration of the self and its circumstances, however, they were not completely free. Except for a few writers,* they imposed some limitations upon themselves, and the limitations more often than not narrowed, even though they deepened, the scope and implications of their work.

The limitations were derived from the supposed demand for naturalism and realism, which had long been acclaimed as the basic criteria for modern literature. Shōyō Tsubouchi's *Shōsetsu Shinzui (The Essence of the Novel,* 1885) first proclaimed these demands in the form of theory. In his novel *Ukigumo,* Shimei Futabatei practiced the theory with fair success. Foreign models included the naturalism of Maupassant and Zola on the one hand, and the realism of Turgenev, Tolstoy, or proletarian literature on the other.

These realistic or naturalistic demands in literature, as they were emphasized by the critics, put needless limitations on the writings of those men who made it their point to describe the small world of their minds and experiences. They did not feel up to such big words as naturalism and realism, which looked more at home in a context like socialist realism. They welcomed the idea of honesty, however, because it had both moral and artistic connotations for them. It meant at once honesty as freedom from hypocrisy and honesty as true-to-life description. Moreover, only by being honest could they make real the relationship between society and their work. They had no well-knit internal society to present in their work as the counterpart of the outside one, which

---

* Shinichi Makino (1896–1936) is one of the few exceptions who did not conform to the naturalistic demands in literature.

would soon reveal the unreality of the inner one. So it seemed to them that honesty was the surest standard by which to judge the value of any work of art. It was the same thing as purity in their eyes. They even hated the word fiction. They hated to tell a lie; telling a lie was the worst profanity against art. So their works, which were called *shishōsetsu* (autobiographical novels), took the form of diaries with no plot or interdependence among the characters. Could diary-writing be called art? As they saw it, there could be true diaries and false diaries. The diary of the man on the street was false insofar as it contained hypocrisy. A writer's diary was true insofar as the confession of his own dark acts hurt the writer and could, if known, cause him to be banished from genteel society. Only a diary of self-incrimination was worthy of the name of art. Ironically, those who wished to be writers, and hence moralists, were obliged to cultivate the darker aspects of their characters in order to have something to "confess." Thus, Shūsei Tokuda, a representative *shishōsetsu* writer, forced himself to engage in illicit love affairs so that he could continue his "honest," humiliating confessions. Osamu Dazai, the greatest of the *shishōsetsu* writers, made successive suicide pacts with two innocent girls. He, but not the girl, survived the first *shinjū* (lovers' suicide), but he was unable to bear the second incident and killed himself as well.

Of Nature, Ghosts, and Beauty

If there is a discrepancy between the ideals that Western fiction strives to attain and those of Japanese fiction, there should be no such discrepancy between their respective poetic imaginations. A poet does not need to visualize the structure of social relationships among his fellow countrymen. He can find symbolic correspondences with the outer world in his own inner world. But the Japanese poet and the Western poet may have quite different perceptions of reality. The Western poet may read in nature a consistent allegory written by an "invisible hand" or see nature as presenting an ideal for the structure of human relationships, an ideal that is to be identified with the ultimate logic of the universe. The Japanese poet may not hear such Platonic preachments; to him, nature has no such pedagogical intent. Though it may sound strange, for a Japanese poet nature does not have the mystical quality that it has for a Western poet; he knows it too well to regard it as "unfathomable," as Shelley described it.

Why should nature be mystical to a Japanese poet who may himself be a ghost wandering in it? There is no clear demarcation between nature and the human world. A girl is *not* pretty like a flower; she *is* a pretty flower that may wilt away at any time. Nature is not an allegory for the existence of some spiritual world beyond, but it may be an allegory for the human world. Thus, for the Japanese poet, there is something prosaic, something routinely static about nature in Japanese literature. There appear no mysterious caves or boats through which or in which the poet pursues the beckoning shadow of Mother Nature as in Shelley's poetry. Nature is not an object to pursue but the environment one lives in. The Japanese poet sees a "stylized" nature; poetic images have a customary form: An *uguisu* (the poetic counterpart in Japanese of the nightingale or cuckoo) *must* sing on a twig of the plum tree. Nature and the human world merge, with nature becoming somewhat prosaic and the human world becoming enchantingly eerie. Nature is not even permitted to be wild or erratic; it must abide by as much decorum as man. Thus, there is not so much distance between prose and poetry in Japanese literature as there is in Western literature. It may be that Japanese prose is a kind of poetry; it is more often than not the tale of a lonely spirit. In this sense, Japanese literature is much more like American literature than European literature.

It is not so surprising, then, that the second wave in the liberation of the Japanese ghosts as I have defined it appeared with the works of the poet-novelist Haruo Satō. Satō's *Denen no Yūutsu (Pastoral Melancholy*, 1918) is at once *shishōsetsu* and poetry in prose. It is in the tradition of *shishōsetsu* because it is an honest description of Satō's daily life in a village in Kanagawa Prefecture where he and his wife moved to weather his time of depression. There is no development of plot as in a novel. There are only two human protagonists: the writer and his wife. The other main characters are two dogs and a cat. But the work is also poetry in prose, as is suggested by the rather romantic title. It was looked upon as very Western and modern at the time of its publication, and in many respects it is. The image of a rose around which the story is constructed is more Western than Japanese. In

early September, the writer finds a rose bush in their garden. It
has neither leaves nor flowers and is choked among the wild
grasses, but he loves roses and says: "Since it is a rose, it will
bloom someday." And he calls it his rose. Apparently, the rose
bush is the objective correlative, as T. S. Eliot defines it, of the
writer's plight. Confident of his gift but living an obscure existence, the writer now has neither leaves nor flowers he can be
proud of, but because he has talent he will someday bloom. He
begins to take care of the stunted rose bush. Summer becomes autumn. His hope changes to anxiety. He feels extremely tired and
wanders aimlessly through the village and in the hills, sometimes
causing trouble among the villagers. One day he finds a little
blossom on his rose bush and rejoices with tears in his eyes. His
wife, who is an actress, yearns for the urban life they had left behind, but nothing can be done about it. He continues to roam
among the idyllic scenes of the area. He loves nature, but he also
finds in it many sinister suggestions. He even has hallucinations,
which make him think of death. Then, one agonizing day, he
finds that his rose, his only hope, has wilted. As he stands there
stupefied at the sight, from somewhere comes a voice saying, "Oh
rose, thou art sick!"

Denen no Yūutsu was undoubtedly influenced by Western literature. Even Furate and Leo, the two dogs who play important
roles, have names that sound somewhat Western. The wild beauty
of nature in which the hero wanders is charmingly reminiscent of
the nature presented in Western Romantic poetry, but the re-
semblances stop here. The nature Satō presents does not embrace
the hero in its kind bosom and heal, as Wordsworth's nature often does, the hero's wounded heart. It is not a self-contained en-
tity, an agency whose independent, guiding logic is always superior to man's logic. Nature in *Denen no Yūutsu* suffers with the
hero. He has a nervous breakdown; nature shares it. It cannot
heal him. Not only is he lost, as a member of the lost generation
after the departure of the Emperor Meiji; nature is also lost and
sick. In this sense he is a ghost, half-demented and roaming
among the hills. One night, he believes he has fallen into a
"soul-dividing" illness. He sees a strange shadow that resembles
him on the road far ahead, and his dogs run toward it gladly
wagging their tails as it whistles to them. He tries to whistle them

back but finds his own whistle is the same as that coming from
the shadow. The idea that the hero may be a ghost is more than
a hypothesis. One even suspects it from the name the hero gives
to their farm house—*Ugetsu Sōsha* ("rainy moon grass-house").
The name is weird enough, but it is all the eerier because it
is clear to the Japanese reader that he has taken it from *Ugetsu
Monogatari* (*Tales of the Rainy Moon*) by Akinari Ueda, a series
of masterly ghost tales of the Edo Period. One may conclude that
Satō was trying to add something to the classical Japanese tradition by liberating the familiar ghosts in its pages. To Satō, nature was not merely something to be contemplated, it was a part
of his own physical makeup in the sense that changes within his
mind brought about a metamorphosis within nature, which in
turn effected a transformation of his mind.

Junichirō Tanizaki, a friend of Satō's, succeeded in enshrining
his own intellect not in an autobiographical work, as Satō had,
but in fiction. Tanizaki wrote about his own deepest feelings, unlike another contemporary, Ryūnosuke Akutagawa, whose overly
distant intellectual approach to his subjects often made the
reader doubt whether he really had worries and aspirations.
Tanizaki's lifelong obsession was a yearning for his dead mother.
Throughout his life, he was never psychologically weaned; he
never grew up. But he knew, unlike the *shishōsetsu* writers, how
to keep an artistic distance from his subject. Except as a fastidi-
ous annotator who explains the historical context, he rarely in-
trudes into a story to pour out his personal, unsatisfied aspirations. An astute technician, he fabricates his stories to resemble a
revolving lantern where three pictures of fetishism, masochism,
and sadism alternate before the viewer's eyes. The lantern pivots
on the image of a physically beautiful and proud woman who
plays a vicarious role as his mother. The force that moves the lantern is not so much inspiration as desire. The images are used to
portray different facets of character; for example, a man who
looks like a sadist at the outset of the story is revealed as a mas-
ochist at the end in *Aisurebakoso* (*Because of Love*, 1922).

There is no doubt that in *Shisei* (*Tattooing*, 1910), his maiden
work, Tanizaki had already discovered most of the techniques indispensable to a writer who wishes to go on writing good literature. The hero of *Shisei* is an artist who had made it his trade to

tattoo beautiful pictures on the backs of men and women. Seikichi always feels "a secret pleasure" in piercing the human skin
with the needle and would like to tattoo a masterpiece on a beautiful woman in Fukagawa, then the prosperous downtown section
of Edo. He finds an ideal girl and cuts a great spider on her
white skin, gratifying both his artistic ambition and his sadistic
impulse. But once tattooed, the pretty but rather reserved girl
turns into a minx who commands men with her beauty. Seikichi,
until then haughty and sadistic, becomes a masochistic, servile
man. In choosing such a hero, Tanizaki was able to express his
love of artistry and his sensuous feelings about skin, which for him
constituted an irresistible obsession. Tanizaki's artistic achievement was to transform his dark sadistic and masochistic impulses
into fiction. *Shisei* is not just a strange, sardonic story of an abnormal artist; it is also the story of artistic creation in general.
The very act of creation cannot but contain within it some abnormal factors: To write is to define and to define is to give things
that have previously had a neutral, impartial existence a character that serves the writer's specific purpose. Thereafter, things
consecrated to art survive those who gave them a new character.

Tanizaki never did abandon the revolving lantern's kaleido-
scopic, deformed images, but despite his initial skill, it took a
long time for his art to mature. His earlier works recall the poor
taste of some imitations of Renoir's paintings—all pink and red.
Works such as *Konjiki no Shi* (*Death in Gold*, 1914) were intended to be exotic and gorgeous, communicating a *fin de siècle*
idea of art, but they lacked something that transforms writing
into art, and this something may be defined as a structure into
which to invite the Japanese ghosts. The walls of Tanizaki's literary structures must have had chinks through which ghosts
could enter, but those who happened to wander in bumped
against the voluptuous, massive body of a painted woman. Of
course, a work not haunted by ghosts is not necessarily a bad one,
but strangely, the absence of ghosts seems to affect Japanese literature adversely. It was not until Tanizaki learned how to stay
away from the gay and lurid while remaining "abnormal" that he
became a great novelist. To say that a work is sober, subdued in
color, and sedately rounded but still "abnormal" is to say that it
may possibly be an abode of the ghosts.

Another work, *Shunkin-shō* (*A Briefing About Shunkin*, 1934), was one of Tanizaki's great efforts, the one that established his name, but it lacks the dazzling tinsel and voluptuous qualities of his early stories. Although it is told by an elderly gentleman who is something of a savant and even has some acquaintance with Zen Buddhism, it is still a grotesque story.

The heroine, Shunkin, the second daughter of a rich proprietor of a drugstore, the Mozu-ya, loses her sight at the age of nine. Her parents then have her learn the samisen* in hopes that music will relieve the tedium of her blind life, but she has an exceptional talent for the instrument. She is found to be a genius, and, in addition, she is a very beautiful child. Everyone spoils her until her parents find it is too late to discipline her to humble gentility. Her willfulness makes her seem a little despot.

The hero, Sasuke, is an apprentice boy at the Mozu-ya. A country boy, he is bedazzled by Shunkin's beauty, which only a rich family in a large city could ever produce. His admiration for her is so great that he even learns to play the samisen. He practices after work in a closet in the loft so as not to disturb the sleep of the other apprentices. The darkness in the closet becomes congenial to him because he knows that Shunkin lives in the same darkness. One day, he is heard fingering the strings and is told to come down and play before the family. He thinks Shunkin has thought of another cruel way to amuse herself; she is going to bring him into general ridicule. After the performance, however, it is arranged that Shunkin will give him lessons.

She seems absorbed in the pleasure of teaching Sasuke, who is four years her senior. The narrator remarks on her childish enjoyment of "play school." She is the severest of teachers. Her parents, unable to get their daughter to abandon her domineering role, allow Sasuke to take lessons from a famed samisen player and teacher of Shunkin, and she is forbidden to teach Sasuke directly. When she is twenty-two years old, Shunkin becomes pregnant. The father is thought to be Sasuke. The parents do not grieve, for they have begun to think that Sasuke would not be a bad choice as their daughter's husband, because she is handicapped by blindness, despite her great talent for music. The

* A three-stringed instrument used to accompany traditional singing.—Ed.

baby is the image of Sasuke but Shunkin denies Sasuke's pater-
nity and shows no love for the child. Her parents are obliged to
give the baby to a childless couple or, as the narrator surmises, to
let someone put an end to it. A while later, Shunkin moves into
a new house to lead an independent life as a samisen teacher,
though it is mostly Sasuke who teaches as an intern. Sasuke's devotion to his mistress continues with the same intensity. They can
no longer live without each other, though Shunkin never wants
the barrier between teacher and disciple to be lifted and never
changes her domineering attitude. One night, someone steals into
the house and pours boiling water over Shunkin's face, so famed
for its beauty, disfiguring it horribly. When Sasuke runs up to
her, she covers her face with both hands and says, "From now on,
never look at my face, Sasuke. You are the last person I want to
see my face." On the day when Shunkin's bandages are removed,
Sasuke blinds himself with a needle. After that Shunkin and Sasuke live on in blissful darkness.

"Like two consecrated Buddha images" could be the last
phrase of this synopsis, or "like two happy ghosts." Indeed,
they had been ghosts from the very first. Shunkin and Sasuke are
almost set apart from the rest of the world. They are even curiously consecrated; they are "saints" in a way, despite Shunkin's
inhuman cruelty and Sasuke's servility. They are lonely figures.
They must, we are made to feel, be souls exiled from the ghostly
world who reside in the human world for a brief period. If Shunkin is the concealed sun goddess, Sasuke may be the moon god,
but the sun must deny their sexual partnership as long as she
stays on the earth and mingles with human beings. The sun is so
bright that it cannot see anything, so Shunkin is blind. The moon
is nothing without the sun; his is an existence to see, not to be
seen. Shunkin, like Juno, bears children, four in all, but refuses
to mother them, exiles them, as it were, into the nether world.
She is an unrequited Juno; she is safe from her son's revenge only
because her feminine fertility somehow seems to render her im-
mune to it.

It is often misleading, of course, to read too much mythology
into Tanizaki's work, as into any Japanese work. Tanizaki is not
an over-intellectualized writer who composes a piece according to
design from mythology. Instead, his work clearly has a "ghost

structure." The fact that darkness is their element seals Shunkin's and Sasuke's obscure identities. There is no development of the story through interaction among characters and between them and the social environment, as there is in most European novels. Shunkin and Sasuke are lonely figures, much like those we see in Western Romantic poetry, but they are far from romantic, or at least their romantic aspirations are mostly concealed from the reader by the method of narration, which, except for Sasuke's last, great leap into perpetual blessedness, puts all stress on physical matters. The narrator recalls the words of an old woman who, when young, served as a maid in their house. According to this woman, Shunkin never washed her hands, even after going to the toilet; she had Sasuke wash her. He also bathed her, and they both enjoyed the physical sensation as his fingers moved caressingly over her body,

> by which time Shunkin would already be out of the tub, and wearing her light bathgown and hood. Meanwhile everything had been done by Sasuke. How would he have gone about it? He must have touched her as sensitively as Shunkin caressed the trunks of the old plum trees —certainly it was no easy task for him. . . . But Sasuke and Shunkin seemed to enjoy the very difficulties, expressing their unspoken love in this way. I suppose we cannot imagine how much pleasure the two sightless lovers took in the world revealed to them by their sense of touch.*

The extraordinary development of the fine arts in Japan has much to do with the "ghost" climate of the Japanese mind, which shows a predilection for such unspiritual matters as clothes, food, earthenware, and so on, rather than for metaphysical quibblings. Enclosed in physical sensations, separated from the communal aspirations that are the foundation of a well-knit society, the artist cannot but dream of making himself into, to borrow Keats's phrase, "a thing of beauty" that is "a joy forever." Even after death, he cannot hope, except for a fortunate moment of Zen inspiration, for ascension to Heaven to join the logic of the universe.

The artist's aspiration toward beauty brings us to the importance of the idea of *bakeru* in interpreting Japanese literature.

* Translated by Jōji Mori.

The verb *bakeru* means "to transform oneself into some other form." The noun form of the word, *obake* or *bakemono,* means "ghost." Of course, as is the case with Western tales, *bakeru* often means to assume an ugly form, but it may mean to become a beautiful thing. To my mind, the latter notion of *bakeru* is more important to an understanding of the meaning or status of "beauty" as the objective or idea to be realized in Japanese literature. Japanese ghosts, denied a metaphysical salvation, aspire to transform themselves into beautiful things, and beautiful objects in Japanese literature may be interpreted as the product of such transformation, that is, beauty is the aesthetic transformation of ghosts. Of course, this hypothesis cannot be proved, but I believe it is valid because it provides us with a perspective on the whole literary scene as well as on individual pieces of literature. We can thereby understand the outstanding characters of literature and trace cultural history with a degree of consistency. The idea of *bakeru* provides, I believe, a clue to aid us in developing a unified picture of Japanese literature if not a clue to its very nature. Thus, by suspecting the existence of Japanese ghosts behind the cherry blossoms of Heian Jingū,* which the heroines of *Sasameyuki* (*The Makioka Sisters*) prize as the most beautiful in the whole of Kyoto, we can see in this undoubtedly beautiful work a larger significance than some critics have accorded it.

The Makioka sisters are lovers of things—cherry blossoms, clothes, *tai†*—and so are Shunkin and Sasuke. Having no social or metaphysical aspirations, and fired with an extraordinary love of things, the souls of the Japanese had no choice but to become ghosts, and then beautiful things themselves. Tanizaki's *Shunkin-shō* is but another example of a good story that turns out to be a ghost story. This tendency seems irresistible. Tanizaki tried to write *Shunkin-shō* as objectively as possible. The narrator, like an astute detective, tries to unravel the mystery of the unbelievable lovers, suggesting different explanations, comparing them, and more often than not leaving the judgment to the reader, but the more he tries to unravel the mystery in a scientific manner, the more enigmatic it becomes.

---

* A well-known Shinto shrine in Kyoto.—ED.

† A kind of fish, much celebrated and appreciated as a delicacy.—ED.

Fragile Sensibilities

The mainstream of Japanese literature from 1917 through 1948 was a procession of grave-faced *shishōsetsu* writers devoted to a fantastic idolatry of "honesty." This worship of honesty has been considered by writers and critics alike to be the basic element in Japanese literature, and for a very good reason. The idea of a mask, or a *persona,* of concealing one's real self behind a social façade, has never characterized Japanese thought. Even Yukio Mishima, who introduced this idea in his thought and work, had to "confess" about his mask (*The Confessions of a Mask,* 1949). To the Japanese reader, a work must always be transparent. He looks behind the work to understand what kind of a man the author is. In such a literary climate, the *shishōsetsu* as a literary form has always been a fort into which writers could retire whenever they felt they had little to write about or when it was dangerous to write about certain topics because of severe military censorship (as in the 1930's). *Shishōsetsu* also offered, unbeknownst to their authors, an abode for Japanese ghosts, because the honesty or truth expressed is that of the ghost in the writers, in the sense that it leads the work into disorderly spontaneity, revealing the writers' innermost, fragile sensibilities. The heroes of *shishōsetsu* works are mostly ugly and devoid of any sweetness of character, but they can dream of becoming beautiful by transforming themselves into, say, white flowers blooming in the dark.

Tanizaki was one of few writers who succeeded in giving objective forms to his dark obsessions, but he did this in a most humiliating, demoralizing way, by presenting himself as having masochistic tendencies. In so doing, he resembled the *shishōsetsu* writers who had made it a point to bare their personal shame before the public. But does the exploration of fragile sensibilities necessarily lead to the moral demand to humiliate oneself? The *shishōsetsu* writers were too much moralists in the sense that, dazzled by the precept of honesty, they had adopted it as the primary artistic value, not recognizing that it alone does not make literature any more than one robin makes spring. Thus, it is not surprising that some *shishōsetsu* writers began to probe into the fragile sensibilities of the Japanese ghosts whom they represented. This new group wrote from their own experiences, as *shishōsetsu* writers had, and even when they began to learn to write fiction they did not stray far from the proper domain of *shishōsetsu*. Their heroes were mostly solitary figures, vaguely reflecting on their obscure anxieties.

> . . . there I see materialization of your original *shishōsetsu*. In the dead of the night, you will be transformed into a slip of a flower. And you will hear the swift flowing sound of the nutritive fluid going up and down the pipe in the stem. Your heavy bud slowly breaks its cups and petal after petal rips itself from the cohesiveness that sticks them together. You will hear the painful cry given forth by the solemn work of opening. The silence that reigns over your world is not the silence of death but hushed words uttered at the critical moment of delivery, words busy, hot, full of intensity. Those who do not know this pain of yours do not tell anything about your art.

This excerpt is from "A Letter to Tatsuo Hori" (1946) by Kiyoshi Jinzai, a critic, novelist, and translator. Tatsuo Hori, one of this new group, which was called *Shin-kankaku-ha* (School of New Sensibility), and one of Japan's most Westernized writers, died six years after this "letter," but his major works had already been written before World War II. Jinzai's letter constitutes a critical commentary on most of Hori's work and is no doubt one of the most informative analyses ever made of it. I have quoted the letter because, despite Hori's Westernism, the letter contains, as key ideas, some metaphors I have used above. This is all the more interesting and significant, it seems to me, because Jinzai seems to share the prevalent opinion that Hori was a writer modeled on the Western pattern. There are some grounds for this view. It is rather easy to discover in his works the traces of such European writers as Raimond Radiguet, Marcel Proust, François Mauriac, and Rainer Maria Rilke. Moreover, the scenes where his stories develop are somewhat Western. One of his favorite places is Karuizawa, a mountain resort first opened by European missionaries who sought to escape the hot, humid summer of the lowlands. Japanese regard it as their most "modern" summer resort. Attractive villas, mountain cottages, and a pretty girl friend who is dying of tuberculosis may be the Japanese equivalent for popular Western novels with a similar setting. However, Tatsuo Hori assimilated only those features of European literature that corresponded to his own sensibilities. In the brilliant analysis of Hori's works quoted above, notice the words, "transform," "this pain of yours." Do they not reveal clearly, if unwittingly, something of the ghost quality of Japanese literature? In Hori's work, there is a persistent admiration for white flowers, especially those that bloom on trees. The plant-flower relationship is obvious and lineal, but the tree with its hard, brown bark and sturdy twigs hardly suggests white, supple, velvety petals. They are phantoms into which the spirit of the tree has been transformed.

Hori's vision is revealed in works such as *Kaze Tachinu* (*The Wind Arose*, 1936), where the spirit of Setsuko, the hero's betrothed who dies in a mountain sanatorium, becomes one with the white flowers, the spirits of the trees or of the snow. After her death, the hero leads a lonely life in a cottage in a mountain village. The seasons pass: Flowers shed their white petals, and snow begins to fall. One night, far down in the valley, he mistakes the light around him for the light of his cottage, but he finds that the light comes from the snow. He realizes, then, that he is surrounded by a light of which he had not been aware but which illumines his life. If this were the light from God, we would have a Catholic novel, but the light comes from Setsuko, who is hauntingly present in nature, in white flowers, in the snow. His solitary life is not "solitary"; she has always been with him.

> Dear Setsuko, I have not once thought that I am leading this solitary life for your sake. I cannot but feel that I am doing as I please, just for my own sake. But do I think that way because I am so familiar with the abundance of your precious love? Have you been permitting yourself to love me so much that I lapse into such a thought, while for your part asking nothing from me?*

This is probably one of the most touching confessions of love in all of Japanese literature. It is even Platonic, but the hero is like the ancient Japanese who looked in the woodland behind his village for the departed soul of his dear wife. The hero does not lead a solitary life in order to practice civil disobedience. He lives a continuation of a half-ghostly life with a girl dying of tuberculosis, the kind of life that "begins at the point people believe to be the end of life." It was a life, we could say, on which

* Translated by Jōji Mori.

death half encroached. And it was a death that nature sheltered in its bosom. In the fifth century, an emperor's consort sang of her yearning for her husband who had gone to hide in nature:

> My Lord has departed
> And the time has grown long.
> Shall I search the mountains,
> Going forth to meet you,
> Or wait for you here?*

The enhancement of feelings of love for someone who has died is a universal phenomenon. However, there are differences between the West and Japan in the nature of these feelings. In his monologue in the graveyard scene, Prince Hamlet only emphasizes the futility of the death of Ophelia whom he had deeply loved. Hemingway's *A Farewell to Arms* is a heartrending love story, but nature is regarded as something of a trapper of love, which is essentially human and belongs to the world of the hero and heroine. The nearest thing to the love expressed in *Kaze Tachinu* is perhaps the love between Jérome and Alisa in *Strait Is the Gate* by André Gide, but Gide's characters are both alive, and both expect to live.

Nevertheless, there is a large area of common ground in Japanese and Occidental literature. But what matters is: Where does this common area lie and from what direction do writers approach it? The area lies along the borderline between the land of death and the land of life. Western literature approaches it from life, while Japanese literature approaches it from death, from the ghost country where men are lone souls who are separated from one another but hope to attain union by transforming themselves into part of the natural world, such as the flora.

If the author of *Kaze Tachinu* lived in the world of trees and flowers, then Kawabata, the author of *Yukiguni* (*Snow Country*, 1937), another member of the *Shin-kankaku-ha*, was a member of the animal world. To say that a ghost is an inhabitant of the fauna rather than of the flora is to say that he is more jealous of his magical powers. Indeed, Kawabata's works are not attenuated ghost stories; they are framed neither in hard reality (as in the documentation of *Shunkin-shō*) nor in psychology (as in Hori's

* Sung by Iwano-hime, the queen-consort of Emperor Nintoku. Translated by Jōji Mori.

Kaze Tachinu) to disarm people who only believe in scientific facts or dramatic necessity. His are aggressive ghost stories; they do not suffer the real world to remain real. They work, so to speak, like chemicals or enzymes, eroding, dissolving, and finally dissipating the core of what we call reality until it becomes transparent and begins to send forth an internal phosphorescent light. We may even say that none of the characters in Kawabata's works is a human being. His heroes have no contours that separate one person from another, as human beings usually have. They have no moral sense in the usual understanding of the word. A father develops a physical relationship with his son's wife with no twinge of guilt in *Yamano Oto* (*The Sound of the Mountain*, 1953). The characters strangely lack a sense of good and evil and have no ear for any commandments. They are confident they will be absolved from any immoral conduct by the one almighty word, *kanashimi* (sorrow). There are several famous passages in which Kawabata refers to *kanashimi*: "After the war ended in defeat, I found no way but to go back to the *kanashimi* of the old Japan";[7] "From now on, I shall sing only about the *kanashimi* of Japan, the beauty of Japan";[8] and "it is only that I have been sorrowing over the Japanese in my own *kanashimi*."[9]

There is something ambiguous about the word *kanashimi*. One may often wonder what Kawabata meant by it. The idea that sorrow is essential in the perception of beauty may show the influence of Edgar Allen Poe. The concept also reaffirms the universal feeling that the good, old, and beautiful Japan is dying with the invasion of Western civilization. However, there is more to the term than a sentimental expression of an ambiguous *angst;* it is more relevant and useful if we relate it to what I have defined as the ghost sensibility. Immoral or amoral acts are pardonable because of the actor's deep *kanashimi*. Chanting the word is like a magical incantation. "*Kanashimi!*" and you are free from your sins. *Kanashimi* is also like a soft, buoyant air cushion; it absorbs the impact of human cruelty. The real world, with its many moral and social liabilities, is separated from the world of Kawa-

---

7 "Aishu," a short essay (1947).
8 Author's comments to Vol. I of *Complete Works of Kawabata Yasunari* (Tokyo: Shinchō-sha, 1948).
9 *Ibid.*

bata's characters by this strangely absorbent *kanashimi*. His characters are freer from social responsibilities than we are, but we know his ghosts are not totally free; they are rigidly bound by an aesthetic code. Even Western ghosts lose their rights if they do not return to their nether abode by daybreak. "I have been the wind and water, too," writes Kawabata in his *Literary Autobiography* (1934), "as the wind comes and the water flows away. I have always wanted to lose myself, but there has been something I cannot lose." These words of Kawabata seem to come from the abyss.

When viewed from the standpoint of novels or of the theory of literature, Kawabata's works cannot but appear as glaring specimens of bad literature. How have such defective efforts come to be prized so highly? His works have neither round characterization nor unity in variety through dramatic necessity, to say nothing of any revelation about what it is in society that supports the actions of his characters. To the last page, we are left uncertain about what kind of a man Shimamura, the hero of *Yukiguni*, is. Nor do we understand Komako, the heroine, or Yōko, the third part in the triangle. Everything is communicated to us through the impressions of Shimamura, who seems to us to have nothing but sensory organs: no heart that precipitates the crystallization of love as Stendhal described it; no mind to reflect on familial or social responsibilities. He is just a trembling nervous system plus a sex organ. He can recall Komako only by his finger; in no other way does his memory retain her. But curiously, because he is a ghost, he is not bound by the fetters of animality. We are informed in detail about the process by which Komako becomes more and more attached to the hero, the process of her deepening *kanashimi* (*kanashimi* because it is an altogether unfruitful love). Because this love is totally unfruitful, the hero and heroine are completely absolved from sin. Here Kawabata's heritage from the *shishōsetsu* writers' morality becomes visible: Thou shalt not be rewarded by anything. Yet even this detail, which is the only reality the novel has, is communicated through the hero's sense organs. He completely lacks the quality of a reporter or interpreter, just as a butterfly hovering over the sea cannot describe it to us. As Naoya Shiga's heroes favored the word *fuyukai* (disagreeable), Kawabata's hero repeats the word *torō* (fruitless). (In *Yuki-*

guni, the word occurs twelve times.) Shimamura is of no mind to accept Komako's love and "burn out in the gale of flame" as Daisuke did in Sōseki's *Sorekara.* To Shimamura, her love is fruitless. It is as ephemeral as the images on the train window described in the first few pages of *Yukiguni.* As they had passed, so must it pass. The train window, which permitted the hero to see two worlds at the same time—the evening views of the countryside outside and the reflection of the scene inside the car—is most symbolic of Kawabata's fictional viewpoint. He never sees things directly, only through a window that also serves as a mirror. The window-mirror merges the human world and the nonhuman world, and its criterion for selection is beauty. To Kawabata, the world is twilight; nothing has clear contours, for all is blurred by dusk. He picks up only what glimmer, twinkle, or glitter is discernible from among the shadowy images in the glass, leaving everything else in the crepuscular chaos. So, when two twinkling lights, one in the inside, human world, the other in the outside, flowing, natural world, meet and burn together for a moment, the author and the hero cannot but tremble with joy at the consummation of beauty:

> The girl's face seemed to be out in the flow of the evening mountains. It was then that a light [out in the mountains] shone in that face. The reflection in the mirror was not strong enough to blot out the light outside, nor was the light strong enough to dim the reflection. The light moved across the face, though not to light it up. It was distant, cold light. As it sent its small ray through the pupil of the girl's eye, as the eye and the light were superimposed one on the other, the eye became a weirdly beautiful bit of phosphorescence on the sea of evening mountains.[10]

A children's version of *Yukiguni* might well be called "The Story of a Ghost Who Visited the Snow Country and Its Spirit." There we are told about a love, but it is a love between the wind and the flowing water. They just graze, passing each other; they never mingle. They are strangely forbidden to consummate true, human love.

Another hero to whom human love is forbidden in Kawabata's works is Kikuji in *Sembazuru (A Thousand Cranes,* 1952). Kikuji

[10] Yasunari Kawabata, *Snow Country,* trans. by Edward Seidensticker (Tokyo and Rutland, Vt.: Charles E. Tuttle, 1957), p. 10.

is never able to enter into conversation with Miss Inamura, who, with her refined manner and her *furoshiki** of a thousand cranes, looks as if she could give him ideal human love. The two are introduced to each other at a tea party given for them by Chikako Kurimoto, a former mistress of Kikuji's dead father. Kikuji hates Chikako, who seems to make it a point to meddle in his life. She has a big, ugly blemish on her chest. At the tea ceremony, however, Kikuji meets a second mistress of his father, Mrs. Ōta, and her daughter, Fumiko. That very day, as if spellbound, Kikuji enters a physical relationship with Mrs. Ōta. Later, after Mrs. Ōta has killed herself, he even embraces Fumiko. He does so in the presence of a *Karatsu* teacup and a *Shino* teacup,† the former a memento of his father and the latter of her mother. Though inordinately irrational, the story somehow conveys the idea that Miss Inamura and the thousand cranes that hover around her are but the benign version of Chikako and the macula on her breast. Chikako, a professional devotee of the tea ceremony, is a guardian of the house of ghosts, and Kikuji, whose father was perhaps a king in the world of the tea ceremony, is a prince who has abdicated his throne by becoming a white-collar worker and a daily commuter between Kamakura and Tokyo. Nevertheless, the former prince has by no means succeeded in cutting his ties with the past. A member of a ghost family, Kikuji had to give up his desire to return to the human world. Moreover, he found his identity and a way of self-realization in living on and acting as one of the elite of the ghostly world.

Postwar Ghosts

When World War II ended in 1945 with Japan's unconditional surrender, it seemed that a new day was dawning for the people of the islands, with a chance for democracy and freedom of speech. The new constitution renounced war as a means of solving international problems. Democratization seemed to appear in every phase of life, public and private.

In literary creation, however, there was no radical change; "the

* A square of printed cloth used to tie up and carry packages. The thousand cranes in this print are a symbol of life and good fortune.—ED.

† The *Karatsu* teacup is large and used only by men, while the *Shino* teacup is small and feminine.—ED.

ghost condition" persists. Japanese literature has shown a remarkable continuity in retaining those features that distinguish
it as Japanese. What looked like change was enrichment; revision
was preparation for movement to a new phase, where the literature's intrinsic character would again reveal itself. To think that
the call of democracy or equality can expel irrational beings from
the house of literature is as naïve as to believe that cockroaches
cannot live in modern air-conditioned buildings. The truth is
that both forms of life thrive in the better climate of modern surroundings. Hence, as social, political, and legal institutions become more "modernized" and "democratized," the antimodern
"ghost-impulse" in Japanese literature becomes more salient. If
there has been a change, it is perhaps that writers have been more
and more stimulated by social demands to depict the contemporary social scene. Simple honesty and the narrowness of the world
they choose to write about are no longer the criteria of quality in
pure literature. Even this change of scene, however, has not given
rise to any fundamental change in writers' attitudes or feelings.
Their characters are still lone creatures who roam about gloomily
and aimlessly, although the landscape is contemporary. The theory of "alienation," promulgated by contemporary theorists like
Marcuse, who reinterpreted Marx to make his thought more relevant today, is curiously resonant with the theory of lonely
ghosts. So here we have another ironical, if not paradoxical,
situation in modern Japanese literature: The idea of literature as
literature of alienation has lured the timid pure-literature writers
into writing about the social scene from their favorite lair, the
small, honest world of *shishōsetsu*. Until this idea appeared, these
writers felt that there was something impure or dishonest about
venturing out of their small world, but the new idea of alienation offers them the possibility of remaining a ghost even in society. It has taught them that society is not necessarily a well-knit
community where everyone speaks up, influences, and is influenced by other members of the community, yet has enough independence to guard his identity and his inalienable rights as a citizen. It has taught them that society can be a form of chaos where
cooperation is impossible, where anxiety hovers in the air, and
frustration is a frequent occurrence. They are beginning to see
that there is no reason to maintain a taboo on writing about a

character in society, because even in society he can keep his eerie identity as a ghost. Thus, in portraying man's sense of alienation, contemporary Japanese literature is perhaps one of the most modern literatures in the world. Indeed, Japanese literature has never been so up to date as it is today; it is even ahead of the times, drawing its inspiration, however unconsciously, from the unfailing ghost classics, the *nō* play.

The decade after World War II saw two trends of writing emerge. One was contained in work by the writers informally called the "intellectual outlaws." The other was promoted by the work of those whose objective was to record their war experiences as realistically and, in most cases, as critically as possible. Among the first group were Osamu Dazai and Ango Sakaguchi. They are descendents of the *shishōsetsu* school in their hatred of hypocrisy above all and in their willingness to talk publicly about the ugly sides of their personalities. In creating their fictional world, they did not depend upon any political theory like Marxism. Of this group, Dazai was the standard-bearer, though the term is somewhat incongruous for those who accepted no external authority. Dazai was a sort of "hypocrite," giving the reader the pleasure of seeing him as a clown who shows his sincerity by depicting his life as a fiasco. According to Dazai, his failure had been predestined from the day of his birth, and it was this predestination that alienated him from people. He was born in a rich landlord family in northern Japan, his father a wealthy member of the House of Peers. He was a bourgeois, not a proletarian, and he called himself "one select" giving the word as sarcastic an overtone as he could. Because he was "select," he was inferior in the sense that he could not share the aspirations of the common people. Like Tolstoy, he could have deceived himself by pretending that he had ties to the common people, and he did to a certain extent, writing resistance stories while a student at one of the national elite high schools at Hirosaki. He even committed himself to the underground Communist movement as a liaison man in the street, very dangerous work in prewar Japan. Yet he knew only too well that even this incriminating activity was no more than what he liked to call *sābisu* (service). He wrote more than once that his life consisted of "service," by which he meant doing things he was not predisposed to do in order to be allowed to live as a member of the human world. As a child, he had learned to smile even when he did not feel like smiling.

Ningen Shikkaku (No Longer Human, 1948), one of Dazai's representative works, begins by introducing three photographic pictures of the hero, which, as he describes them, have no touch of humanity about them; they are cold, artificially posed, and idiotic. He defines the hero, whom we have every reason to know is the author, as a clown who, in a literal translation of the author's words, is "trying one last wooing of humanity with his desperate service." Applying the interpretation I have suggested, he is a ghost who, ashamed of being a ghost, is desperately asking for membership in the human race, although he knows he cannot have it. His only hope is to pretend to have it, making every effort to look human by participating in such "most human" activities as illegal, underground Communist work or living with a girl, unmarried, and even attempting a murder-suicide with her because of a love in which he did not believe.

Dazai's first work, *Gyofuku-ki (The Setting Sun*, 1939), is about a girl who lived with her father, a woodcutter, deep in the mountains beyond a waterfall that Dazai had visited one summer. Her father loved her, even treasured her, but one snowy winter's night when drunk with sake, he had raped her. With great sorrow in her heart, the daughter had thrown herself into the pool at the base of the waterfall and become a fish. There she was, still swimming, with her white scales glistening when the author visited. It is a symbolic story of frustration and decline which elegantly and sorrowfully suggests the beauty of ruin. It is a story of alienation from creation, of inability to give birth. The girl, living deep in the mountains, had yearned for city life and people but could only return to the mountain waterfall, condemned to stay there eternally in her sterile beauty.

Later works of Dazai are more sanguinely human. Kazuko, the heroine of *Shayō (The Slanting Sun*, 1947), is the daughter of a peer who had lost his title with the end of the war. She throws away her scruples and becomes pregnant by a man who already has a family but whom she cannot forget after just one kiss. But the raciness of the story, if such it is, comes not from the rather banal plot of an illicit love, or from the portrayal of a "new woman" who had the courage to sever herself from the feudalistic ways that often still poisoned Japanese life, but from the weird-ness of her background, where all forces converge to bring ruin and depravity. (Her younger brother commits suicide the morn-ing she is with her lover.) Her adventure is almost an attempted escape from the castle of the ghosts. Her castle is now rundown, and its ghosts are dying of exhaustion born of malnutrition. How can a ghost survive? It can go down to the human world, select a human mate, and conceive a child.

To present a fair picture of postwar Japanese literature, how-ever, a section should be devoted to the other group, those men whose objective was to record their war experiences as realisti-cally and critically as possible. This is a varied group of writers in terms of temperament and convictions. Some, like Shōhei Ōka, who wrote *Furyo-ki* (*How I Became a Prisoner of War*, 1952), in keeping with the tradition of *shishōsetsu*, had no social theory by which they judged their particular experiences and placed them in a larger, impersonal frame of reference. Ōka's only concern was his individual state of hunger, physical pain, fear, humilia-tion, and the like. Other writers, like Hiroshi Noma, the author of *Shinkū Chitai* (*The Vacuum Zone*, 1952), were deeply in-volved in the sociopolitical situation, believing that such involve-ment was a necessary part of the human condition. After having been abandoned by his platoon in the Philippines, Ōka had wandered, exhausted, among the hills and fields, often fainting from the fever of malaria or from hunger and thirst. Yet, as he did so, he thought to himself, "I hated the military authorities who had dragged me into such a hopeless war, but it seemed to me that I had no right to protest against them for the fate I was suffering then insofar as I had made no attempt at my own risk to stop them." Soda, one of the heroes of *Shinkū Chitai*, thought he had such a right and asked himself: "Where can one find the way to destroy this artificial, abstract society in which I am now forced to live?" Each of these men succeeded, in his own way, in em-bodying his agonizing wartime experiences in a convincing artis-tic form. They were writing not as ghosts, but as human beings with all the features of humanity—an interest in personal rela-tionships, a love of clear thinking, and a hatred for nightmares, whether psychological or circumstantial. These authors were working on the same literary terrain as their Western counterparts. With their emergence, Japanese literature seemed to have escaped at last from its preliterary age, the ancient abode of exasperatingly equivocal, unreasonable ghosts, and to have struck the true vein of literature in which all stories are told in terms of humanity and society is seen as the reflection of humanity. Yet, ironically, each of these realistic or humanistic works is the story of a crisis that ordinary life would never produce. The heroes of these stories, confronting their physical and psychological limitations, never dare to bring forth man's finer aspirations from the darker region of the mind. Their situation is so mad or extreme in itself that the hero is outghosted by it. Just as a patch of light pink looks almost white against a lurid red, so does a ghost in an extreme situation begin to look like a very reasonable human being. Japanese writers, with rare exceptions, have successfully introduced characters who convey a real sense of humanity, a willingness to cooperate with others, and a freedom from ghostly impulses, only in such extreme situations. One such work is Toson Shimazaki's *Hakai* (*Broken Commandment,* 1906). In this novel, the hero, in order to live a fully human life, in the end ignores his father's deathbed desire that he never reveal that he is a *burakumin* (an outcaste).* Yet the novel also depicts an extreme situation; few people, fortunately, are untouchables. But the novel might also be considered a social version of a ghost story: The status of ghost is symbolized in the untouchability of the hero.

Other works, set in less extreme situations, have not attained similar fame as pure literature. Roka Tokutomi's *Omoide No Ki* (*My Memoirs*), a Dickensian novel about a boy's aspirations told with much humor, and Tatsuzō Ishikawa's many works with thoughtful, kindly heroes are well-written stories, but somehow they do not achieve the status of first-rate literature. In their fiction, society- or humanity-oriented Japanese writers have therefore instinctively favored the portrayal of an extreme situation; only there can they write from the same perspective as Western writers. In writing *Shinkū Chitai,* for example, Hiroshi Noma

---

* *Burakumin* is a euphemism for the technical term *eta,* which Westerners use (the Japanese almost never use it) to designate a substantial group of people (several hundred thousand) who have long been discriminated against in Japanese society. Originally the stigma resulted from occupational status associated with slaughtering animals.—ED.

found himself in an unusually fortunate situation for a Japanese writer. As a soldier, Noma experienced the intrigues that self-interest, vanity, and psychological strife render so common in army life and that cut across the army's rigid class distinctions. His position in the army made it possible for him to describe that social world much as Pierre Choderlos de Laclos's position in the society of his time had inspired him to write *Dangerous Relations*, or as Radiguet had been inspired to write *The Ball of the Comte d'Orgel*.

However, the circumstances that brought Japanese fiction close to Western fiction soon passed away, at least in the field of pure literature. Although they were still in love with extreme situations, society-oriented writers learned to introduce some aesthetic distance between themselves and their subjects in their works. Removed from the direct impact of harsh experience, the heroes resumed their old, ghostly weirdness.

Another important writer in the socialist group, Rinzō Shiina, has been groping for a new type of proletarian literature. His fiction incorporates a dash of Dostoevsky, Sartre, and the Christian idea of love in works of social concern and does so with fair success. His books, though they are the products of social consciousness, are very different from Dos Passos's trilogy *U.S.A.* or Sholokhov's *And Quiet Flows the Don*. They are not sketches of people at work in society; they are the stories of men almost crushed with the "weight of life," in Shiina's favorite words. His characters are proletarian ghosts. Shiina himself had received no education above junior high school and had been a common worker until he became an organizer of a Communist cell and was arrested for that in 1931. He began to write later, after abandoning the official Communist line. Immersed in a nihilistic mood after his departure from the Party, but still having much sympathy for the oppressed laborer, he was absorbed by, and deeply anxious about, the heaviness of life. In *Omoki Nagare No Nakani* (*In the Midst of the Heavy Stream*, 1947) he writes: "I am nothing but a heap of ruin.* I feel myself heavy with the consciousness that I have been a ruin from the very start." In *Shinya No Sakamori* (*The Midnight Banquet*, 1947), he hopes for

* The term *haikyo* means, literally, "ruin" and carries a nuance that cannot be conveyed adequately in English.—ED.

"liberation from all that is heavy" through transformation (*ba-keru*) into some strange beautiful thing and not through endurance. To my mind, Shiina's works are limited in that he only seeks liberation in the images of common, ordinary things that are eternally secure, like the tangy smell of *miso* soup boiling over the pot in the cool morning air. It is all too clear, however, that he is no less a ghost in spite of his lack of the means of liberation. Yasuta Sunagawa, the hero of *Eien Naru Joshō* (*The Eternal Preface*, 1948), is described by the author as a gawky "janitor of a graveyard." The sense of heaviness, felt not only in outside objects but also in oneself, is one of the key terms in the vocabulary of ghostdom.

Many works, in addition to Shiina's, which are intrinsically ghost tales, are more often than not misinterpreted as resistance or left-wing literature by social- or humanist-oriented critics. *Kuroi Ame* (*Black Rain*, 1966) is a glaring example. The author, Masuji Ibuse, had been known as a humorous writer who sought to convey the bizarre quality of a comical situation. (His first work was the story of a giant salamander who cried, "What a mistake!" on finding he had outgrown the hole leading out of the rock cavity in which he had been living.) But the later work, *Kuroi Ame,* gave the critics some evidence that a conscientious writer is also concerned about human misery. It may be so, and I hope it is, but a dose of sublime principle, or an acceptable sociological thesis, does not necessarily promise a writer literary renown.

Kuroi Ame is a detailed record of the hellish week suffered by the people of Hiroshima who had been scorched by the atomic bomb. It was written a quarter of a century after the disaster, but it is still a shocking, detailed record of the holocaust. *Kuroi Ame* has every qualification to be one of the greatest works of antiwar literature ever written, the more so because its tone is far from that of propaganda literature. (No one in it cries: "Out with American Imperialists!") I believe it can be best recommended to readers in the Pentagon or the Kremlin. Yet, I still believe that, along with its merit as antiwar literature, it is the "ghost impulse" that gives the work its quality *as literature*. It seems to me that the author even relishes depicting skin dangling from flesh that is swollen and watery with lymph and limbless people still twitching as they die. Wounded people, most naked with their clothes burned off, aimlessly, dazedly roaming among the ruins are a picture of hell crowded with ghosts suffering the agony of eternal damnation. Some may say the author's fascination with the event is a mere coincidence; he really wants to end *all* war, because war will produce the hell he depicts. I am in perfect agreement with him about ending war, but as a literary critic I am afraid I must deny that this is the basic point his book makes. The cue lies in the author's attitude toward two men who early in the book go fishing every day and later launch a fish-farming operation in a pond they have purchased. They cannot hold regular jobs because they suffer from leukemia caused by the atomic bomb in Hiroshima, but they have to earn their livelihood some way. Also, in the last scene of the book, the hero gazes at hundreds of thousands of baby eels in a little stream at the back of a factory yard while other people listen to the radio as Emperor Hirohito announces the end of the war. With the sheen of their backs, fresh from the sea, these elvers leave an unfading impression on the reader of the strangeness of their presence. Why should there be such irrelevant absurdity at one of the most important moments in the history of Japan, which till then had never lost a war? Was this not the moment for the hero to stand up and denounce the military who had ventured on such a foolish war or the American bombers that had unleashed the atom? Even if we hold that the author abstained from injecting a propagandistic note because it would only have blunted the edge of the story, is it not still pointless to stand and admire baby eels in a backyard stream at such a moment? I believe we should rather consider the story again in terms of the basic image of fish. Were the people, their skin watery with lymph, also fish? Did they change into eels, cooling their scorched skin in fresh, pure water on the day of the surrender of Japan? Or is it that the two ghosts, the men at the fishing farm, were cultivating the people who had changed into fish and selling them? I leave it to the reader to ponder these cues.

Now we are ready, I believe, for a discussion of the greatest names in contemporary Japanese literature, Yukio Mishima*

---

* This essay was written before Mishima's ritual suicide in November, 1970. —Ed.

and Kenzaburō Ōe, but in a sense I am afraid we may even be too ready for it, because any reader who has followed the details of my argument will instantly perceive why they are the ghostliest of Japanese ghosts, especially Mishima, whose works are the better known abroad. However, my worry stops there, for there is no typical ghost in Japanese ghostdom; each one has its own features, problems, and idiosyncratic weirdness with which to frighten us.

To say Mishima is a ghost and to say what kind of a ghost he is are quite different matters. Much evidence tells us that he is a ghost. First, Mishima is not adept at constructing works that reproduce an organic society in the sense the great European masters have been. However, Mishima likes to think of himself as a lyrical poet who sings for lonely souls. He selects for his heroes characters almost overwhelmed by complexes, which he helps them overcome by ritualistic processes accompanied by magical prayers. Second, the entire body of his work operates in terms of a strategy of beauty. In this sense, we may liken Mishima to Oscar Wilde, but, unlike the Irish aesthete, he has the unique propensity of a ghost: the desire for transformation into a beautiful thing. Mishima feels somewhat dissatisfied even after seeing beautiful things; his dream is to become one with them. His physical training through body-building and *kendō* (Japanese fencing) is dramatic evidence of this. By means of such techniques, he seeks to remake his body into a beautiful thing with resilient sinews and hot blood, so that his body will convey his thoughts. Thus, he is necessarily an admirer of Greek classical beauty as it is expressed in sculptures of beautiful youths. Necessarily again, he is an admirer of the classical form of literature as it is expressed in the four-act symmetry of the tragedy. Third, despite all his idolatry of beauty and Greek sculpture and drama, Mishima is no Platonist. He does not believe in intellectual beauty as Shelley sang of it in his "Hymn to Intellectual Beauty," nor does he believe in an "invisible hand," or some unseen scheme of the universe that eventually accords with Reason. He is certainly not apocalyptical in the usual sense of the word. But it is true that, because of his unparalleled imagination and intensity of aspiration for beauty, Mishima looks, more often than not, like a Platonist. However, let us call his Platonism "pseudo-Platonism"

to distinguish it from the real thing. The key to a better understanding of the structure of Mishima's fictional world, I believe,
lies in understanding his pseudo-Platonism.

It seems to me that the source of inspiration that guides Mishima's creative efforts, perhaps unconsciously, contains a great
paradox: Like those ghosts-to-be, the ancient Japanese, he sees
continuity between life and death, but death *is* an unmistakable
phenomenon of life, and science tells us that it ends life in every
possible sense of the word. Consequently, irony is at the core of
Mishima's creative efforts; he writes from the assumption that the
pattern of life he presents is only feasible insofar as the continuity between life and death can be realized on this side of death,
that is, within the life that ends in death. This paradoxical situation may look rather normal in the Western tradition: Christian literature is written as if man had an eternal soul. But this is
a mere surface resemblance. In Mishima's world, there is no problem of salvation and damnation or grace. Even with these problems unsolved, Mishima remains untroubled because he is a
ghost. He will keep his identity even after death, a sensate identity, as a part of sensate nature where logic, or logos, remains un-
revealed by the dead who have found another abode in trees or
flowers.

These points are not made just to have a consistent interpretation of the whole history of Japanese literature in terms of
Japanese ghosts; I propose them because I believe they help unravel the mystery of the two kinds of beauty that the hero of *Kin-
kaku-ji* (*The Golden Pavilion*, 1956) attributes to the pavilion.
For the protagonist, immortal beauty exists on this earth only as
a memory (this is why I call Mishima pseudo-Platonic). As long
as death exists, beauty must be mortal for it to appear and appeal
to mortal man as beauty. Beauty really worthy of the name must
dissolve the moment it is born. "The Golden Pavilion must be
burned down," mutters the hero of *The Golden Pavilion* after
"the courage to face whatever one has reached, an almost immoral courage," is born in him. Man can enjoy both life and
beauty, because beauty is a momentary thing, but when beauty
finds a secure abode in, say, the Golden Pavilion and thrusts its
eternal existence upon the lives of the people who admire it,
there arises a great dilemma: How can man enjoy life if beauty

is not mortal? So the hero, whose peculiar psychological burden
of stuttering impedes normal self-expression, is motivated by
three urges, conscious or subconscious, in burning down the Pavilion. The first is to expunge the venomous influence of an eter-
nalized beauty and recover the possibility of living the life from
which he has been alienated. The image of the Pavilion has always intruded and restrained him from partaking of his few
opportunities to taste the honey of sex. The second is to awaken
beauty and restore its perfection by rendering it mortal. The
hero had found the Pavilion more congenial in wartime when
bombing constantly threatened to destroy it by fire. The third is
to execute an act of beauty. The burning of the Pavilion is an act
of self-expression that can never be repeated; its uniqueness in
time realizes the very nature of beauty.

In Mishima's world, the beauty of one-timeness seems to be
firmly linked with the beauty of physical love. In *The Golden
Pavilion,* the hero's heart throbs at the loveliness of a white shirt
slung across a school fence. The shirt belonged to a student in the
Naval Engineering School, an earlier graduate of the junior high
school that the hero had attended. The white, sweet-smelling
shirt, damp with the sweat of a young body, and the dirt on the
shining gold embroidered case beside it look like the "relics of
a young, legendary hero." Even a bee comes to rest on the shirt,
mistaking its whiteness for that of a flower.

The white torso of the Young Saint Sebastian, as Mishima per-
ceives it in Titian's painting (*The Confessions of a Mask,* 1949),
is another example of the link Mishima sees between the momentary nature of beauty and erotic love. The martyrdom of the
young saint by hanging from a tree only emphasizes the physical
beauty of his white skin. The first orgasm of the hero of *The
Confessions* occurs in the presence of the picture of this torso.

In Mishima's work, eroticism and violence are also entwined.
Physical love always tempts violence; it is erotic because it may
be raped by violence at any time. A person who embodies sexual
beauty must be killed. Saint Sebastian was to be martyred not
for his faith but for his physical beauty. A young prince who is
killed because his body is as noble as his mind and a young out-
law whose white loincloth turns red with blood when the villain
stabs him in the abdomen are Mishima's inevitable images, and

they seem to have an irresistible allure for him. Etsuke in *Ai No Kawaki* (*Thirst for Love*, 1950) kills a young gardener with a hoe because she loves him. Through a hole in the closet, Noboru, the boy hero in *Gogo No Eikō* (*The Afternoon Wake*, 1963) witnesses a sailor consummating the act of love with his (Noboru's) mother. He kills the sailor to preserve the beauty of that moment and to protect from the mediocrity of common love the "sacred" relationship between the mother and the sailor. The boy cries silently to himself: "This is the one thing no one is permitted to break. If this is broken, the world will end. To hold back such a thing from happening, I would do anything, however cruel it might be."

Mishima's works may be defined as the songs of innocence and experience of a young ghost, an aesthetic version of D. H. Lawrence's *Sons and Lovers*. The problem dealt with throughout his works is: How can a ghost wean itself from the memory of beauty and find a way to exist in this world full of abstract, unaesthetic ideas? Of course, he cannot forget beauty, and one means to solve the problem is to harmonize beauty and life by making beauty momentary. However, Mishima's alienation from life is too thorough; he feels that the equation of beauty, violence, and sex, often expressed in homosexuality, is the only thing that supports the lonely ghost's existence, exiled as he is in human society. The ghost cannot participate in the human experience that contributes to the making of a family or a community; he is visited and harassed by the memories of beauty. But as long as he lives, he can see death as people see it. To behave as if the acceptance of death (perhaps by *harakiri*) takes extraordinary courage is his only way to make himself believe that he is not a ghost. But this make-believe is all for naught, as his obsession with death testifies.

If there is any reason to regard Kenzaburō Ōe as a better writer than Mishima, and not a few people think he is, it is perhaps because the structure of Ōe's works offers more substance than that of Mishima's for reflection on the situation of modern man. Paradoxical though it may sound, however, Ōe does not describe society any better or more fully than Mishima. In fact, he does not so much describe it as leave it untouched. Yet his very assumption that a clear, tangible society exists outside of his world of fiction makes his work more "real" than Mishima's. In Mishima's writing, the outlines of society are blurred, even dissolved, by his intensive rhetoric. This tends to obscure rather than illuminate the identity of things in society. Ōe's work, on the other hand, like a highway bypass, leaves a large area where ordinary citizens can build their city. The effect is to make it possible for each world, imaginary and real, to become a commentary on the other. His work is so constructed that normal society, which he never introduces except as an occasional intruding element, serves as the wall of his fictional world, which is a nightmare. In other words, the outside human world, which may at any moment surge in and inundate the inside world, supports the work's reality. The homosexual party in *Seiteki Ningen (The Sexual Man,* 1963), is a ghost situation; and the village boy who runs away from it crying, "I've seen it! I've seen it!" represents the unfavorable façade of the world outside of Ōe's fiction. The medical report at the end of *Kojinteki Na Taiken (A Personal Matter,* 1964), which makes it clear that the hero, Bird, had been mistaken in believing that his newborn baby was a deformed monstrosity from which he must escape at whatever social or moral cost, represents a benign façade of the society that Ōe permits to continue outside of the ghost situation depicted in the work. Curiously enough, Ōe rather respects the ordinary world whose firm dependable walls give a sense of security to both the work and the reader. For example, Bird never thinks ill of his wife's father, whose social status as a professor of literature makes him the most respectable man among the characters. Some readers think that Ōe's attitude toward the real world limits him as a writer, but it saves his work from becoming pretentious bravado.

Ōe's world is also the world of young ghosts or of ghosts who have never succeeded in growing up psychologically. It seems appropriate that Bird's favorite book should be *My Life in the Bush of Ghosts* by the African writer Amos Tutuola. Young, immature ghosts have enough breeding to respect certain aspects of society even if they cannot support it as a whole; but insofar as they are ghosts they have their own way of life, which often makes them antisocial. They are lone souls; they have inordinate, dark pride and an excessive sensitivity to humiliation. Sex is their only real passion and the only drive that presents any idea of concreteness to their minds. Thus, when they are balked in having normal sexual relations, they think nothing of becoming homosexual. They are inhabitants of the fauna; they are all small, wounded animals, like birds or rabbits, with timid hearts. Being weak, they are too busy with their minute worries to discover the idea of cooperation. If there is any possibility of cooperation, it is the kind seen among animals assaulted by their enemies. Any social participation beyond this mutual defense is not prompted by their spontaneous will to make some contribution but by a blind desire to escape from a worse situation. Thus, the boy hero of *Seventeen* (which has the same title in both Japanese and English; 1961), in order to escape the tormenting sense of solitude, the harassing sense that people's stares accuse him of his secret habit of onanism, joins a right-wing gang whose aggressive, violent activities seek to exterminate "the Reds" and reinstate the Emperor's Way.* *Seventeen* is a ghastly description of the process by which a would-be victim turns into an assailant as his introverted eroticism turns into an extroverted one. He becomes as sexually aggressive as he had wanted. In a Turkish bath, which occasionally takes the place of the brothel Japanese law now prohibits, he has himself masturbated by a young woman who silently behaves like an obedient slave girl. At the climax, his semen spatters over her face. It is then that he feels for the first time a strange but strong power to conquer rise up within him.

Seventeen is a criticism of life in that it points out that sex can be a danger to society, especially when it is connected with a will for political power. This criticism has much poignancy, because, according to Ōe, and I think we must agree with him, sexual feelings represent the weaker side of humanity, in that they are accompanied by the fear of antagonism and the desire to subjugate oneself to another. In ordinary situations, sexual feelings want peace, but so much so that they may serve even a dangerous will. It is also true, however, that outside of the world of *Seventeen*, there still exists the ordinary, sane world which the hero avoids. If this outside world did not exist, his internal world would lose the wall that supports it, because one of his subcon-

* In Japanese, Kōdō, a purposely vague term used by right-wing fanatics to describe the system they support.—ED.

scious but strong wishes is to be punished by society. If there is no possibility of punishment, his obsession cannot be realized (and indeed many of Ōe's works end with punishment). So it may be said that Ōe's works present Japanese ghosts in confinement.

Ōe's first work, *Shisha No Ogori (The Pride of the Dead,* 1957), strangely corroborates the saying that a writer's first work is his best. In this novel, the hero is not so much the narrator who comes to work in the morgue of a medical school to get money for school fees as the dead who lie there. The dead seem more alive than the narrator and others who work in the morgue. Their confinement in the morgue is an extreme situation which permits the Japanese writer, like his Western counterpart, to bring relationships between characters into dramatic tension. By depicting such situations, Ōe often achieves dramatic tension, but the tension never extends beyond the small world in which his characters are confined. And because of the weakness inherent in the characters, his crisis is also a ridiculous one, unlike the genuinely extreme situations of wartime that have been described by such senior writers as Shōhei Ōka and Hiroshi Noma.

In portraying the ridiculous, however, Ōe is one of the few Japanese writers with a gift as a humorist. In this sense, he has something in common with the British humorist Evelyn Waugh, even though the two writers differ strongly in other ways. For one thing, the humor in Ōe's work is the sweeter for his perception that the human heart has the gentleness and sensitivity of a small animal. English culture sets a high value on humor, and Waugh is in this tradition. Paradoxically, even though Waugh, like Ōe, wrote a great deal about mad situations, English tradition worked against him, because he could rely upon the English language which is, I believe, the most humorous language in the world. Ōe has no such tradition; he cannot depend upon the Japanese language; I do not even think he was trying to be humorous. His awkward situation as a ghost and his timid heart have made his humor unwitting. He is all seriousness, even trying to outgrow his ghostly madness. As Ōe writes in a collection of his essays, *Warera No Kyōki O Ikinobiru Michi O Oshieyo (Tell Me the Way to Outgrow Our Madness,* 1969), the title of which he took from a verse phrase of W. H. Auden:

It seems to me that "our madness" is the madness of the times which assaults us from outside; or it seems to me that the madness emerged from within myself, my own existence from which I cannot escape because it is rooted in my past with a bondage of blood. And the meaning of "outgrow our madness" sometimes comes to me as "outgrow it by conspiring with it"; at other times as "outgrow it into our right mind resisting it."*

But Ōe will never succeed in "outgrowing" his madness "into his right mind." If he does, he will lose his identity as a ghost.

Ghosts fill the pages of Japanese literature as they fill the lives of Japan's writers. The ghostly principle I have proposed provides a clue to the nature of the creative impulse in the literature of Japan.

* Translated by Jōji Mori.

4

Lying in Wait

Shintarō Ishihara

The land was darker than the sky. Dusk had already settled over the ground where we landed. The light saffron of the setting sun that we had seen in the distance during our twenty-minute flight was no longer visible.

As soon as the two helicopters had spit out the fifteen men that made up our unit, they rose and left as though even that brief repose were unendurable. It made me apprehensive to watch them chopping homeward through the evening sky, like birds returning late to their nest. With that, daylight died.

I looked around me but there was nothing much to be seen. A cleared field that until recently must have been cultivated stretched before me, dotted with waist-high brush thickets; beyond the field was a luxuriant mangrove forest.

Master Sergeant Grey, our squad leader, stood nearby, nodding his head as he checked the field map. Having gotten his bearings, he said, "Let's go!" and started walking straight ahead.

We crossed a narrow creek, advanced about 200 meters beyond it, and came out into a small clearing in the middle of which stood a clump of four or five rubber trees. In one corner of the clearing a trench had been dug and banked with sandbags. The

Translated by Noah S. Brannen and William I. Elliott.

sergeant nodded when he saw it, took another look at the map, and beckoned to the men as if to say, "On the double!" We cut across the clearing and walked along the edge of the mangrove forest. The sergeant looked over his shoulder at a Negro corporal who was lugging a light machine gun: "The platoon that dug that trench was all killed." With that, he let us know what we were in for. And what the job was that had to be done.

About three weeks before, thirty-four men had been sent out to patrol this area. They were ambushed and slaughtered, all but one. When their buddies came along to recover the bodies they found they were three bodies short. Maybe those three had been taken prisoner. Every last weapon was gone. Later a report came in that the ambush squad had turned up again in the same area. Twice in the last ten days the Americans had sent search platoons, but so far they hadn't been able to find anything. The photographer and I belonged to the third effort.

We had moved about a kilometer from where the helicopters had dropped us, trotting along as though we were chasing the dusk that with every second was deepening over the land. The sergeant suddenly stopped us and had us retreat about 100 meters. There in the darkness, where we had to imagine rather than really see a sparse forest ahead and behind, he deployed the squad. They seemed to know exactly what to do. They fanned out, grappling in the dark, and lay down.

Sergeant Grey wrapped his long arms around the photographer and me and pushed us along until he sat us down beside a knee-high shrub. Then he shoved us down on our bellies as though teaching a dog tricks. Before leaving on this mission, we had had to promise to obey his every word, and so I lay there docilely on the wet dirt and grass, which were faintly alive with some foul-smelling herb. The sergeant settled down 2 meters to one side of us, and on the other the corporal, Winston, crouched with his machine gun. No sooner had the men dug in than darkness came full, and every trace of them vanished. My luminous watch said 7:15. "We made it on time," the sergeant whispered. That was the last word, the last human voice we heard that evening. Silence and darkness came together.

7:30. The darkness had become impenetrable. I squirmed and tried to see something. There were no stars. Above me, about my chest, at my side, before my eyes, and even at the tip of my nose there was only darkness. Why was everything so black? I contemplated the obvious: There was no light, no brightness anywhere. Yet, more than that, the darkness that closed in on us had somehow a quality different from the everyday darkness we were used to. It was not just that objects were now no longer visible but that darkness came as a positive presence, replacing those objects. Nor was the silence merely stillness—not the simple absence of sound but in place of sound a positive silence, heavier than a stone, pressing against us. Silence was darkness and darkness was silence. I felt I had entered a completely unknown world, a world I had never even heard of. It robbed me of my five senses and of orientation in time and space. I felt as though I were in a dream, and while I still understood thus-and-so, I wasn't really sure that I did.

In this stony silence and darkness, I pricked up my ears and strained my eyes, trying unsuccessfully to reaffirm myself. It was so unsettling that I started swallowing my spit and tried to depend on that act for reaffirmation. But with only that going for me, I was no better off than I would have been in a dream. Nothing came out when I tried to whisper. It wasn't the same as trying to cry out in a dream and being unable to—no, something inside me was actively suppressing even my whisper, and only that "something" could explain where I had come, and why.

Suddenly I remembered. Still glued to the ground, I slightly raised that body that was being swallowed up in the hard and heavy silence and darkness, and pivoted to the left. It was an awful effort and I could barely move an inch at a time. I felt my chest scraping the dirt. *That* was not darkness. That was certainly the dirt. Twisting, still prone, I reached out my left hand and was shocked: What I was looking for surely had to be there—somewhere—it couldn't *not* be there! Like a pilot navigating at night without a gyrocompass, my hand lacked direction. My frightened hand frantically scratched about the ground and finally grabbed what it was looking for: The photographer was there.

Anxiety poured out of his fingers. He was at once startled and reassured. Or was the anxiety not his at all? He gripped my hand. The two hands fumbled, awkwardly trying to seize each other without being sure of how to do so. But grasp at last they did.

Can a simple handclasp carry so much human strength and assurance, and so clearly help a man find himself? It can and does. He was there and I was here. That was a fact.

I thought to myself that I had long ago experienced much the same feeling. Was it my mother's hand I looked for and found when I was a child? No, I had a feeling it was long before that that I had tried to confirm my existence. Now the two hands, not knowing when to let go, remained clasped on the ground. At length, the photographer turned a little to face me and released my hand. Yet, even though our hands had come apart, I could make out his movements. And then for the first time I could feel the presence not only of the photographer but of the others around me, Winston on one side and the sergeant on the other, by the path. At last, this special world I had entered loosened up a bit and grew larger.

Shortly after 9:00 it started raining. The rain seemed to rend the heavy silence and darkness it was falling through. It struck my neck and back and upturned face. The force and weight and coolness beating against me also brought sound, brought proof that this place was a world that could expand and be penetrated by my five senses. I tried looking left and right. I wanted to see the rain and so once more confirm the fact that I was here.

And then I saw it as well as heard it, for lightning tore itself out of that unseasonal downpour. The stony darkness was ripped apart by purple cracking, and in that split second the shape of rain was visible. Over my head crashed a rent and falling darkness. For once and that once only I did what I wasn't supposed to do. I half-raised my head to take a look at the world I was in. The purple crack and flash yielded up the presence of Winston and the sergeant and the photographer, and the others, lying as solid and immovable as rocks in the brush. That momentary spectacle reminded me of a fable about some people who were placed under a spell and were eternally petrified. I looked hard, but everything I saw was frozen. In one of the flashes, I saw my own shadow. I wondered why the sight of it made me feel like someone out of the past. I felt like a rock assaulted by rain.

In the unreality of color and time under that eerie light, I again wanted to reaffirm something about my selfhood, but the flash and thunder left no room for reflection. When the sky fell silent, the rain and darkness that produced the violent light and noise seemed to return much heavier than before.

The darkness pelted us with rain. When it let up I had the feeling that something had passed over me. Not a raincloud. During that brief time, as I lay perfectly still, I felt that a segment of my own fate had passed over, and not necessarily a lucky segment either. Nor was I very optimistic about the immediate future. Because after the rain came the cold and, with the cold, fear. I kept recalling the last drop of rain that fell on my back. It landed on my right shoulder, which was slightly raised as I lay propped on my elbows. The rain had stopped. But for some reason the sensation of that very last drop remained for a long time. After the rain, I realized that something new was in store for us. It was a kind of premonition that, compared with what had happened so far, the things to come would be pure hell.

During the rain, I had worn a vinyl poncho zipped tight around me, although even before the rain I was soaking wet from crawling over ground that stood in water, and lying in it. Every time I raised my head and peered more *at* the darkness than into it, the poncho bit into my neck. And every time it did, I recalled a closeup shot I'd once seen of a Marine. A battle had been fought in the rain, and across his helmet he had scrawled, "War is hell." That was a good photo. I wondered how I myself must look right now. If the photographer by my side were to have snapped me, what sort of expression would I be wearing? It would doubtless be a face that even I wouldn't recognize.

When the rain had stopped, I looked up and still couldn't find a single star. The darkness had become, if possible, yet heavier and thicker. And, incredibly, time had hardly passed at all. But in such a monolithic darkness even the passage of time was distorted. As my body grew colder, the heavy darkness filled me with fear, and again I felt myself absolutely isolated in an alien world. I badly wanted to get up and look around just to see what was hidden in this oppressive darkness and silence.

My body was flush with the ground and I was wet and cold. I was lying a little unevenly, though, because one side had lost most of its feeling. I knew that eventually the walls of the internal organs would go numb and then, one by one, the organs themselves, and then the stomach and the lower half of my body. My circulation seemed virtually nil. And I was unable to pound or massage the numb parts.

The air was getting colder and so was my body; darkness and silence compounded one another. The relative assurance I had had when we set out on this mission finally turned to uncertainty and then to acute fear. What would happen, I thought, if things continued in this way? I was irritated at myself for knowing the answer—and knowing, at that, absolutely nothing. I was angry. And then I became resigned to my predicament and alone with a fear I couldn't get rid of. And yet I didn't really know what I was afraid of. Cold and fear didn't cancel each other out—they became one thing.

I am convinced that a man dying of burns clearly feels the coldness of fear. Certainly my every experience so far, when it came to a crisis, was a cold one. The times when I had cheated death at sea were always in wintry storms. In a yacht race six years before, a cold front blew through the Sagami Straits, shredding the water as though with razor blades, and killing eleven of my mates. I was so cold on the watch, straining my eyes for all they were worth, that I was tempted to dive into the warm December water that sprayed my face.

Again, near Oshima Island, off Ryūo Point, a freezing wind once threatened to dash our ships against a breakwater. And some terribly cold gusts, blowing off Mount Amagi near Inubashiri Island off Itō, cut our jib to shreds and tried to run us onto the reefs.

It was also cold in Alaska. One time, in a sort of primeval forest near Sitka, I ran smack up against a brown bear that loomed up 3 meters in front of me like some nearsighted monster. That was the first time anything like that had ever happened to me. I was frozen in my tracks; I could feel paralysis overtaking my legs. My toes seemed frostbitten. We were crossing a channel that flowed out of an icy river when that monster appeared.

And once when we went walrus-hunting with some Eskimos, with the camp far behind us, the ice field suddenly started heaving and crumbling, the cracking chasing us like a herd of elephants and we running with kayaks on our backs. The fury of that ice was cold.

Yes, fear is always cold. Still, somehow the present fear was different. My body had begun to freeze, but I was scared in a way I had never been before. Or maybe I began to panic only because some known ingredient of fear was missing from this experience. Fear I had known before, but it had never driven me to panic. Something was different. And only by deliberately reminding myself of the strange difference was I able to endure my fear. What was I afraid of? Was it the proximity of the enemy? Awareness of what was about to happen? No. Neither of those. I had heard all about those things and was prepared for them. Can a man really be afraid of something he is prepared for? Compared to winter storms at sea and brown bears and heaving ice fields and even death itself, the enemy and the things that would happen when they appeared would really be frightening—horribly frightening. But if it were the enemy and slaughter that I feared, I would have been able to control my fear, because I was prepared for such things; in fact, I had come out anticipating just that. Then was the thing I feared merely this stony silence and darkness? Why was the darkness fearful? Whatever the explanation, I was scared to death.

Then I recalled a weapon I had seen at the infantry training center back at the base. As though to summon evidence in order to explain my fear, I recalled it clearly. It was a simple gadget that the enemy commonly used when they were engaged in an ambush. Knives they had, and clubs, and even bows and arrows. But I remembered something else—could almost feel another weapon I had held in my hands. It was an instrument of death fashioned out of two sticks and an attached length of piano wire. One of them would sneak up behind you out of the pitch black and in one swift motion wrap the wire around your neck and draw the sticks tight in opposite directions. I had tried wrapping it around my own neck. The wire seemed soft and pliant and felt different on my neck from ordinary wire. Ordinary wire was hard, like a mink's claws; this wire was as soft as fur. And with just the slightest pressure it would bite with almost a pleasant feeling into my neck. The instructor's assistant explained that if full force were applied it was quite a simple matter to cut clean through the neck and so behead your victim.

That was it! That was what my fear was all about. I had an image fixed in my mind of the enemy slipping up from behind, falling on me suddenly like rain in the dense blackness. And I was merely waiting, passively waiting for the attack. That was it! That was why I was so damned scared. The helpless waiting terrified me; the waiting—and the fact that I had no alternative. In the darkness, I had stopped breathing and was just waiting—only that and nothing more. Never before had I just waited. At other times, when some enemy had suddenly attacked, I had tried either to escape or to defend myself. But here, even though the battle had begun, I was reduced to mere watching.

To the attackers, I, a Japanese, was no less an enemy than the sergeant who crouched beside me in the darkness. I was his ally and thus their enemy. But actually that wasn't so. At the base, the photographer and I had refused the weapons that they offered us. They had their reasons, I'm sure, for offering them; in principle, though, I was just an observer of these operations. My status was one of noninvolvement. Yet, having come on this mission, shut in by darkness and waiting, I realized my mistake. They were right when they blinked at our refusal to carry weapons. No one in such a situation as we were in could be noninvolved. Enemy or ally, the killer or the killed—it had to be one or the other.

The enemy is about to appear, and here we are, waiting. And I am a part of the "we." They are coming after me too, coming at me from behind with the deadly piano wire in their hands, and the photographer and I, though in theory justifiably noninvolved, are without weapons. Was there any alternative to waiting? Always before I had been able to do something, whether it was running away or fighting it out. I had always been able to choose some form of resistance.

In the offing beyond Ryūo Point, after the cold front had passed, the wind and waves pushed us along and were still so turbulent that we were on the verge of running aground on a shoal close to shore. Then the wind quit altogether. I hoisted the sail again, stood the crew in the bow, and with a keel-length boat hook tried freeing the ship by pushing against the rock.

Even when a squall engulfed us during the race around Mikimoto Island, there amidst the reefs in the offing beyond Tsumeki Point, where current and tide swirled and scattered the phosphorescent sea creatures, we nevertheless rowed that twelve-ton ship with the oars from our lifeboat and even made use of the boat hook.

Something, no matter how desperate, could always be done. I

had always hit on some way to ward off and escape the object of my fears. Even if a particular way was known to be useless, the fear was broken by the simple act of doing something.

In the offing beyond Habu and again off Tsumeki Point, what if those fishing boats hadn't appeared like angels and cast us towlines? Even if we had gone aground, we wouldn't have been too scared.

And in the Alaskan forest, when I ran into that huge enemy of a brown bear that couldn't use language, I had a mountain knife ready at my hip. If the bear hadn't been nearsighted and had seen me, no doubt I would have lost but I would have tried my damnedest to do something with that knife.

But what if a man walks straight into terrific danger and can't do a blessed thing about it—then what? And on top of that, I had actually chosen to go on this mission!

The moment I regretted my decision to come along, my fear doubled. When I understood that I couldn't defend myself or save myself, and as a matter of fact could do nothing but wait and pray for that good luck that may or may not exist, fear seized my chest and I thought I was going to retch. "What in hell did I come to this godforsaken place for?" Like a fool, I kept asking myself the same question. I think that for the first time in my life I took a good look at my real self. Before setting out, I had probably assumed that I was a lucky guy. I'm not sure. Anyway, now I was angry at myself because I had no way of guaranteeing it. I was terrified.

The men had repeated the painfully obvious fact that the enemy was one hell of a crafty fighter. This fact now seemed to twine about me in the darkness and silence. In a way, I had a common sympathy both for the enemy that was coming and for those of us lying in wait, in spite of which I wished I had a pistol in hand. I wanted to kill that bastard who would pounce on me from behind with his wire. No matter what, at that moment the enemy who was coming was *my* enemy. That was a fact. Again I looked at my watch. Time seemed to stand still. It dragged. Only with considerable effort was I able to keep from yelling out. I squirmed again and tried to touch the photographer, and each time I was reassured of his presence I felt also the feeling of the condemned who watch each other ascend the execution platform. When I touched him, I could almost hear his whole body responding, stirring on the ground. When I touched his back, his response told me his thoughts as clearly as if they had been my own. He also was feeling the touch of the piano wire. In that moment, our fear was mutually canceled out, for each of us felt the fellowship of the condemned.

I wanted to get my feelings across to him, and so with my finger I wrote on his back, "afraid . . . afraid." His body nodded assent and his hand reached over to write the same word on my back: "afraid." At that, my world grew larger again. There was a moment of peace in knowing that this fearsome darkness was shared by another human being who had exactly the same feelings I did. I gathered strength and wrote on his back, "long . . . night." Each of us confirmed the immediate presence of the other fearful person, and it was only in this act of writing that we momentarily surmounted our fear. He replied, "long . . . long . . . neck . . . choked . . . by . . . piano . . . wire . . . afraid." And then, to let him know the thing I was really afraid of, with a fear I thought I alone might be bearing, I wrote out, "they . . . come . . . from . . . behind." He understood and stirred. I sensed that he was looking behind us. For a second or two, I relaxed and wondered whether I was a coward. A coward is one who, when there is something to do, does nothing. But what could the photographer and I possibly have done?

"Fool," he wrote. "I'm a fool."

"Why?"

"Can't take pictures."

He was right. It was pitch black, and here he had hauled along three cameras. I chuckled to myself. He was good-natured, slight of build. Somehow or other, I felt sorry for him.

It was only while we were writing that our predicament amused me. How wonderful it is to realize that one is not alone. After all, a man's feelings are for the sake of others.

Now his hand touched not my back but my shoulder, went along the nape of my neck and finally stopped before my face. The luminous dial on his wrist showed midnight. "Half," he wrote. The mission was half over. We both thought of the remaining half, and our fingers fell silent. Yet even in that silence I knew that another human was with me. Then again, I thought, so what? One or two of us—what's the difference? It wouldn't make any difference to the enemy. For a while, I thought about getting out of there. He and I might make it back to where the helicopters had landed, not far from the trench. One way or the other, it was equally risky. Anyway, it struck me that our chances of survival would be greater if we were moving instead of just lying helplessly on the ground.

Before long our "salvation" arrived from an entirely unexpected quarter. Where they came from is beyond me, but mosquitoes and ants found us before the enemy did. Our insect repellent had been washed away by the rain, and no sooner had the mosquitoes begun biting than the ants came crawling over the ground. They sneaked in around my sleeves and collar and began biting in earnest. Since noise was taboo, I couldn't slap at them, so I warded off the mosquitoes by waving my hand and, when they tried to light on my face, by screwing up my lips and blowing. I could do nothing about the ants save slowly rub my body. The stinging produced a slight sensation of warmth in a body that was cold, where any feeling still remained. I felt my dead flesh come to life again. The ants swarmed all over me, biting at will until I was just one big itch. I could distinctly follow all their inroads: Some moved from my side to the middle of my back and others from my right thigh in the direction of my stomach; one stopped on my right biceps and another was vigorously trying to get in through my sleeve opening. Those that tried to get in under my collar I could have brushed off. They got in because I stayed very still. At least, the ants let me forget for a while the predicament I was in. While they were crawling over my side, I didn't give much thought to the piano wire. And I thought that by the time they had worked over my entire body and had their fill it would at least be dawn. For some reason, though there was no connection, I believed that as long as the ants were at my flesh the enemy simply wouldn't appear. I gave myself over to those tiny ants, which I could feel, if not see, and at the same time I was afraid I was going to fall asleep.

How long was it? Hordes of ants were enjoying my body when suddenly the sergeant, whom I had completely forgotten, gently kicked my foot. Before I could respond, he had drawn alongside, turned, pressed his lips to my ear, and said, "They're here." He thrust his ultraviolet binoculars at me.

Even while I understood what he had said, I wasn't especially impressed one way or the other. I figured nothing could make matters any worse. The binoculars were heavy. I pressed them to my eyes with no idea where to look. The darkness in front of me floated spottily into view on a dim screen. It was a shade above total darkness. I couldn't get any sense of depth; whether I was looking at the thicket or forest or what, I couldn't tell. Now that my eyes had adjusted to the darkness, the view on the screen appeared not as the actual reality hiding out there but as something else. While looking through those binoculars, I recalled that the name "Starlight" was printed on them.

I turned them and looked, still ignorant of what I was supposed to see. And then at once I held them still because I distinctly saw something that wasn't simply the result of my own hands' movement. In that dim field of vision I knew I had seen something. Lacking the dimension of depth, what I saw was like a blurred shadow or something moving in a thick fog. It was upright and faintly wavering. At any rate, this was a figure and substance different from what I had seen so far in the silence and darkness. I lowered the binoculars and tried to hear something. Just as I was about to inch over and give the photographer a look, the sergeant took the binoculars back—as though he were swiping something, I thought, that had been entrusted to me.

"They've come," I wrote on the photographer's back. To myself, however, I said it must have been a mirage. Then, for the first time, I heard the sergeant swallowing his spit. That clarified the issue. Then the sound of feet came thundering out of the distant darkness. Marking time with my drumming pulse, I counted out the approaching steps one by one. Something was indeed coming toward us out of the darkness. In another moment, I would be able to see it clearly enough, and hear it, and even feel it. And now I was no longer just waiting. I was unafraid. I placed myself on the perilous boundary line between reality and dreaming—a dream I wanted to wake up from and couldn't. Once more I was disoriented.

On the other hand, although I had no idea how powerful the binoculars were, I tried to estimate the distance between me and the shadows I had just seen. In any case, the conclusion (foregone?) was at hand. My consciousness, as when waking from sleep, was divided into the two layers of numbness and seminumbness.

I felt myself floating and it made me mad, for I was neither enraptured nor drunk. At this point—I can't be sure—I may have drifted off into sleep.

My confusion exploded and shattered. "Fire!" A voice close to my ear yelled, and the darkness was obliterated. A flare fired by the sergeant exploded right between my eyes as with the swift parting of stage curtains, and the darkness gave way to upright figures steeped in the orange footlights of the blinding midday sun. At that point, my fear had no relation to the enemy. Instead, I was enraged at the immensity of the hard darkness that until then had hidden them.

Rifles were fired on all sides and after that another flare. In its light, I had a good look at the face of an old man in short pants, standing paralyzed as he cried out in anger, his hair in confusion. The old man screaming was reminiscent of the unreality of a movie run in slow motion. Of all of those who were pulling back, crawling away on their bellies, only that old man was yelling—without uttering a sound, like an actor who has forgotten his lines and stands there paralyzed. Yelling in that way, the old man was straining frantically to see me, his eyes out of focus.

I know what curse he yelled at me. He cursed the immensity of the hard darkness that until now had hidden us. No doubt. And in the next instant, like a film that jumps its track, he popped out of focus and disappeared. Why, I don't know, but when that happened, I laughed with a kind of brittle, brutal yell. I scooped up some dirt from under my chest and flung it his way, still laughing.

Someone was laughing in reply. It was Winston. In the midst of that horrendous rifle barrage, I saw him dragging his machine gun cartridge belt and heard him violently yelling and laughing.

Then another flare was fired, this one pure white. It exploded higher up than the others. The firing ceased. Under the sputtering, falling brightness I still trembled, but as the rifle fire died out I felt the rebirth of that awful silence. All I could hear, even after the silence came full on us again, was the huge voice of Winston, laughing through the confusion of a lot of screaming.

Darkness descended again and our squad withdrew to the vicinity of the trench. When we started walking, I had the impression that in the absence of light the darkness had acquired a shape of its own. We moved perforce cautiously, awkwardly, and now and then I stumbled into the men before and behind me. When that happened, I realized that for no justifiable reason you could believe in and trust your fellow human beings. Yet that realization, I confess, did not take into account those who had just been killed. While we walked along, I was brushing the ants off and crushing those that still infested my clothing.

We got to the trench and waited there for dawn. The rain fell once again briefly. Dawn, when it came, came extremely fast. Watching the sky whiten, I could at least say to myself that I had finally eliminated whatever it was I hadn't understood. No matter how hard I tried, though, my misgivings stuck with me and made any sense of satisfaction impossible. I guess I still regretted my decision to join the mission. Even now, I still don't have the slightest idea why I had joined it.

When it was light enough, we all returned to the fateful spot where we had lain in wait. Along the way I said to the sergeant, "There was an old man among them." He just inclined his head. He didn't remember.

Along the narrow trail running east and west, eight corpses were scattered. They were less than 10 meters away from where we had lain. Sergeant Grey alone had kept watch through "Starlight." He said they had converged all of a sudden right before our eyes from bypaths to the left and right.

The clouds broke up and the corpses were faintly reflected in the early sun. Tattered hunks of bodies lay strewn everywhere, the blood washed off by a squall. These corpses just seemed suddenly to have blossomed wildly on the ground like overambitious flowers out of season. I searched for the face of the old man whom I was sure I had seen, but, when the soldiers started turning over corpses and lining them up, he wasn't there. In the end, the corporal who had worked the grenade launcher came in, toting the head of a corpse of whom precious little else remained. Probably the corporal himself had done that one in. A right arm and the fragment of a left hand dangled precariously from the jacket he had been wearing.

"Just this much, but it's heavy, man," the corporal said. And holding it by a remarkably well-preserved jacket lapel, he held it up and placed it at the far end of the line-up. The old man was last to answer roll call. His face was supported by a scrawny shoulder and a skinny right arm. He was lying aslant the others, face up. Considering the surprise and suddenness of last night's fight, his expression was remarkably calm. In fact, none of those dead faces bore more than a mere trace of shock. The old man seemed calm, I suppose, mainly because his eyes and lips were very lightly shut. If I had to describe his expression, I would say it was resigned. His half-white hair had been washed clean by the rain. When compared to the whole wide explosion that went on around him, it may have been fairly easy for him to endure his own limited experience.

"Well, there was an old man in the bunch after all," the sergeant said, hunching his shoulders as he surveyed the lot. Odd, I thought, as I looked up and down the line, that I couldn't muster much interest. The photographer was busy snapping pictures, but I could see from his expression that it was an anticlimax. I felt the same way.

Then one of the men came in dragging a wounded guy who with his chest torn had managed to crawl off about 100 meters into the brush before he fell unconscious. I looked down on that motionless prisoner. Loss of blood had stopped him, though he was still breathing. "Good!" I thought, "Good!" If it hadn't been them it would damned sure have been us. And since that prisoner was obviously a goner anyway, the sergeant lined him up next to the remaining half of the old man and shot him through the head. Only a little blood trickled out. The prisoner was a corpse, his facial expression exactly the same as before. "Good! Thanks to them I managed to survive!"

What I was thinking about was not those dead guys lined up at my feet and not the other soldiers looking down at them. I was thinking about myself, an observer of both groups. I started thinking about my own fate but stopped just as quickly because I thought it was no good thinking about such things. Yet, somewhere down inside, I still was sorry that I had chosen to accompany this mission.

Sergeant Grey said, "Let's go!" The soldiers began shouldering their arms. Starting to move out, he turned to me where I still stood by the head of the old man. He winked at me as though beckoning. As we walked along side by side, he said, "Well, what ya think?"

After a moment I said, "Once is plenty."

5

Poems

THE BIG SHADOW
Tsutomu Fukuda

When it is fine,
A tall apartment building
That has recently raised its square height
Close by
Casts its big shadow
Upon my house and heart half of the day,
Calling back to my memory
The vast waste land of Texas
Where I watched the vermillion sun
Sinking cloudless thousands of miles away,
Not a single object obstructing my sight
As I gazed on its solemn, gorgeous fall.

Translated by James Kirkup

MY WATCH
Tsutomu Fukuda

My watch is tearing away
Every second of my life.

I repent of having done everything
To make it go faster while young.

Translated by James Kirkup

CYCLE OF THE MONTHS
Shuntarō Tanikawa

1

within her someone prepares a banquet   within her someone
carves an unknown son   within her someone is wounded

2

the palm of god
injured clumsily in the act of creation
   still finds it difficult to forget

3

"with such accurate regularity   florid funerals
occur within me   they are mourned in the color of
celebration   they continue, unwounded and unable
to die, to return to nothingness   my children who
are overly young . . . a ripe moon is falling   there
is no one to receive it   I am waiting   I am alone
squatting in a chilly place and waiting   for someone
to sow the moon   for someone to deprive me of this
rising tide   with a wound, lost to the memory of
all, within me that is outside the reach of healing"

. . . while alluring those who will to live toward the
shore   the tide flows full within her   there within her
lies a sea calling to the moon   and as the moon revolves
around   there lies within her an endless calendar . . .

Translated by Harold P. Wright

EARLY IN SPRING
Kiyoshi Akiyama

The beggars push aside
the snow in front of the crematorium.
They sit on straw mats in a sunny place
with their bundles and crutches
and gaze at the sky—it looks more like snow.
They're sunburned and runny-eyed
indifferent
to the cars that splash muddy slush.
The women have towels wrapped around their heads.
The beggars glance coolly at the passers-by
but call to the mourners
who are walking out of the gate
or carrying the bones away in taxis.
Then they rake up the thrown coppers.

Translated by Atsuhiro Sawai

WHITE CLOUD
Shinkichi Takahashi

with my arm
     I'll smash through that white cloud:
countless airplanes making a roar
will probably be flying out.

Translated by Harold P. Wright

STONES
Kyōzō Takagi

O, my twisted mind!

Stones, stepped on, are mute.
If I kept silent,
Could I also become a stone?

This wretched life: under the kitchen sink
We can see earthworms crawling.

Isn't there anyone who
Will toss me up into the sky
Like a stone?

Translated by Michio Nakano and James Kirkup

HAMMER THROW
Shirō Murano

Look!

In a world circumscribed by iron
A poor dynamo is panting momentarily

Set in a white circle.

Translated by James Kirkup and Shōzō Tokunaga

SUNLIGHT
Tsutomu Fukuda

Robbed gradually of sunlight
By the new houses built around,
I look for it
Whenever I can, and
Wherever I go,
Like a stray dog
Looking for something to eat.

Translated by James Kirkup and Shōzō Tokunaga

HANDS
Shuntarō Tanikawa

hands
they feel
hips of women
hands
they tease
hair of boys

hands
they squeeze
hammers
hands of friends
hands
they seize
daggers
hemlines of lives

hands
they strike
a father's face
hands
they stroke
inkslabs

hands
they create
they destroy
they take
hands
they give
they hold
hands
they release
they open
hands
they close
hands

ceaselessly do something
ceaselessly do nothing

hands
they indicate in vain
thickly luxuriantly
        like leaves in summer

hands
wide open they wither

Translated by Harold P. Wright

PART TWO

Society—Politics—Economics

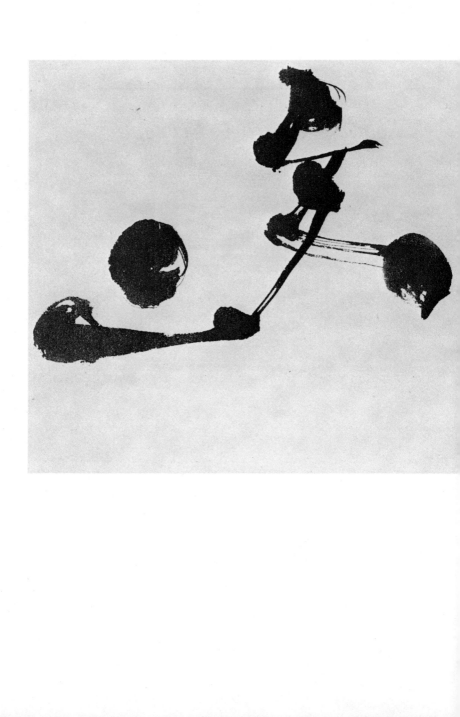

6

Basic Notions in Japanese Social Relations

Toshinao Yoneyama

Introduction

When an American says "hi" to other Americans, he expects a response to this form of greeting. If others do not respond properly, he will be upset. This sort of expectation in everyday conversation, or in communication in general, requires a sense of sharing the same system of values and attitudes expressible by commonly shared words. When we are in cross-cultural situations, we cannot and usually do not expect the same response from others as we do from people in the same culture, and therefore we tend to tolerate their strange manners, because we know we do not share the same notions about communication with each other. The word "hi" will work throughout the United States today, but it may not work the same way even in other English-speaking communities. In the case of the Japanese language, the sound "hi" (*hai*) does not mean "hello"; it means "yes." Thus, to express a greeting in Japan, we would use the word *yaa* or *yā dōmo*.

We all recognize this kind of difference in language, and when we get more deeply into a foreign language we realize that, besides the differences in the sounds, words, and grammar of language, there are differences in the frame of reference for each expression. For instance, the word "spring" in English is one of four nouns used for the four seasons. These four seasons are the frame of reference for the word "spring." Within this frame of reference, we can associate the word with many other related matters. Such a frame of reference, that is, a set of words related to each other, is what I shall call a *basic notion*. Considered in this way, for instance, the basic notion of the four seasons cannot be assumed in a country or region where there are only two seasons, dry and rainy. In such countries, there are usually more subtle differentiations of words than simply the idea of two seasons to describe seasonal succession. In monsoon Asia, the set of words or the basic notion related to seasonal succession is different from that in English, and it would be misleading to attempt to use the basic notion of the four seasons among such people. It is clear that we have to find out what the basic notions are in each cultural context, for they vary from one culture to another. In order to describe the peculiar character of a particular culture, it is important to know its basic notions. I once used this hypothesis of basic notions in order to describe the ways of thinking of a culture in East Africa. I tried to describe basic notions of the culture in relation to some objectively measurable aspects of life such as 24 hours, 365 days, or the life span of an individual. This study eventually led me to outline both the sacred and the secular worlds of the people, making a diagram of related notions they held. In the same way, it should be possible to describe Japanese culture by examining the basic notions held by the people of Japan.

This article attempts to describe some basic notions commonly shared by Japanese today in their social relations. We will limit our discussion to aspects of social relations in Japan, although other elements in the culture are, of course, just as important as social relations. Japanese culture is complex and can be divided into many subcultures by various indices such as regions, social strata, occupations, or even sexual and generational differences. The basic notions in each subculture will show distinctive features. Furthermore, each individual has basic notions that are to a certain extent unique, since his experience and background are different from those of others. However, we will not deal with these subcultural differences or with individual variations but will restrict ourselves to the most common basic notions of the national culture in contemporary Japan. I have selected words from standard sources and have sometimes given more than one English equivalent so as to show the range of meanings of the notion.

I and Others: The Importance of Nakama

One dimension of social relations can be described by starting from an ego or "I" center of reference. In a Japanese cultural context, *jibun* and *tanin,* or self and others, are important categories. This dichotomy is important in other cultural contexts as well, but the meaning is different in the case of Japanese culture. The word *jibun* literally means one's own share, and although it usually refers to oneself as an individual, it may also include others than oneself if they are closely related. The word *tanin* means other people and also can be a single person or many people who do not belong to one's own group.

This dichotomy between I and others leads to two different phases of social relations: One is the relationship between "we" and "they," and another is the relationship between the private and the public. Both aspects are significant in social relations in everyday life in Japan.

The first aspect, the "we" and "they," is classified by a pair of notions: *mikata* and *teki,* or allies and enemies. In any explicit conflicting or competitive situation, this pair of notions is commonly used. However, in a less hostile situation, the more general pair of notions—*nakama* and *tanin,* or one's fellows and others— is used. In either case, the pairs of notions create a social boundary between two groups as viewed from the "I" perspective. When one is with one's allies or fellows, one can be more informal, more relaxed, while when one is with enemies or people other than those of one's group, one needs to be more cautious in behavior. In ordinary life, even when there is no explicit conflict, the idea of "one's own group" and "others" seems important. In fact, the *nakama* (one's own group) might be the most crucial notion in all Japanese social relations.

The world where a Japanese usually lives is the world of *nakama* and includes his relatives, friends, peer groups, and other fellows with whom he can identify closely for some reason. With them, he can feel at home, and yet, at the same time, there is always the potential danger of being excluded from one's *nakama* if one behaves wrongly toward them in some way. *Nakama-hazure,* or "being shunned by one's fellows," will sometimes endanger one's social or economic life or might even mean losing one's reason for existence.

One of the most stable *nakama* is one's family and relatives. This group is often referred to by another term, *miuchi,* or relatives. A proverb, "blood is thicker than water," is often quoted when social relations are discussed. The term *miuchi* can be applied to peers other than one's real relatives as a kind of metaphor. However, we should not exaggerate this metaphoric notion as some scholars of Japanese culture do. The term "familism" or "familistic organization" is very often used as a core concept in Japanese social relations, but this concept is often misleading. It is true that the mutual dependency of a family or relatives is important, but conflicts do sometimes start within the real kinship group. One's brother may not necessarily be a *mikata* in a particular conflict situation. Another proverb, "strangers begin with brothers," is used to explain such situations. In reality, both *nakama* and *miuchi* vary in membership according to the situation, although the importance of blood ties is generally accepted.

It may be worthwhile to add a word on the Japanese family here. The structure of the family in Japanese culture is actually a bilateral system, giving almost equal weight to the social relations on both the father's and the mother's side. In this sense, the Japanese kinship system is by nature closer to European than to Chinese patterns where clan relationships have developed to a considerable extent. In recent times government pressure forced family relationships into a more patriarchal, lineal pattern, but since World War II the older norm in Japanese society has re-emerged.

If we realize that the emphasis on familism is given less weight in Japanese society, the notion of *nakama* becomes a more distinctive idea in social relations in Japan. A list of words that appeared under the heading of *nakama* in a standard Japanese-English dictionary will show the wide variation in the meaning of the term when translated into English. It includes: a company, a party, a set, a circle, a coterie, a companion, a fellow, a mate, a comrade, a colleague, a fellow worker, an associate, a fellow trader or a fellow craftsman, a partner, a gang, a confederate, and an accomplice. It also gives the following examples of usages: *nomi-nakama,* a boon companion; *asobi-nakama,* a playmate; *daraku-nakama,* a fellow profligate; *gakkō-nakama,* schoolmates; *bunshi-nakama,* the literary fraternity, and so on. From the list in English, we can see that the notion of *nakama* is not directly related to the ties formed on the basis of blood, nor of territoriality, although it can include close ties formed by such groupings as a family or kindred or a community. Also, it is clear that some *nakama* last for one's lifetime, and others are ephemeral. *Nakama* are important in establishing one's life pattern; some form one's basic peer groups throughout life.

Nakama can exist within larger social groupings in such places as the formal organization of big companies or public administrative units. When the *nakama* is organized for political or economic reasons within a larger organization, it is called *batsu* or *habatsu,* that is, clique. There are many cliques within a larger organization representing common interests. The bases for *batsu* are varied; there are *gakubatsu,* or academic cliques; *kei-batsu,* or matrimonial nepotism; *kyōtō-batsu,* or parochialism; *mon-batsu,* or lineage influence, and so forth. The *gunbatsu,* a military faction as a political pressure group, and the *zaibatsu,* a financial combine, are well known as prime causes of World War II, and they were very much a part of this notion of clique or one type of *nakama.*

The term *nakama* was used during the Tokugawa Period for some privileged groups of merchants or guilds, such as traders associations, which were called *kabu-nakama* (literally stockholding fellows) in Edo (Tokyo) and Osaka at the end of the seventeenth century. However, this kind of grouping can be traced back to groups of some new religious sects or of market-keepers found everywhere in Japan even prior to the thirteenth century. They were, again, based neither on kinship ties nor on community ties, but were formed for a specific function or purpose. Thus, the *nakama* is by its nature an association. We should recognize that there has been the notion of *nakama,* together with the notions of blood or territorial ties, throughout Japanese history and that this neither-kin-nor-territorial relationship has played an important function in Japanese social relations for a long time.

It is an established tradition among scholars of Japanese studies that Japanese society is firmly based on "familistic" notions. The relationship between *oya* and *ko,* or parents and children, has been considered one of the most important and can be extended to other social relations beyond the family. In fact, the ultranationalists during World War II emphasized this relationship as a central concept of the state. Using the analogy that the emperor is the father and the subjects are all children, they attempted to interpret the nation as if it were a family. The study of *oyabun-kobun* (boss-protégé), the patriarchal nature of Japanese social organization, the familistic nature of large business enterprises, and so forth all presuppose "familism," or blood-tie analogy, to be the core of Japanese culture. It is, of course, important, but if we try to interpret Japanese social relations entirely through this term it is rather difficult to explain how Japan could form a modern national administrative system and a modern military machine so rapidly with relatively few instances of real nepotism or localism. The whole process of technological and industrial modernization in the last hundred years cannot be explained by a "familistic" theory of Japanese social relations. The notion of *nakama* will explain more clearly the factors of change in Japan.

Reciprocal Obligations: Giri and On

The most extensive analysis of Japanese notions in social relations can be found in *The Chrysanthemum and the Sword* by Ruth Benedict. One of her major efforts in that book is to focus upon the reciprocal system of obligations among Japanese in terms of *on* and *giri,* or, according to her definitions, "a category of incurred obligations" and "a category of total obligations." She devotes three chapters of the book to discussion of these two notions and related concepts in the Japanese social context. Her presentation of a "Semantic Table of Japanese Obligations and Their Reciprocals" seems to be an excellent summary of her assessment of reciprocity in Japanese social relations.

However, there are several things we must note in her description of the idea of reciprocity in Japan. First, both terms, *on* and *giri,* are not originally Japanese but are derived from phonetic renderings of Chinese characters. The term *on* is from the Chinese *en,* and the term *giri* is from the Chinese *i-li,* and we can find examples of their use in the ancient Chinese classics. They do not appear in an ordinary Japanese context, especially on the popular level, until the Tokugawa Period (1603–1868). The counterpart of the concept *on* in Japanese is *megumi* (a favor, a benefaction, kindness, or mercy) or *nasake* (sympathy, compassion, fellow-feeling, pity, mercy, benevolence, or love) or *omoiyari* (sympathy, fellow-feeling, compassion, mutual consideration, delicacy, or thoughtfulness for others and their feelings). *Megumi, nasake,* and *omoiyari* are all important notions often used to express sympathetic consideration for others, but it seems to me that their meanings never crystalized, unlike the term *on,* which came to mean a debt of gratitude or, in other words, to suggest a context of reciprocity. Moreover, the notion of *on* as a debt for one's lord's favor or for parental love (both aspects are emphasized in this way by Benedict) became an important one for social norms among the warrior class when that class seized political power and attempted to use Confucian doctrines as an explicit moral base for their political control.

Almost the same historical process can be observed in the case of the term *giri,* which has a clearer history. Professor Shōtarō Sakurai, an historian, points out that the word *giri* was not used during the Heian Period (up to A.D. 1200) and, although it first appeared in a writing of Nichiren (the founder of the Nichiren Sect of Buddhism in the Kamakura Period, 1184–1333), he used the word simply to denote "reasoning," which is the original meaning of the term in Chinese. Sakurai says that the concept was originally a Chinese social idea and, during the Sung dynasty (A.D. 960–1279), was applied specifically to the relationship between the ruler and his subjects. The idea was adopted by the ruling warriors, especially in the Tokugawa Period, as the designation of a subject's obligations to his lord. Among commoners, however, the concept had different meaning. Saikaku, Chikamatsu, and Shunsui, the great writers and exponents of "merchant culture" in the Tokugawa Period, have written many stories and dramas using the term *giri,* but for these writers of urban background the word simply meant either (1) to return a favor, or (2) to keep *yakusoku* (a promise, an engagement, an appointment, a pact, a contract, an agreement, a condition, or a date). It

is interesting to note that for these great writers the theme of reciprocity between lord and subject was not an appealing topic, and
there are few cases when they used such a theme in their writing.
Saikaku's *Buke Giri Monogatari* (*Stories of Warriors'* Giri), for
example, contains twenty-six short stories; all of them deal not
with relations between lord and subject but with reciprocal relations between fellows.

Among peasants, on whom direct subordination to their lord
was enforced, there was some tendency to follow *giri* in the same
sense it was used by the warrior class, but many scholars have
shown that the term *giri* was not popular among them. Professor
Tsuneichi Miyamoto, an expert on rural history, says that among
the peasant class the sense of *giri* became important after the introduction of a cash economy in the Meiji Period (1868–1912).
There was a strong sense of reciprocity and mutual aid among
peasants living in the same locale as members of a community,
but this was not identical to the term *giri*, which expressed the
warriors' conception of their moral obligation to their lord. Sakurai suggests that this notion of *giri* penetrated the rural vil-
lages through the Kabuki drama that circulated in the countryside after the Genroku Period (1688–1704).

From these points, we can conclude that the notions of *on* and
giri have not been consistently and pervasively used in Japan
throughout time but have rather recently developed since the
eighteenth century. Benedict is not wrong, because the concepts
of *on* and *giri* were important in prewar Japan, at least as explicit
cultural norms that had been emphasized by rulers for many
years, but we should note that both notions emerged from the
warrior-class subculture and were adopted into the national culture; they were not really widespread ideas initially. Benedict's
interpretation of Japanese culture tends to make the warrior subculture an explicit pattern for the whole of Japanese culture.
Many students of Japanese life, both in Japan and abroad, tend
to have this sort of misunderstanding. Similarly, it would be misleading if we took Zen Buddhism or *bushidō* (the warrior ethic)
as the essential core of Japanese culture. They are certainly well
developed and sophisticated approaches to life and have played
important roles in Japanese history, but they are neither representative nor typical aspects of Japanese culture as a whole. To

attempt to explain Japanese culture as a whole from such narrow specific bases would be to fly in the face of much contrary evidence.

Reciprocity Within Nakama: Tsukiai

In order to understand the fundamental notions about social relations among the Japanese, we have to examine the relationship of individuals within their *nakama*. As we noticed, the *nakama* is usually a primary group, although the cause or the reason for its formation is very functional. Its maintenance usually requires face-to-face relationships almost daily. On the other hand, when people need to cooperate with others for some purpose, they will voluntarily commit themselves through the formation of a *nakama,* even though they are physically located at a distance from each other. In this case, physical distance is not the primary criterion of the *nakama,* because psychologically the individuals are close enough to feel primary ties. Thus, even though the *nakama* relations are functional and purposive and the individuals' participation in a *nakama* grouping is partial, such a *nakama* can still be defined as a primary social grouping.

Since the *nakama* is a primary group relationship, there is a concrete network of bonding or reciprocity. This reciprocal relationship among members of a *nakama* must be maintained even when they are living at a distance. Thus, for example, the exchange of New Year's cards and other means of seasonal greetings become important. The exchange of New Year's greeting cards is now a very popular custom, and, despite the criticism which appears every year, the practice is increasing. The Ministry of Postal Service offers special greeting postcards, conducts a lottery, and provides a special delivery system on January 1. Some people even consider the number of cards they receive on New Year's Day to be a measure of their influence and prestige. The more *nakama* one participates in the more greeting cards one will receive.

The various exchanges of gifts among the Japanese are another example of reciprocity within the *nakama*. Traditional observance of *chūgen* (now July 1, but originally the fifteenth day of the seventh month of the year according to the lunar calendar) and *seibō* (the end of the year) are the two peaks of gift exchange. Linked to these are the semiannual dates for paying debts. Again, in spite of the official prohibition of gift exchanges for government employees and the wider public criticism of the custom as a "bad tradition," all stores and shops are busy at these two periods delivering gifts ordered by their customers. Other opportunities to exchange gifts are the occasions of rites of passage, such as weddings, births, funerals, or birthday celebrations for older people. The forms and materials of these exchanges vary, but the fact that these occasions are observed primarily by members of *nakama* is very consistent. Insofar as the exchange is carried out within the *nakama,* it is not considered to be bribery, and if one attempts to use these occasions as a kind of bribery to get a favor from someone, the public reaction will be strongly negative. We should note that there is a latent but clear notion that gift exchanges at these times are almost exclusively within *nakama.* It is possible, therefore, to conclude that the custom of exchanging gifts is a chance to reconfirm and reinforce the bonds of the *nakama.*

Participation in activities of the *nakama* is another important aspect of *tsukiai* (association with members of one's in-group). If a salaried man does not join his *nakama*'s get-togethers, such as drinking and chatting for a couple of hours after work and before going home, he will be considered an asocial person. The pressures for conformity within the *nakama* are very strong in this respect. Sometimes, one has to sacrifice one's individualism for the sake of maintaining proper ties in the *nakama.* "*Tsukiai* is special" is a phrase of the great writer Saikaku, and it means that one must be aware of the importance of *tsukiai* and must always respond to its demands. It is clear that this notion is pervasive in its effects among Japanese today.

The importance of *tsukiai* illustrates the nature of the other-directedness of Japanese culture. We should note that this other-directedness is not a new phenomenon revealed after industrialization or the emergence of a so-called mass society. It has been a traditional notion in Japan incorporated in the concept of *nakama* for at least several centuries. One wonders why this is so, and we will return to the question later.

Another aspect of *nakama* is the system of sanctions practiced within the group. The *nakama* is ultimately an egalitarian group, although once it is institutionalized hierarchy and status may appear within it. Sanctions within the *nakama,* either positive or negative, vary in each group, but all of them would include praising a member who has made some contribution to other members or to the *nakama* as a whole, and shunning the member who takes action detrimental to others or to the group. Every member of a *nakama* will recognize his rights and obligations toward the *nakama.* If it is merely a group for playing chess or for dancing, one can take these activities lightly and the sanctions will be less serious, but if the *nakama* has some grave importance for one's life, such as a *nakama* at a working place or where one lives, one will take the sanctions of the group seriously and they may well be heavy. One's rights within and obligations toward one's *nakama* can be expressed in terms of the *on-giri* dichotomy. We have already pointed out that *on* and *giri* in the Tokugawa warriors' sense were not widely shared notions. However, if we take the two notions in the sense that Saikaku used them or if we designate them as two notions operating within the *nakama,* they can be used to describe *nakama* relationships. The dichotomy of *on-giri* is thus neither the vertical, status-oriented notion expressed among the warriors nor a universal expression of relations of affection. It is a pair of mores embedded in the *nakama* group expressing the reciprocal relationships of members.

Public and Private: Another Aspect of "I" and "Others"

Another important element in social relations in Japan is the distinction between private and public. Public affairs are called *ōyake-goto,* or simply *ōyake,* and private matters are usually referred to as *watakushi-goto* or *shiji.* There is another pair of notions related to them: *kōjin* and *shijin,* or a public man and a private individual, which is illustrated in such expressions as "I will support it as a personal matter, but not in a public capacity." In public speeches, Japanese often use phrases like "excuse me for being personal" when they refer to their own affairs or other private matters. One's sentiment, feeling, affection, and sometimes even personal opinions are all considered to be private matters, and normally they should not be discussed in public or mixed with public affairs. The clear separation of one's public duties from one's private interests is considered a very important requirement in social relations. For example, government officials usually maintain strict impersonality in decision-making when they are at the office. Public administrators must be neutral and objective in their tasks, and to a large extent this rule can be applied to all administrative matters even in private enterprises. There are many examples of this. Although the customs procedures in any port of entry to Japan may be inefficient and beset with red tape, little corruption is found there. Bribery in administrative matters is practically impossible in any office. Police are often too rigid in their attitudes toward minor violations of regulations, but they are very punctilious in their interpretation of regulations and restrictions. They seem almost cold, and it is very difficult to establish personal rapport with them.

This separation of public affairs from private matters will sometimes lead to extreme situations in which one's private interest is sacrificed. An episode concerning a high-ranking government official just before the end of World War II is illustrative. The man was appointed to be governor of Okinawa when the prefecture was about to become a battlefield. Although he could have rejected the appointment, he dutifully went, leaving his family behind in Tokyo, and died in Okinawa. Another famous example is that of a Minister of Finance in a currency emergency caused by inflation after World War II. When he took action to freeze all old-yen currency and to allow a limited exchange quota for old yen into new yen, he never mentioned this impending government action to his family. As a result, the family suffered serious financial losses. These examples of *kōjin* behavior (a man in a public capacity) demonstrate the clear separation between public duties and private interests. The Japanese simply could not mix the two. Such traits, really ethical principles, are apparently derived from the ethics of the warrior class during the Tokugawa Period, when it was no longer engaged in military pursuits but its members had become administrators for their respective feudal lords. This depersonalization and the attempt to deal fairly in public matters have been maintained among government administrators, as well as in private enterprises.

However, public action often leads to ambiguity in responsibility since responsibility for a particular act does not rest with a single person but with many related persons in the bureaucracy. When the War Crimes Trials were held in Tokyo after World War II, there was much discussion among the Japanese about the nature of personal responsibility. Since most decisions are made by a group of people who are in charge of a matter rather than by an individual, it is difficult to single out the person responsible in the system of Japanese decision-making. This situation is symbolized by the series of seals required from individual officials from top to bottom of the bureaucracy that may be found on any official document in Japan. This illustrates the fact that, among Japanese, public affairs are not the concern of an individual but require a consensus among related people.

The notions of public and private can be traced back beyond the Tokugawa Period to an earlier time, when they were elaborated by Confucianism. Public matters, especially those related to political affairs, are called *matsurigoto* in classical Japanese. The word means government, administration, or politics, but it is derived from the word *matsuri* (a festival, a fete, a gala event, or worship) and *koto* (matter or thing). This shows that in ancient times political affairs were inseparable from ritual events. Therefore, politics was a sacred event that should be separated from the ordinary events of everyday life. Thus, the pair of notions, public and private, is related to the dichotomy between sacred and profane, or extraordinary events and ordinary matters. For sacred and profane, the Japanese used to have dichotomized terms: *hare* and *ke*. They are no longer used in common parlance except for a few vestigial terms like *haregi* (one's holiday dress, one's gala dress) or *hare-no-basho* (a public place, a ceremonial place, a formal place). If we use the traditional dichotomy, the public is always *hare,* or sacred, extraordinary, and formal, whereas the private is usually *ke* or profane, ordinary, and informal. While the former requires tension, formality, fairness or justice, and logic, the latter provides relaxation, informality, and personal expression of sentiment and passion.

Even today it is patently clear that Japanese are keenly aware of this distinction between the public and the private. One sees it in the fact that whenever people go out from home they will dress rather formally, will speak in a more circumspect, modest way, and will carry themselves in a more formal manner. At the same time, in a public place one can behave in a very impersonal way. Thus, along with a certain formality of manner, we also see at the same time some openly expressed aggression or hatred or ignorance of manners in public.

The Field of Social Relations

A combination of the two dichotomies, *nakama* (one's own group) as against *tanin* (others), and *ōyake* (public affairs) as against *watakushigoto* (personal matters), will produce four columns, and from the point of view of the individual, the "I," these four columns represent four different types of people toward whom one might act differently. Let us sum up the four categories.

1. *People who are both* nakama *members and related in private matters:* One's family members or close relatives are classified in this category, though blood ties are not a required condition. The term *miuchi* is used for people in this category. Their relation to the "I" is usually permanent, or at least persistent over a long period of time. One can expect to find intimate mutual bonds, and persons within this group are so close to each other that formal exchanges of gifts or greetings are not necessary. This is a basic unit of social life, cooperating primarily for consumption.

2. *People who are* nakama *members and related in public matters:* Most peer groups and corporate groups are in this category. In other words, all the various *nakama* one belongs to, except one's *miuchi,* can be classified in this category. These are the most important people for the individual, since they will define and essentially determine his role in life. The length of contact may vary, but it is usually long-term. The exchange of gifts and seasonal greetings is important to reinforce the relationships and is commonly practiced. The *on-giri* type of reciprocity of rights and obligations is revealed in this category, for there is more than a ritualistic relationship involved.

3. *People who are not* nakama *members and are related in private matters:* People like a crowd of commuters of whom the

individual is one are classified in this category. Reciprocal interaction is minimal, and relationships are often impersonal and
sometimes hostile. Especially in metropolitan areas, apathy toward others is the prevalent pattern. People in this category may
not even be recognized as human beings as far as one's social life
goes, because they are mere strangers or men on the street with
whom one has no relationship.

4. *People who are not* nakama *members but are related in
public affairs:* People like policemen at a crossroad, an official in
a revenue office, a salesman visiting one's home, or a lecturer at a
meeting one attends are included in this category. Such people do
not have any direct relation to the individual as members of his
nakama, yet he has to maintain a certain relationship on specific
occasions. The attitude of the individual toward such people will
be formal and often impersonal, though he needs to establish certain positive relations with them. No exchange of gifts or greetings, except the minimum manners of formality and politeness,
are required in the public setting. Relations with them can be ritualistic and without personal content.

If we adopt these categories, we can see that the most important social relations among Japanese are the first and second, and
if we exclude one's familistic ties, as they are an almost universal
category in any society, the second will be the most important
category of Japanese social relations. In fact, we may say that people in Japan are only related to the outside world through this
nakama category. In a sense, Japanese effectively live only within
the *nakama* group.

For the Japanese, the world (*sekai*) is an unpredictable, floating, ever changing complex rather than a clearly definable en-
tity. The only concrete area where he can trust others and can
feel he is living is the *nakama.* Thus, the *nakama* as a field of social relations becomes the prime element among Japanese, and
most social actions of individuals are focused in this plane.

There are many Japanese terms that specify some field or profession. Examples are *seikai* (world of politics), *kankai* (world of
government officials), *zaikai* (world of finance), *gyōkai* (world of
business), *gakkai* (academic world), *bundan* (the literary world),
kadan (the world of Japanese poetry of thirty-one syllables), *hai-*

dan (the world of Japanese poetry of seventeen syllables), and the like. Each such "world" is more concrete than the world in general, because each forms a *nakama* grouping or a federation of them, and so the word "world" is used to suggest a set of specific relationships. Formal organizations in Japan are, in general, mechanical entities, and the real operations are usually carried out by several *nakama* groupings within organizations. Japanese society can be conceived of as an aggregated mosaic of various kinds of *nakama* groupings.

Good relations within one's *nakama* provide all kinds of benefits and conveniences to one's life. A letter of recommendation, for instance, can be very powerful when it is sent from one member of a *nakama* to another, whereas when used outside of the *nakama* the letter will be a simple formality. When one needs to make contact with a stranger, one will seek to establish contact with someone from one of the stranger's *nakama* who is a member of one's own *nakama*. Through this kind of contact, people can extend their world. Thus, *kankei* (relationships) or *konekushon* or *kone* (both derived from the English word connection) among *nakama* groupings are crucially important notions in the system.

So far we have seen some important aspects of social relations in Japan in terms of two dichotomies. We should not ignore other aspects of Japanese society, such as its social strata or allocation of authority, but it seems that the core of social relations is not in these but rather in this egalitarian grouping of *nakama*.

Some Causes of the Basic Notions

One might question, however, whether this kind of associational grouping is any more than an expression of a kind of universal phenomenon in the modern world, which eminent sociologists have already identified (e.g., Tonnies's "Gesellschaft" or MacIver's "association" or even Riesman's "other-directedness"). I would argue that the very nature of such social relations, which is often referred to as typifying the "modern" character of society, is a deeply rooted characteristic of Japanese social relations. There are, I think, four reasons for this "modernity" in Japanese social arrangements.

First of all, we should note the generally homogeneous character of Japanese culture. We all know that race, language, and culture show different, independent distribution in the world. We have to draw three separate maps to illustrate these three aspects of life. For example, Great Britain can be divided into several cultural traditions, which are sometimes antagonistic to each other, and the United States has many ethnic groups that make the country heterogeneous in character, although both countries use English as their national language. Thus, we need to see ethnic and cultural distributions separate from linguistic affinity. It is rather difficult to find a national culture in which the three elements overlap, and Japan is an exceedingly rare case in which the overlap is almost complete.

Although the Japanese as a physical race are a mixture of many different elements, and, in fact, there are considerable differences among them, the Japanese themselves tend to think they are all alike. They never wonder when they see, for example, a man who looks almost like an Indonesian and another who resembles a North Korean sitting side by side on a train, because they take the difference in their looks for granted within the range of how Japanese should look. Although there are local variations of dialect, and Japanese will joke about them, the phonemic structure of the Japanese language is basically the same in all parts of the country. Despite the local and subcultural variations of custom, Japanese culture is fundamentally homogeneous. We can assume that these similarities are largely due to the geographical isolation of the island chain, physically detached from neighboring countries, and to the unified nature of its historical background since the seventh century. We have in addition to notice particularly the political as well as the geographical isolation during the 250 years of relatively stable peace of the Tokugawa Period. That period clearly reinforced the internal homogeneity of Japanese culture. This cultural homogeneity was able to support such general concepts as *nakama* or *tsukiai* and made them universal notions that go beyond the subcultural as well as status differentiation. If the country had not had a homogeneous cultural background, egalitarian ideas could hardly have been accepted throughout the society.

The second factor that has given a particular cast to Japanese social relations is the demography of the country. One-thirtieth of the world's population lives on the Japanese islands, a space smaller than California. The aggregation of a mass of people in such a limited space creates, even as does the physical setting, an environment different from that of a less populated area. In order to survive, Japanese have to make special social arrangements, avoiding conflict as much as possible and permitting effective human cooperation. As the population is homogeneous in terms of its ethnic, linguistic, and cultural background, exploitation of or despotic control over one group by another could not work as it has in other countries where those elements could easily be used as reasons for conflict or control. In a sense, the Japanese have had to develop a society like that of herbivorous animals, not like that of carnivorous ones. The *nakama,* or associational group, was the response of the Japanese to the social need for co-operation in order for individuals to survive. It was a result of Japan's unique demographic situation.

The third cause of this kind of notion was the relatively early development of urbanization. Although the transformation of cities in Japan into modern industrial metropolises took place after the middle of the nineteenth century, we have to realize that there were large urban centers in early eighteenth-century Japan. For example, historical data show the following urban populations: Kyoto in 1719, 341,494; Edo (Tokyo) in 1721, 501,394; and Osaka in 1721, 382,471. If we compare them to 1801 statistics for Paris, 547,000; Berlin, 170,000; and London, 864,000, we have to conclude that urbanization took place in Japan at a relatively early date. Apparently, notions such as *nakama* or *tsukiai* emerged among city dwellers who needed associational ties rather than kinship or territorial (community) ties, and partial participation in groups for certain functions rather than lifetime commitment to ascribed groupings. Early urbanization seems to have been one stimulus to the development of certain key notions in social relations.

A fourth cause of these basic notions is related to secularization and the emergence of a relativistic point of view in Japanese ways of thinking. The emergence of sects in Buddhism during the Kamakura Period, including Jōdō, Zen, and Nichiren, was evidence of the process of popularization of Buddhism in Japan, but at the same time it also constituted a protestant movement against the established orthodoxies of the older sects that were protected by the medieval government. Dogmas of the new sects were generally more inner-directed and stressed direct relationships between people and the Buddha or the sacred elements of religious life. In a sense, they were a reaction against the trend to secularization under the older Buddhism. During the sixteenth century, especially in 1571, when Nobunaga Oda burned down Enryakuji, a great temple complex near Kyoto that was a religious sanctuary as well as an academic center where all the new sect leaders had studied, the older authority of religion was almost completely destroyed. After the Tokugawa regime was established, all religious institutions were put under the control of the government, and local temples became civil registration offices in each locale. The role of priests was limited to the ritual observance of funerals or ancestor cults and to teaching children to read, write, and use the abacus, rather than to spiritual preaching. Although there have since emerged several evangelical religious movements both in Buddhism and in Shinto, the general trend in society has been toward more practical and more pragmatic secular activities. The process of secularization has been going on in Japan for many centuries. One significant characteristic of this process is that people tend to think about matters more in relative than in absolute terms. One might believe in a dogma, but at the same time one must admit there are many other ways of looking at or of thinking about things. This has created a context in which one's own *nakama* can coexist with those of others and has made it possible for an individual to participate in more than one *nakama* at the same time.

In this discussion of basic concepts in Japanese social relations, I have singled out as central the notions of *nakama* and *tanin*, and of public and private. They are important in ordinary life, and they are caused by historical and geographical factors, such as homogeneity of cultural background, demographic conditions, early urbanization, and early secularization. I have attempted to stress the associational instead of the familistic tendencies in Japanese society. By doing this, it is possible to examine many aspects of Japanese society from a new angle, and we may be able to see more clearly a model of social arrangements that has emerged in a densely populated, urbanized, and secularized society. Viewed in this way, the model of basic social notions in Japan may be useful as we attempt to analyze other contemporary societies which, today, have a setting comparable to that out of which Japanese society has grown.

7

The Disharmony of Form and Substance
in Japanese Democracy

Mitsuru Uchida

The perennial question of the last two decades has been, "What is the status of democracy in Japan?" To answer that question, it is necessary to focus on specific attitudes and behavior by looking at Japan's basic political structure and the ways in which the Japanese have participated in that structure in recent years.

The Conditions of Japanese Participation in Politics

The foundation of parliamentary government in Japan was laid in the last decade of the nineteenth century. In July, 1890, the first general election took place, and the first session of the Imperial Diet was opened five months later. In that election, a mere 1.1 per cent of the population—450,000 out of 39,900,000—were entitled to vote, because only male citizens twenty-five years of age and older who also met a high tax qualification were eligible. The tax qualification was gradually lowered, and in 1925, with the passage of the Universal Manhood Suffrage Act by the Diet, all men aged twenty-five and older became qualified as voters regardless of their tax status. Finally, a few months after the end of World War II in 1945, the election law was drastically revised, providing for women's suffrage and lowering the voting age to twenty. With this, needless to say, the number of eligible voters expanded enormously and today slightly less than 70 per cent of the population—some 70,000,000 people—are entitled to vote.

There are six kinds of elective public offices in Japan and a total of almost 81,000 elected officials. These include the 491 members of the House of Representatives (Lower House), 250 members of the House of the Councilors (Upper House), 47 prefectural governors, 2,700 prefectural assemblymen, 3,300 mayors, and 74,000 municipal councilmen. While it may be true that Japanese voters do not have as many opportunities to exercise their right at the polls as American voters do (there are about 800,000 elective public offices of various kinds in the United States), this is a superficial comparison: In the United States, elections do not occur so frequently because the terms of office of public officials are longer. Thus, with respect to elections, Japan can safely be said to be as democratic as any other nation with a democratic system.

Moreover, Japanese participation in politics is, of course, not limited just to voting. In prewar Japan, civil liberties were curtailed to an extraordinary degree by the Peace Preservation Law which was enacted in 1925 simultaneously with the Universal Manhood Suffrage Act. The former law ruthlessly suppressed all socialistic or antiestablishment movements. This notorious law was abolished after World War II, and the postwar constitution of Japan, promulgated in 1946 and put into effect in the following year, guaranteed "freedom of assembly and association as well as speech, press, and all other forms of expression."

Under such conditions, constitutionally speaking, political participation in Japan is as democratic and open to all as in the United States or Great Britain. The rise of interest groups and the flourishing development of mass media in the postwar years attest to this. For example, during the war, labor unions were disbanded one after another, and when the war came to an end virtually no union had survived. With the war's end, however, the ratio of participation in labor unions literally soared. By mid-1946, it was already 40 per cent of the labor force. It then leveled off and has now dropped slightly. According to a survey conducted in 1969 by the Ministry of Labor, 11.25 million workers and laborers—35.2 per cent of the whole labor population—were organized participants. The General Council of Trade Unions of Japan (Sōhyō) was the largest federation of labor, having 4.25 million members; the Japanese Confederation of Labor (Zenrō), the second largest, had 1.96 million members.

Japanese Political Participation

Having looked at the form of Japanese politics, we might ask the questions: Are civil rights and liberties exercised as satisfactorily by the Japanese people as was hoped by the architects of the constitution? Are Japanese citizens participating in politics actively and voluntarily? In seeking answers to such questions, several aspects of political behavior need to be explored. The first of these is the percentage of those who vote among the population eligible to vote. The highest percentage in the postwar Japanese general elections was recorded in 1958, 77 per cent. The lowest was 68 per cent in 1947. In 1969, the percentage was 68.5, the second lowest.* The average voting percentage for eleven postwar general elections is 73.1. As this figure shows, the Japanese have been as active as the Americans or the British, if not more so.

However, if we look more deeply into the meaning of these facts, we cannot interpret them too optimistically. First of all, the voting percentage has been higher in rural districts than in urban ones. For instance, in the general election of 1963, the percentage was 71.1 on the average throughout the country. In some thirty districts in rural prefectures such as Shimane and Tottori, far from metropolitan centers, however, the turnout of voters was much higher than the average—more than 80 per cent, while in urban districts a very low percentage was recorded, with such areas as Tokyo, Kanagawa, Osaka, and Kyoto recording not more than 62 per cent.

The low voting percentage in urban districts probably has something to do with the process and progress of urbanization. As one American scholar has pointed out, "the more mobile the population, the greater the barrier to participation residence re-

* In the December, 1972, elections, 73 per cent of those eligible voted.—ED.

quirements become."[1] In our 1967 survey in a city of Kanagawa Prefecture (next door to Tokyo), we were unable to locate about 10 per cent of our intended interviewees because they had moved to other places, although their names remained in the official electoral registration books of the city. We have to assume that few of those who moved were active enough to take the required steps to vote by mail.

At the very least, we must caution that a high percentage of voting in rural districts is not necessarily indicative of nor correlated with political awareness. On the contrary, the rural voters seem to be less aware politically than urban ones. For example, a 1960 election survey conducted in selected rural and urban districts pointed out that 42 per cent of the urban respondents could not express any definite opinion about the most controversial issue in the general election—the United States–Japan Mutual Security Treaty—but that in the rural district 54 per cent of the respondents were indifferent to this issue.

A second aspect of political behavior is concern with issues. We have evidence that about two-thirds of the Japanese voters are not seriously interested in vital political issues in any election. In other words, the number of issue-oriented voters is not so large as it is often expected to be. And this is especially the case with rural voters. In our 1960 survey, among the rural respondents 31 per cent were party-oriented voters and 40 per cent were candidate-oriented, while among the urban respondents 33 per cent were party-oriented and 35 per cent were candidate-oriented. It seems clear that a great many Japanese voters are casting their ballots not in support of particular policies, but rather in support of particular candidates. In this, their voting decision is very often greatly influenced by the opinions of their leaders.

Of course, we should recognize that American voters are also considered to be enmeshed in the web of personal influence. As a case in point, an Erie County voting study done in 1940 by a group of political sociologists from Columbia University found that personal relationships are potentially more influential than the formal media of communication, and that personal influence flows horizontally among the voters. That is to say, American

[1] Lester W. Milbrath, *Political Participation: How and Why Do People Get Involved in Politics* (New York: Rand-McNally, 1965), p. 93.

opinion leaders who occupy a mediating position between their followers and the organs of mass communication are mostly from the same socio-economic status.[2]

In Japan, however, although personal influence is just as vital in the electoral decision-making process, the influence tends to flow vertically, with political communication going more often than not from men of higher social standing to men of lower standing. Actually, social standing has been cumulative in Japan. We frequently find that a mayor is, at the same time, the president of various social and cultural associations, and his wife, in her capacity as the mayor's wife, assumes the presidency of a women's society or the community PTA. It is very probable that political communication and influence on voting behavior descends from the leaders to the rank-and-file members of these associations.

The third aspect of Japanese political life that needs attention is the organizational characteristic of interest groups. As noted above, the rise of interest groups in the postwar years has been phenomenal. However, membership in Japanese organizations is frequently not a matter of free will or choice. The Agricultural Co-operative Association boasts a huge membership embracing more than 90 per cent of all the farmers in Japan. However this statistic may mean that most farmers have not been active enough to "contract out." The same thing can be said of the Zengakuren or the National Federation of Student Self-Government Organizations. Technically speaking, in Japanese colleges and universities where student government associations do exist, there is no student who does not pay his membership dues, because a student is automatically a member of the student association whether he likes it or not, and the dues are collected for the student association by the university bursar, together with other student fees, and then turned over to the student association.

All of this evidence suggests that there is incongruity between the form and the substance of Japanese democracy. It is true that Japan has been substantially democratized in the postwar years, but not in the full sense of the word. Japanese democracy suffers

[2] Paul F. Lazarsfeld, *et al., The People's Choice: How the Voter Makes Up His Mind in a Presidential Campaign,* 2d ed. (New York: Columbia University Press, 1948).

today from its dual structure: democratic form and tradition-oriented behavior of the people.

Is the Nation Divided?

At this point another question might be posed: If the form and the substance could be made consistent, would Japanese democracy be free from other strains? Here, we must remind ourselves that in the nineteenth century and even as late as the 1920's, when female suffrage was provided for the first time in the United States and in Great Britain, most political writers and philosophers assumed that if a democracy was not functioning well the remedy was not to set limits to the democracy but rather to try to establish democracy on a larger scale and on a more secure basis. "More democracy" was a sort of battle cry in those days, and one of the methods deemed most important for realizing it was to extend the franchise.

However, it has turned out that even after universal suffrage has been established or a society has become more democratic in form, democratic processes do not necessarily become more stable, nor do they function more effectively. Universal suffrage and civil liberties were constitutionally established in Japan just after World War II, but the political system has been rather unstable and tensions have been great not only because of the lag between form and substance but presumably also, in a sense, because of progress in the development of democracy itself. E. Pendleton Herring once said, "A democracy inclines toward chaos rather than toward order. The representative principle, if logically followed, leads to infinite diversity rather than ultimate unity."[3] Even so, the state of affairs in Japan seems much worse than he assumed it to be, because the Japanese people appear today to be considerably polarized in their political views. It is very frequently remarked with much regret that there are two nations in Japan, or that the Japanese are badly split in their ideas regarding the national future. Such a situation is considered by many to be damaging to the effort to achieve a national consensus on key issues.

[3] E. Pendleton Herring, *Public Administration and the Public Interest* (1936, reprinted, New York: Russell & Russell, 1967), p. 377.

It is widely accepted that the Liberal Democratic Party (LDP), which has long been in the majority, is the party that advocates the maintenance of the *status quo* or the group that most resists change. In contrast, the Japan Socialist Party (JSP) and the Japan Communist Party (JCP) aim at a revolutionary change of the *status quo* or at least at basic structural change. These two groups are, so to speak, denying each other's right to existence in the political arena. From another point of view, we might say that the LDP is the party of the establishment or the party whose aim is primarily to conserve the "traditional" value system of Japanese society.* On the other hand, the JSP is an antiestablishment party, one that strives to break down the traditional value system. At the very least, we should say that the center of gravity of the LDP would be found on the side of the establishment forces and the center of gravity of the JSP on the side of the antiestablishment forces, with the Democratic Socialist Party and the Kōmeitō lining up in between.

The Japanese people are frequently aligned along these party lines, embracing different or opposing views of the society and the polity. They are embracing what we call different *Weltanschauungen*. Moreover, with the recent uprisings of antiestablishment-oriented students and young workers, this national schism has seemingly been further aggravated. Many factors might be enumerated as having brought about this phenomenon. Just a few of them can be touched upon here.

Socially, in the postwar years the overturning or loosening of the hold of the traditional value system should be noted. In prewar Japan, for instance, selfless devotion to the country was the most valued commitment in life. The whole came first and the individual came last, or, on the scale of values, society or the state was at the highest point and the individual was at the lowest. In the postwar years, however, a kind of reversal of the value system took place, putting the individual at the highest and society or the state at the lowest on the value scale. Second, there is a marked difference in level of education between the old and the new generations. In the prewar years, only a small percentage of the college-age population attended colleges and universi-

* The LDP platform stresses the need to preserve and revitalize the family system and calls for the enhancement of the Emperor's status—Ed.

ties (3.01 per cent in 1940). After the war, however, the percentage has risen continuously, and in 1969 it was 21.4 per cent (26.6 per cent for boys and 16.1 per cent for girls).

These two factors, reinforcing each other, have made it very difficult for parents to convey their values positively and confidently to their offspring. This leads to a situation in which political socialization cannot proceed smoothly and effectively. This has very serious implications for the healthy working of the Japanese political system, because it is assumed that "the persistence of some kind of system may in part be dependent upon the success of a society in producing children most of whom acquire positive feelings about it."[4]

Politically, we must note the monopoly of governmental control held by the LDP in the last two decades. The same conservative group has been in power continuously since 1948. What is worse, there is little prospect for a change of government in the foreseeable future. Under the circumstances, the ruling party has tended to be all-powerful politically, and the opposition parties have expended their energies solely to oppose the majority. Thus, rule of the majority has disintegrated into rule of the majority party. Here is one reason for the instability of Japanese democracy and for the persistent allegation that Japan is a divided nation. It is generally held to be essential to the stability and success of a democracy that there be occasional changes of the party in power. Japanese democracy, unfortunately, has lacked this healthy condition.

The situation being what it is, is Japan inevitably to continue as a divided nation, as has often been asserted? To my thinking, this is not necessarily the case. Indeed there are deep and serious splits of opinion among the Japanese, for instance, as regards the United States–Japan Mutual Security Treaty. The pro and con groups appear to be completely incompatible with each other. However, the following fact suggests a different story. It is clear that no political party is a monolithic group with its members and supporters all of the same mind. Party lines are blurred, and there is not the sharp cleavage between them that we might expect.

[4] David Easton and Jack Dennis, *Children in the Political System: Origins of Political Legitimacy* (New York: McGraw-Hill, 1969), p. 5.

According to the 1967 survey in which I participated, the division of opinions among the respondents with respect to the Mutual Security Treaty was as follows:

Opinion	*Percentage*
(A) The treaty should be maintained	23.2
(B) The treaty should gradually be discontinued	29.2
(C) The treaty should be discontinued immediately	11.8
(D) No definite answer	35.8

Generally speaking, A is the position of the LDP, B is the position of the DSP, and C is that of the JSP and the JCP. However, our findings show clearly that all of the LDP voters did not always agree with A, while JSP voters did not necessarily hold opinion C. As a matter of fact, among LDP voters, 32.2 per cent responded with A, 25.5 per cent with B, and 4.4 per cent with C. In the same way, among the socialist voters, although 20.5 per cent answered C, 34.2 per cent answered B, and 15.1 per cent answered A.

Another fact to be taken into account in this connection is that there are a considerable number of people in Japan today not affiliated with the parties. When we conducted our survey in 1967, one of our questions was: "Is there any party that you support generally in your daily life?" To this, 48.7 per cent of the respondents answered in the negative. The LDP was supported only by 20.5 per cent of the respondents, the JSP by 18.6 per cent, the DSP by 6.6 per cent, the Kōmeitō by 5 per cent, and the JCP by 0.6 per cent.

These facts might work to check or alleviate a head-on confrontation between the parties and between groups of citizens with distinctly different ideas of the world. Or we could say that, although these conflicts of opinion make it very difficult to achieve a national consensus, the situation is still not so serious as to be fatal to Japanese democracy. This is because there are substantial numbers of voters who cross party lines and are not so strongly committed to any party that they support its policy positions unquestioningly.

Changing Factors in Japanese Political Life

We have suggested that Japanese democracy exists today far more in form than in substance, and that the progress of democracy in form has led to serious tensions in which the nation itself appears to be divided and a national consensus difficult to achieve. While I agree that there are serious problems to be faced and that political tensions and division are severe, we need not despair of democracy in Japan. We must face these tensions and attempt to alleviate them.

Under these conditions, it is rather natural that the younger generation should be fed up with the *status quo* of society and the polity in Japan. One reflection of their feelings is the eruption of student activist demonstrations, which have of late become more and more violent in tactics. Another reflection of the mood is that growing numbers of the younger generation have become apathetic to politics. In the general election of 1969, voters in their twenties seemed the most reluctant to go to the polls. According to a survey conducted at that time by the Ministry of Home Affairs, the worst voting percentage was recorded by the voters between twenty and twenty-four years of age, and the second worst by the voters between twenty-five and twenty-nine, the percentages being 57.6 and 61.9, respectively. In particular, voters in their twenties who lived in the seven largest cities turned out in the fewest numbers, with a majority of them staying away from the polls.[5]

However, the situation is not necessarily without hope. We can point to at least two factors of change that could help to overcome the difficulties and ease these tensions. One is the appearance in the political arena in substantial numbers of a new generation of voters. In 1969, about 40 per cent of the voters had been born after 1935, and it is estimated that by 1975 this new generation will form the majority of voters. This has great meaning in Japan, because these young voters have few or no memories of World War II. They have had most or all levels of their education in the postwar educational system, and consequently they have substantially different values from their elders. They are likely to be more free from the pressures and flow of traditional personal influence in politics.

The other factor making for change is the unceasing progress of urbanization in Japan. Urbanization tends to reduce the influence of traditional patterns of personal relationships and to make

[5] *Asahi Shimbun* and *Mainichi Shimbun,* March 23, 1970.

the flow of political communication more horizontal. In other words, urbanization is accompanied by an increase in the number of voters who are independent of the ties of blood and land.

All things considered, the future of Japanese democracy may be viewed with modest optimism. The Japanese must vigorously attack the problems in our political life, using wisely our accumulated experience and applying common sense to the issues. We have had substantial success in the past, but much remains to be done. Much depends upon the attitude and behavior of the new generation of voters. For this, we shall have to wait and see.

8

Making Democracy Our Own

Makoto Oda

"Of the people, for the people and by the people." In those famous words, Abraham Lincoln expressed so concisely the basic principles of democracy. Each of the three democracies means something different, and the importance of each distinction between them is, I believe, becoming more and more evident these days. Let us, as Japanese who have just passed through a swift postwar history of democracy, examine the importance of these distinctions. In the postwar years, democracy enjoyed a hospitable reception in Japan. To a surprising degree it spread rapidly among the Japanese people, and there is no disputing the fact that it spread deeply as well. The reason for this was that democracy responded directly to the desires of the people. It was a time when each and every Japanese had to struggle for himself to stay alive. Ruling elites, including of course the government leaders, suffered an unprecedented diminution of their authority during the postwar period. The only existing authority was the Occupation Army, and it was this group alone that constituted the basis for democracy—in the sense of political system—in postwar Japan.

There were factors at work in the immediate postwar years that conspired to mislead the Japanese about the true nature of democracy. In the first place, the defeat meant that the Japanese people lost all confidence in their government. More importantly, however, they were able to ignore their government in those years. The Japanese people had only a dim understanding of the nature of the new democratic institutions that governed them. For example, they tended to ignore the fact that, whatever else democracy means, it also implies state power capable of coercing individual citizens. In addition, Japanese were so preoccupied with the problems of simply keeping alive that abstract questions of any kind were of secondary importance. As a result, there was a natural tendency for Japanese to look upon democracy as a system that provided tangible benefits to the people. They were more concerned in those years about the rights and privileges of democracy than the responsibilities. For the time being at least, the benefits provided by democracy seemed real while the threat of state power acting against the interests of the people was perceived only vaguely if at all. In this situation, there was an inevitable tendency to regard democracy as simply a system, to emphasize its methods and techniques while losing sight of its essence.

What do we mean when we talk about democracy "by the people" (*jinmin ni yoru minshushugi*)? To my mind, "by-the-people democracy" stands somewhere between "of-the-people democracy" (*jinmin no minshushugi*) and "for-the-people democracy" (*jinmin no tame no minshushugi*). On the one hand is the essential spirit of direct democracy, which we associate with "of-the-people democracy." On the other hand are the more concrete aspects of democracy, which we associate with "for-the-people democracy" and which in fact tend to be something like enlightened monarchism. Or, to put it simply, "by-the-people democracy" is a matter of the mechanics of democracy, a question of systems. Of course, in the West even the mechanics of democracy were not something that existed apart from the basic principles or spirit of democracy but rather flowed from those principles. In the case of Japan, however, we were simply handed a democratic system as a finished product.

Democracy and the Progressive Movements

It was, I believe, unfortunate for the subsequent development of democracy in Japan, as well as for the student movement, that

the Communist Party was "discovered" and came to take a leading role in the postwar democratization movement, because the
Japan Communist Party (JCP) did not attempt to get to the
heart of what is meant by "democracy *of* the people." Instead, it
created among progressives a tendency to attempt to see everything and solve everything in terms of a mechanical conflict
between bourgeois democracy and proletarian democracy. This
tendency was doubly mistaken or, more correctly, doubly irre-
sponsible.

First of all, Japan's progressives should have realized that, even
assuming that a system of proletarian democracy would be established, it would still be necessary to come to an understanding
of the basic principles of "democracy *of* the people." (I am
aware that the following may be an overstatement, but I believe
that the importance of understanding *"of-*the-people democracy"
—even under a system of proletarian democracy—can be seen in
the tendency of the present generation of Soviet youth to seek
freedom from state controls. It can also be seen in a tendency
toward direct democracy in the Great Cultural Revolution in
China. The 1968 incident in Czechoslovakia is the most exact
and dramatic illustration of what I am pointing out here.)

Secondly, this mechanical juxtaposition of bourgeois and proletarian democracy tends to give rise to the facile conclusion that
all problems, all contradictions, have their origins in bourgeois
democracy. As far as the progressive forces in general were concerned, their main emphasis was shifted to the "for-the-people"
aspects of democracy. From the foregoing, we might conclude
that, because everything evil was blamed upon bourgeois democracy, the progressives failed to tackle forthrightly the most basic
questions of democracy.

A number of unfortunate results have come from all this. One
example is the undemocratic tendencies evident even within the
progressive camp; even today, we hear the members of progressive
parties clamoring for the "establishment of democracy" within
their own parties. Another is the lack of spontaneity or democratic ways of thinking among the masses. An even more important result is the ready, all *too* ready, willingness of the progressive forces to define the goals of its "democracy for the people" in
terms of material goals sought by the masses of the people. This

attitude gives rise to the view that every struggle must be rooted in questions of livelihood. Or, to put it another way, we have a situation in which the progressive forces manage to rationalize practically every struggle they mount—from wage demands to election reforms—in terms of the world situation. When issues are not tied to matters of daily concern for the average citizen, the movement tends to be weakened, as we have seen in the early stages of the anti–Vietnam war movement. I was astonished to read some university student movement handbills which proclaimed that students were somehow assisting the people of Vietnam by struggling against tuition rises.

There is still another pitfall in identifying progressive movements too closely with the needs of the masses. I have already discussed how a certain "democratic order" (*minshushugiteki chitsujo*) is formed when the ruling elite finds it useful to support the masses in its demands for "democracy *for* the people." In this connection, there is a danger that the progressive forces, almost without realizing what is happening, will also support the masses' demands for "democracy *for* the people" and consequently, in effect, link themselves to the "democratic order" that supports the purposes of the ruling elite.

The logic that the progressives have employed, to put it simply, is based on the notion that there is a juxtaposition between two different kinds of democracies. For a time, at least, this kind of logic was amply appealing as far as the realities of everyday life were concerned. However, the persuasive force of the argument began to weaken as the living standards of the masses rose. As a result of relatively improved living standards, the old Marxian formula is now inapplicable. That is to say, the descent of the masses into total misery is no longer with us and thus can no longer be expected to produce the sudden dramatic historical changes anticipated by Marx.

A further weakening of the argument put forth by the progressives occurred as undemocratic tendencies within the progressive camp itself became more and more evident as a result of the disclosures of Stalinist excesses, the sensational expulsions within the ranks of the Japan Communist Party, and, finally, the splits within the peace and student movements.

In response to the obvious fact that the masses are to a certain

degree sharing in the general economic prosperity of the nation
—that they do have something more than their chains to lose—the
theory of "structural reform" was devised.* This theory should
certainly be given due credit for its reassessment of the notion of
"democracy of the people" in the context of the present situation. However, up until now its formulators have not created
programs sufficiently appealing to win mass support. Furthermore, I doubt whether the theory of structural reform is capable
of attracting the masses away from the present order and developing a new order. I am inclined to think that what we might
indeed have is a union movement that is exceedingly powerful in
terms of its ability to achieve its economic demands. In all other
matters—for example, in its stance on the Vietnam war—it would
probably be similar to the gigantic labor union movement in
America. It would neglect to a criminal degree the task of creating a new order in place of the present one, and, indeed, in some
instances the labor union movement would serve as a powerful
bastion for the maintenance of the *status quo*. Of course, it is not
impossible to awaken the American working class to the need for
political action on matters such as the Vietnam war. But this is
not something that can be accomplished through the juxtaposition of proletarian and bourgeois democracies.

Growing Emphasis on Democracy "for the People"

There seems to be a growing universal trend to emphasize "democracy *for* the people" rather than "democracy *of* the people."
The trend seems to accompany the burgeoning of the population
in democratic societies everywhere. It also appears to accompany
the burgeoning of social control functions—that is, the growth of

* The theory of structural reform is associated with Saburō Eda, who, as
Secretary General of the Socialist Party, presented it to a Socialist Party con-
vention in October, 1960. Briefly, it represents a revision of orthodox Marxism,
which proclaims the futility of social reform without revolution. Eda's social
reform theory, based upon policies developed by the Italian Communist Party,
holds that, although bourgeois democracy is an extremely limited form of democracy, it does at least guarantee to the proletariat certain rights that should
be utilized to advance the interests of the proletariat. Similarly, just as the
laboring class must exploit the existing political system, it must also improve
its economic position by reforming the present economic system rather than
seeking to overthrow it prematurely.—ED.

the state—and the expansion of systems to provide for the needs of the people. The welfare state provides for the needs of the people and gives us a fine illustration of this trend toward emphasizing "democracy *for* the people."

Let us examine what happens as "democracy *for* the people" begins to receive greater emphasis than "democracy *of* the people." It is only natural that the true essence of democracy—the spirit rather than the letter of the concept—tends to be increasingly ignored as a democratic system and certain procedures are established in any society. Consequently, the more the *system* takes hold, the more the essence of democracy becomes devitalized. Consider, for example, the case of ancient Athens, where a strong flavor of "democracy for the people" was evident, especially with regard to the nameless masses of the population. In his famous funeral oration, Pericles spoke as follows of Athenian democracy:

> Our form of government does not enter into rivalry with the institutions of others. We do not copy our neighbors but are an example to them. It is true that we are called a democracy, for the administration is in the hands of the many, not of the few. But while the law secures equal justice to all alike in their private disputes, the claim of excellence is also recognized; and when a citizen is in any way distinguished, he is preferred to the public service, not as a matter of privilege, but as the reward of merit. Neither is poverty a bar, but a man may benefit his country whatever be the obscurity of his condition.[1]

One can look upon this as simply an expression of the views of the ruler. One can also say that the situation in Athens was not all that glorious. There is, however, no doubting that both the rulers and the ruled in Athens regarded Athenian democracy as a model political form. One gathers that Pericles felt Athenian democracy was splendid because the citizenry enjoyed prosperity guaranteed by a magnificent state system. When I was studying in America in 1958, it was because of the similarities I found between American and Athenian attitudes toward democracy that I was often reminded of this speech of Pericles and marveled at democracy in America because it was a total way of life there

[1] *Orators of Ancient Greece*, vol. 1 of *The World's Orators* (New York: G. P. Putnam & Sons, 1900), p. 49.

(just as it had been in Athens). Surely this accounts for the tremendous strength the men of both countries exhibited in their courageous defense of their democracies against foreign enemies. It is truly awe-inspiring to observe Americans defending their fatherland. Their view of democracy includes an almost limitless trust in the government they have elected, and that too was something remarkable to observe. For Americans, democracy is a transcendental, self-evident truth that, in all its aspects, is absolutely undebatable. On the other hand, I was just a tiny bit uneasy about the attitude of the Americans. After all, only a few years after Pericles made his illustrious oration, Athenian democracy degenerated into mobocracy. What happened? Was not Athenian democracy itself at fault? The immediate cause of the transition from democracy to mob rule was the failure of the Sicilian expedition, but the basic cause lay with the Athenian people. When the Spartans defeated the Athenians in the Sicilian expedition, Athens's time of peril began. Can we say then that Athens's enemy had been a foreign enemy? Or was it not that the enemy was an internal enemy?

It seems that the same kind of phenomenon is occurring in contemporary America. It was democratic America that began the monstrous evil of the Vietnam war. On second thought, perhaps it is more correct to say that the blame for the war can be laid to American democracy itself. The people elected a President and they elected a Congress in accordance with democratic procedures, and then the President and Congress decided on war in Vietnam—all of this on the pretext that it was the will of the people. The end result was that the will of the President and Congress was forced upon the people in the form of a war in Vietnam.

The first to involve America in Vietnam was the "mainstream liberal," Harry S. Truman. Following him was Dwight D. Eisenhower, the "moderate liberal." And after him, it was John F. Kennedy, the great white hope of American liberalism, who deepened American involvement in the war. It was, of course, the American people who elected all of these liberals by democratic procedure. Truman and Eisenhower had helped to bring Nazi war criminals to trial on the grounds that human beings everywhere must obey a law of mankind that transcends the law of nations. They then turned around and ordered the American people to participate in the evil war in Vietnam, saying that it was their duty as citizens, something they had to do in order to protect democracy. When faced with that kind of an appeal, what is the citizen supposed to do?

In this connection, I find an analogy to the invasion and slaughter that democratic Athens perpetrated upon Melos in the Peloponnesian War. Before the battle, the Melians asked the Athenians: "But must we be your enemies? Will you not receive us as friends if we are neutral and remain at peace with you?"

To this the Athenians responded: "We shall endeavor to show that we have come in the interests of our empire, and that in what we are about to say we are only seeking the preservation of your city."

Because Melos failed to agree to the Athenian terms, the Athenians commenced hostilities and in the end defeated Melos and "thereupon put to death all who were of military age and made slaves of the women and children."

Every time I reread this passage of Thucydides, I am reminded first of all of my good-willed American friends and acquaintances and, secondly, of Socrates. To his death Socrates believed that, above all else, the democratic decisions of the people had to be respected. And yet this same Socrates had on two different occasions risked death by acting in opposition to the Council of Five Hundred. What then would Socrates have done if he had been ordered by law to participate in the massacre of the Melians as a member of the expeditionary army? American citizens are in very much the same predicament as Socrates would have been. When I was in Moscow and observed the absolutely unlimited trust of the Russians in their government, I was again reminded of this passage from Thucydides. Itsurō Sakisaka has written, "What deeply impressed me on meeting Soviet people was the confidence they had that 'Whatever our government promises to do, it does.'" I had the same feeling after meeting the Soviet people, although, in contrast to Sakisaka, my feelings were more of apprehension than admiration. With the exception of a very few, everybody talked about the aid that the Soviet Union was giving to North Vietnam but said nothing about their own willingness to participate in any kind of an anti–Vietnam war movement. It was a perfect example of the "if our government promises to do something, it does it" attitude. The problem is that it also did just what it promised in the case of the Hungarian rebellion.

The People, the State, and Power

There is a tendency when defining democracy as "government of the people, for the people, and by the people" to become captivated by the "of the people, for the people, and by the people" part of the definition and to overlook the hard realities that are implicit in the first word, "government." But as I have repeatedly pointed out above, democracy means the government and the state, and they mean power. The state is guided by its own internal logic as it strives to maintain its power, and on occasion it ruthlessly ignores the democratic principles on which it was founded. I cannot help feeling that there are two kinds of democracies—not only in Japan but in the whole world. Though it is perhaps an awkward expression, one might be called "state democracy" (*kokka minshushugi*). The other is "democracy *of* the people."

In the case of "state democracy," the people are simply objects to be ruled by the state. State democracy interprets "democracy *by* the people" (that is, institutional democracy) mainly in terms of "democracy *for* the people." As far as "democracy *of* the people" is concerned, state democracy regards that as a matter of somehow reflecting the will of the people in elections. In other words, it is simply a problem of mechanics or systems. Or to put it another way, the people are the implements that construct the sacred Diet and government; they are simply the "stuff" (*sozai*) of the state. The people are not only stupid, they are so disorderly that they must be instructed in moderation by the Prime Minister.

Nevertheless, even state democracy, if it is to live up to its claims to being a democratic system, must tolerate many ways of looking at a question. If the *system* is to survive, these different viewpoints must be tolerated. Yet it is clear to me that the spirit of democracy can be devitalized by the system. When democracy becomes devitalized, or formalized, different viewpoints, protests, opposition movements, demonstrations—all these become just so many institutional accessories indispensable for a stable "democratic order." When such activities go beyond being accessories, or when the government decides that they have exceeded their accessory role, then the government declares them to be "excessive" or "disorderly." Nor does this kind of devitalization occur in bourgeois democracies alone. I recall telling a young Soviet citizen whom I had met in Moscow that I had participated in an anti-Vietnam demonstration in the Soviet Union. He deprecated it as meaningless and futile. "Ah! Another government-sponsored rally," was his immediate response.

As societies become larger and more complicated, state democracy (as opposed to democracy of the people) generally becomes more and more prevalent. When I talk about state democracy, I am not simply referring to bureaucratism (*kanryō shugi*). State democracy involves much more basic problems of democracy, and the connotations of the phrase are much broader than bureaucratism. It is in this sense, therefore, that I believe that the Cultural Revolution in China has great meaning. One can detect there the outlines of an effort by the revolutionists to confront the problems of state democracy in China. That, at least, was the intention of Mao Tse-tung and the Red Guards when the movement was launched.

At that time, Mao called it the "seizure of power." This strikes me as interesting for two reasons. The first is the fact that there had taken root within the immense structure of proletarian democracy a powerful state democratic system in which Mao himself was severely constrained. That much is indisputable, and I would go further and say that to that extent Mao's course of action was appropriate. Of course, it was appropriate only insofar as the "seizers of power" were meant to be the people—on behalf of "democracy *of* the people"—and not simply Mao alone.

However, judging from the present state of affairs in China, and especially from such things as group recitations of the *Quotations of Chairman Mao,* I fear that the net result of the Cultural Revolution will be to create a Maoist state democracy to replace the existing state democracy.

My belief is that the only effective way of countering state democracy is to return once again to the principles of "democracy *of* the people." Once that is done, the ultimate goal of "democracy *for* the people" is within reach. If we proceed in that order, it will be clear that the emphasis up until the present has been just the opposite, that is, on the creation of "democracy *for* the people" as the initial step in the process. By starting with "democracy *for* the people" and then constructing a system of "democracy *by* the people" appropriate to it, "democracy *of* the people" becomes absorbed in the framework of the state democratic system, and the will of the people can be expressed only in ways sanctioned by that system.

Naturally, it is perfectly appropriate to utilize the customary pipeline of voting as a first step toward revitalizing democracy. Nevertheless, we would do well to keep in mind that there are serious flaws—almost inherent ones—in this approach. To put it simply, the flaw is that the voting citizen is said to have "entrusted" his political will to a certain candidate by voting for him, and the candidate is thereby said to "represent" the political will of the voter. The problem, however, is that the scope of the citizen's "trust" is nowhere clearly defined. To be sure, the time limits of the "trust" are spelled out in most countries; in Japan, for example, the limits are four years for members of the Lower House and six years for members of the Upper House. But does a vote cast because one approves of a certain candidate's stand on the public utility rates, for example, necessarily imply approval of that candidate's stand on the Vietnam war? Of course not. But in actuality it is taken for granted by everyone that it does.

Let us also consider the time factor, which somewhat complicates the question. In some cases, a certain issue might not even have developed at election time. Or, in other cases, the issue might not have assumed much importance. At such times the voter obviously cannot imagine how the candidate for whom he is casting his vote is going to represent his political will. But in fact, the Diet member always behaves as if he *is* representing the political will of his constituents.

We see fundamentally the same thing if we turn from the individual Diet members to political parties. But even here we know that simply because a certain party ably represents the will of a voter on domestic issues, it does not follow that it also represents his will on matters of foreign policy. We should switch, therefore, from an election system in which elections are held at certain predetermined time intervals to a system in which new elections are held in response to new issues. For example, if more than one-third of the total membership of the Diet should oppose the government on a certain issue, we would automatically have a new election. At any rate, unless some procedure is devised whereby important issues are submitted to a popular referendum, we will always have the danger of our democracy's being turned into state democracy. According to the public opinion polls of several newspapers, the opponents of the United States–Japan Mutual Security Treaty greatly outnumbered the proponents. And yet the Liberal Democratic Party supports the treaty on the pretext that it has the support of the people. There is no more perfect example of state democracy than that. Can we not also say that the Diet ignores the wishes of the vast majority of the Japanese population by its failure to declare its opposition to the war in Vietnam?

"Democracy *of* the people" is a way of thinking that starts with a recognition of the importance of the individual. For one thing, it is a way of thinking that recognizes that each individual lives just once and there is no substitute for that life. This outlook holds that a man can die from one bullet just as well as from nuclear war. It is a powerful refutation of the notion that, while we abhor nuclear wars, we can bear up under ordinary wars, a notion that has taken hold of our minds almost without our being aware of it. (I refer to it as a "nuclear mentality.") This recognition of the importance of the individual also points up a serious question about war and revolution, a question that is summed up in the assertion that there is really no difference between the mass slaughter perpetrated by the Americans in Vietnam and the terrorism perpetrated by the North Vietnamese in their war of liberation. Such an outlook may be completely wrong, but it is still an important argument that we dare not ignore. It is an argument already faced by the people of Vietnam and, in a sense, by the blacks of the American South. It is a question of how long and in what situations to persevere in a policy of nonviolence in the face of an overwhelming use of force by the establishment. In this connection, I must add that I cannot help but feel somewhat apprehensive about the naïveté of the younger generation of antiestablishment revolutionaries who, compared to the earlier generation—the "old left"—have not experienced the horrors of war and therefore may be inclined to resort to violence too quickly.

Also at the heart of the recognition of the individual's importance is the fact that, in the midst of the rapid acceleration of progress, the individual who appears to be an insignificant cog in a wheel is paradoxically becoming ever more important. (If this is not yet true, I would guess that it is what the future holds.) After all, as the mechanisms of our civilization become more and more complicated, that one little cog can cause the entire mechanism to come to a halt. If, for example, the veto power, a device appropriate to "democracy *of* the people," is exercised, the machinery grinds to a halt. To take an extreme example, we know that a small minority of individuals have the decision-making power with regard to the use of nuclear and hydrogen bombs, and yet, if this or that individual staff member refuses to push the button, the world may yet be saved from nuclear holocaust. As the individual citizen becomes aware that his increasing importance as an individual can be a powerful weapon, and as he translates this awareness into personal action, a vital step toward the achievement of "democracy *of* the people" will have been taken.

This outlook is based upon the premise that, as civilization advances and society becomes more complicated, the requirements of individuals tend to become more standardized on the one hand and more diversified on the other. Where we had total poverty (or something approaching it), the needs of one person tended to be the same as those of another. "Give us bread!" was the cry. I think we must acknowledge the basic fact that diversity of needs is an inevitable feature of contemporary life—and that the diversity is not merely one of means to attain goals but a diversity of the goals themselves. We must be aware of the fact that different individuals have diverse requirements and needs, and in some cases these requirements are mutually exclusive. We must also recognize the fact that there are different notions of what "democracy *of* the people" really is. Somehow, then, we must decide how we can convert these individual awarenesses of "democracy *of* the people" into a system of "democracy *of* the people" that functions on the national level and at the same time avoids being swallowed up piecemeal by state democracy.

This calls for some consideration of appropriate methods. Movements should be constructed in response to each individual issue for which a basic consensus of at least a fairly large number of people can be attained. An example is the anti–Vietnam war movement. Let me give you some of the thoughts I had before I inaugurated the Beheiren movement.* First of all, I felt that Beheiren should not have a permanent organizational structure but should be temporary and *ad hoc*. Next, the movement should address itself to a specific problem and not try to achieve such grand goals as the "protection of democracy." If we identified ourselves with such all-encompassing goals, many people might well join the movement, but each person would have a different interpretation of what democracy was, and in some cases those differences of opinion would be fatal to our movement.

Third, I believed that we should not incorporate every last issue into the movement. Major defects in the postwar antiestablishment movement in Japan were, first of all, that it emphasized grand-sounding goals like "protection of democracy" and, secondly, that it tried to accomplish too many tasks—everything from ending the Vietnam war to preventing increases in public utility rates. This was a fine way of mobilizing large numbers of supporters, but people do not all think alike all of the time, and to take for granted that they do is to ignore human nature. Moreover, by giving equal emphasis to all problems at all times, the movement lost its focus and strength. (I do not mean to overemphasize this point. I am aware that it is possible to channel the energies of a movement too exclusively toward one single issue.)

A fourth principle is a corollary to the third. That is, while we must be wary of tying too many causes together, we have to realize that a movement like the anti–Vietnam war movement will be strengthened only if it is joined to other directly related causes.

Fifth, we must not believe that our goals can be realized overnight but must consider them as long-range goals. Sixth, while we do consider alternative courses of action, we must avoid the

* Beheiren (League for Peace in Vietnam) is a citizens' antiwar group conceived, launched, and directed by Oda. He attempted to avoid ideological commitments and to seek the widest possible participation by individuals.—ED.

pitfall of vacillation. And, finally, the last principle, which I considered basic to founding Beheiren, was the interaction between the long-range, unchanging philosophy of Beheiren and the tactics of the organization, which would be flexible and geared to the moment.

One pattern of action that we have often seen in the antiestablishment movement is for intellectuals or civic groups to appeal for support and then, in response to that appeal, for labor unions to join the intellectuals or civic groups in a united front. While this method has not been tried in the United States it has been tried extensively throughout the advanced capitalist nations of the world. I certainly do not deny that the united-front technique is useful and still worth trying, but at the same time I believe it is necessary to form various movements in response to different problems among laborers, the general citizenry, or a combination of the two. There is today an all too common tendency for labor unionists to act only when their labor unions take action—a situation that leads to grave problems concerning the principles and functions of labor unions. It is a colossal error to continue to regard labor unions in themselves as a progressive force. I am not referring to the fact that most Japanese unions are company unions. Let us remind ourselves that American unions, which, on the one hand, are capable of waging a powerful economic struggle, are, on the other hand, extremely conservative in their political behavior. Far from being progressive there seems to be a worldwide trend toward labor unions' becoming very powerful instruments of state democracy. The trend is evident in the Soviet Union no less than in America. Therefore, laborers—as individuals—must endeavor to form politically progressive organizations just as the intellectuals and the man in the street do. If the laboring man does this, he will help to rid the labor movement of the elements of state democracy and turn it into a device for bringing about "democracy *of* the people."

Finally, we must extend our consideration of "democracy *of* the people" to the level of international democracy. The big powers have established a system of international democracy (or at least something that appears to be international democracy) "for the numerous nations of the world" and "by the numerous nations of the world." Once the system has been established, the various small countries of the world become so much "stuff," existing only for the sake of the system. The system of international democracy must be reorganized so that it exists *for* the small nations of the world rather than the other way around. In order to do this, it is necessary that there be profound appreciation of the notion of "democracy *of* the people" by all peoples, including the peoples of the big powers that are now oppressing the smaller nations of the world. Let us imagine a factory worker who is somehow involved in the production of goods that America uses in prosecuting the war in Vietnam. If that factory worker lacks an appreciation of the notion of "democracy *of* the people," then he will find it difficult to see that at least a part of his life is made possible by denying democracy to the people of Vietnam. Thus, while this laborer is a victim exploited within the system of state democracy, he is at the same time an exploiter vis-à-vis the Vietnamese people.

The peoples of the world, especially the so-called advanced peoples who have had long experience with a "system" of democracy, have reached a new stage: They must now take another look at democracy. They must re-examine the true meaning of democracy and remake democracy so that it is their own. I believe the Japanese people are no exception.

9

The Japanese Economy

Yasuo Sakakibara

The Economy and the Society

A school play produced and directed by a junior high school student in Kyoto last autumn started with the familiar phrase: "Once upon a time, there lived an old man and his wife. . ." But in this version, Momotarō* was not born from a peachstone floating in the clean water of a brook but was instead a sudden mutation of the species caused by mercury-contaminated mud in the river. When he grew up, he took a dog, a monkey, and a pheasant with him (as in the legend) to attack the paper mill and chemical factory upstream. Company officials were depicted as demons, and Momotarō won the battle against the demons, at least temporarily.

One doesn't have to be a junior high school student to see the extent of pollution in Japan. Those who live in the Tokyo-Yokohama area can count on one hand the days of the year when they can see the blue sky. To the question, "What does Tokyo not have?" on a television quiz program, the correct answer was "sky." Riders on a commuter train in the Osaka-Kobe area have to hold their noses so as not to smell the stench when the train crosses over the Kanzaki River.

Cleanliness may have been a traditional virtue for centuries

* Momotarō is the hero of a Japanese folk tale born out of a peachstone (*momo* means peach) to an elderly childless couple.—ED.

in Japan, but it seems to have been forgotten, at least for most of the postwar period. Or one might say that the Shinto regard for cleanliness and purity has been submerged into the Buddhist characteristic of self-denial and withdrawal. In any case, the Japanese have tolerated pollution because they have been concentrating their efforts on rapid economic growth. After all, the only thing the Japanese could be proud of, after the destruction of the Imperial Army and Navy, was their economic achievements, capped by the world's fastest economic growth rate.

Not only in the air and in rivers but also in other matters vital to decent living, Japanese have seen little improvement in spite of the country's well-publicized economic growth. Twenty-five years after the end of World War II Japan still had an acute housing shortage. Indeed, housing is so short that it has changed the pattern of courtship in the cities. A proposal of marriage these days is not considered official unless the man tells the girl where they will live after marriage. Even those lucky people who can live in their parents' house or can buy a house find their housing situation utterly inadequate. They may have a color TV set or even a car, but still they live in a small house with no flush toilet, not to mention central heating and hot running water. The housing shortage is caused in part by the internal migration of the population to cities and by the growing independence of the nuclear family. However, it cannot be denied that it is also caused by the governmental lack of concern for the environment.

For the average Japanese, it is and always has been almost impossible to buy a piece of land on which to build a house. Between 1955 and 1964, land prices rose more than 20 per cent per year, and they rose more than 10 per cent per year from 1965 to 1969. However large a percentage a man saves of his income, he can hardly catch up with the steep rise in land prices. On the other hand, prices of other consumer durables have been declining because of increased productivity. So Japanese can save enough to buy TV sets or cars, but they cannot buy a piece of land. Moreover, only a limited amount of consumer credit has been available to the Japanese consumer, because most of the money gathered by banks has been invested in plant and equipment.

Thus, most Japanese in cities have been forced to live in places far distant from their work. In the Tokyo area, a man who can find a place to live within two hours' commuting distance is considered lucky. This situation also aggravates the urban transportation problem. During rush hour on a commuter train a man can hardly breathe, the crowding is so severe. In winter, the problem is even worse than in summer: Trains can carry fewer people or must pack them in even tighter, because each person, with his overcoat, takes more space. On crowded runs, commuter trains with more than a dozen cars leave the station every two minutes. A Japanese sociologist has commented that the Japanese are commuting the distance between the number-two ranking of the Japanese gross national product in the free world and their number-twenty ranking in per capita GNP.*

The Japanese may have cars, but they don't have the roads on which to drive them. Road construction has not kept pace with the increase in automobiles. Today every seventh Japanese has a car, and soon every fifth will. If we placed all the cars in Japan on paved roads, the distance between each car would be only five meters; soon it will be only three meters. Accident rates are naturally very high, and nearly 20,000 people were killed on the roads in 1970.

Education is another area of life that does not seem to show any improvement with rapid economic growth. More and more students are going on to higher education, but investment in schools has been minimal. Since 1955, the ratio of junior high school graduates entering senior high school has increased from 48 to 78 per cent. The proportion of senior high school graduates going to colleges and universities has risen from 15 to 24 per cent. Japan today has more than 500 colleges and universities, including junior colleges. Many of these colleges were established after World War II and are derided as "box-lunch colleges." To accommodate increasing numbers of college students, Japan depends on private institutions. In order to meet higher costs, colleges accept more students; to accept more students, colleges have to build more buildings, and in order to build more buildings they have to accept more students. Meanwhile, the faculty-student ratio

---

* By 1970, Japan ranked eighteenth in per capita GNP (calculated at the rate of 360 yen to the dollar). The recent revaluation of the yen has raised Japan's rank further.—ED.

goes down and the quality of education deteriorates. Private universities, which are surviving on a hand-to-mouth basis financially, cannot give thought to what type of university graduates society is demanding today. To compound the trouble, the business community does not contribute to the universities and seems to be satisfied with the situation as long as it can secure enough college graduates. The government has avoided taking responsibility. The end result has been riots on campuses.

Are all these inconveniences the result of our highly cherished "fastest economic growth?" Do we have to sacrifice ourselves to this extent to achieve economic miracles? Can't we now afford to have some improvements in these items, sacrificing instead the high rate of economic growth? The Japanese have started asking questions, and things have started slowly to change.

Students, newspapers, government officials, Marxists, and even businessmen are now all talking about the threat of pollution, dangers on the roads, and the deterioration of education. Students who lost the campus fight last year are particularly ready to fight against what they consider social evils, even though some have the agonizing thought that the fight against pollution is not as exciting as that against the Vietnam war and Mutual Security Treaty revision. Many of the leading economists have written articles denouncing the use of the gross national product as a measure of economic growth. Government officials and businessmen, sensing the coming of the inevitable, are proposing various measures to improve the situation.

The Japanese Economic Miracle

When the price paid is ignored, Japanese economic achievements are remarkable indeed. From shambles and dust, Japan has striven successfully to build an economy whose size is second only to the United States in the free world and third in the whole world. Even today, the expansion of the Japanese economy never seems to stop. Its GNP increased from 1960 to 1965 at the rate of 9.9 per cent annually in real terms, and from 1965 to 1969 the rate was 11.7 per cent. This means that, out of $160 billion GNP in 1969, 27.2 per cent is attributable to the increase in the first half of the decade and 46.9 per cent to the increase of the last four years. National income per capita increased from $382 in 1960 to $1,290 in 1969.

I am sure if there were a hundred economists in Japan, there would be a hundred different ways of explaining the reasons for such rapid economic growth. But I have my own pet theory, the "good-luck-and-the-ability-to-grab-good-luck" theory. I do not think that we can deny the existence of good luck as a factor in the development of any country. Whether we can exploit it or not is another matter, because people often do not even realize its existence or, realizing it, let it pass them by because of ill-timed policy. For example, we have seen a constant decline in ocean shipping costs since World War II as a result of technological innovations in shipbuilding. Ships have become larger, in fact gigantic in terms of the prewar standard, and further, specialized bulk carriers are now being built and used. Larger and more specialized ships have reduced the cost of shipping, thereby giving Japanese products a geographical advantage. The Japanese are lucky in the fact that technological innovation occurred in shipping, not in land transportation, and Japanese businessmen have been shrewd enough to exploit their improving geographical advantage. If this were not the case, how could Japanese steel, whose production requires Indian ore and American coal, be shipped to the United States and still be competitive? Without the decline in shipping costs, the Japanese economy would have had a lower ceiling on economic growth.

Though the geographical advantage the Japanese economy has been enjoying does not seem likely to disappear in the near future, all other possible reasons for rapid economic growth seem to be losing or are expected to lose ground.

Economic theory tells us that two important determinants of economic growth are the rate of saving and the efficiency of capital invested. Throughout the 1960's, Japanese savings accounted for 33 to 40 per cent of the GNP—a very high proportion indeed. Domestic capital formation (which is equal to saving) grew 18 per cent annually in the 1960's and had exceeded $80 billion* by 1970, second in volume only to the United States.

* Calculated at the 1970 exchange rate of 360 yen to the dollar. Under the rate that became effective in December, 1971, this figure was about $95 billion. In February, 1973, the dollar was again devalued and the yen was floated.—ED.

Out of total capital formation, 34 per cent was saved by households, 44 per cent by corporations, and the remainder by the government. Household saving has been the most important because it has been the component that made total saving high in Japan. It increased in the 1960's at the annual rate of 17 per cent, higher than the increase in consumption. No one knows for sure why the Japanese have been saving so much, but the following seem to stand out among many possible reasons: (1) the traditional Japanese virtue of thriftiness, (2) the inadequacy of the social security system, (3) the need to save for children's higher education, (4) the bonus system, and (5) the lack of consumer credit.

Most economists doubt, however, that these factors will continue to be significant in the 1970's. Traditional values, such as self-sacrifice and individual restraint, are quickly disappearing as the Japanese come to be interested more in yen than in Zen. Consumption is becoming a competitive virtue, especially among the younger generation. Thousands of women swarm through the department stores in the daytime, and men hunt bars at night in the back alleys of the cities. The social security system may continue to be inadequate, but the Japanese are becoming increasingly optimistic about the future, making households less concerned about saving for rainy days. The Japanese will continue to be education-minded, but students' fees for universities, especially national universities, will also continue to be low. The bonus, as a form of wage payment, was significant in the 1960's because roughly half of it was saved, on the average. However, as the starting wage for new school graduates rises because of the labor shortage, the relative share of the bonus in the total income of a household may decrease. Optimism may also increase the propensity to consume the bonus because of the expectation of future bonuses. In the 1960's, the Japanese had difficulty in obtaining bank loans to finance major consumer durables and houses, hence they had to save money to purchase them. Most economists and businessmen agree that credit conditions will ease in the 1970's. All this suggests that Japan's already high household saving rate will not increase and may actually decrease.

Corporate saving has grown fast—especially since 1965—because of the extended boom, but it is doubtful that it can continue to do so. Over-all corporate earnings are unlikely to increase as fast as they did in the past, because a larger share will have to be spent on labor and on research and development. Government savings are difficult to forecast, but possible increases in defense expenditures (currently less than 1 per cent of GNP) and improvement in the social security system can be significant factors restraining the growth of government savings. Thus, total savings (including household, corporate, and government) relative to GNP are likely to decline in the future.

Unusually high capital efficiency has been maintained so far in Japan. Among many possible reasons for high efficiency, the following two seem to be most relevant:

(1) Japan has not had to spend a lot of money in research and development. It could readily import new technologies, developed mostly in the United States, with a relatively small amount of royalty payments. It could even choose the best among available technological developments. Since the efforts of Japanese firms after the war have been concentrated on catching up with the West as quickly as possible, they have found imports of technology much cheaper than trying to develop their own. Though investment in research and development will pay off in the long run, in the short run it has a low efficiency of capital.

While Japan has had a relatively large reserve of scientists, they have had a meager amount of research money. If we have had any comparative advantage in research and development, it has been in the areas that require manpower rather than money, such as electronic appliances and optical apparatus. Japan has spent little money on "big science," such as aerospace, atomic energy, and military hardware, where efficiency of capital is even lower.

However, Japan today has reached a Western level of technology, and it is expected that in the next decade its investment in research and development will rise. Already many big corporations have large-scale laboratories manned by top scientists, and they are allotting increasingly larger percentages of income for research. Further, the Japanese Government is also expected to spend more money on "big science" as a matter of national pride, and this will also reduce the efficiency of capital in Japan.

(2) There are many lines of investment with varying degrees

of capital efficiency. For example, investment in machines is more productive than investment in offices and thus increases the GNP faster. In the same way, capital efficiency would be lower for sewerage systems, housing, education, road construction, and the like, as compared with plant and equipment. The Japanese have neglected the lines of economic activity that have a lower efficiency of capital and have concentrated on machines. Even in road investment, Japan has built highways that would facilitate the movement of goods rather than improving local roads, since the latter have lower efficiency.

In the sense that the economic miracle of Japan has been based on the neglect of areas vital to a decent living, the anger of the middle class is well justified. In the near future, when this neglect becomes politically dangerous to the ruling Liberal Democrats, Japan will be forced to invest more in sewerage, housing, education, and roads.

A brief survey of the two important determinants of economic growth, saving and efficiency of capital, suggests that the growth rate of the Japanese economy will fall in the future. Furthermore, there are other possible bottlenecks to rapid economic growth in Japan, a mishandling of which may bring serious consequences.

Factors Affecting Japan's Future Growth

Rapid economic growth would have been impossible if Japan had not had an efficient, well-educated, hard-working, and relatively abundant labor force. On the other hand, the stereotyped description of Japanese workers as people who are loyal to the company and receive low wages with long work hours is, of course, wrong. They are human beings with the same earthly desires as other workers. They want higher pay and shorter hours, and prefer easier work to hard work.

In the 1960's Japan, for the first time in its history, faced a serious shortage of labor. It is said that there are now about five job openings for every new entrant to the labor market. Most Japanese firms today think of the labor shortage as their most pressing problem. Indeed, many small firms have gone bankrupt, not because of the shortage of demand or of capital, but because they could not secure enough workers. The pamphlets for recruitment issued by various companies always show beautiful dormitory buildings with a TV set in each room, delicious menus with sukiyaki twice a week, and various recreational activities, including swimming and ski trips at company expense. Yet, many companies still face the problem of unutilized production facilities due to lack of manpower.

In the foreseeable future, there is no prospect that the labor shortage will be eased. The over-all population growth rate has been down to 1 per cent per annum for some time; it is only natural that Japanese parents who live in a small apartment want to buy a car before they have a baby. As a result, it is estimated that the working-age population will grow by only 3 million in the next decade. The spread of higher education is another factor behind the labor shortage, especially of blue-collar workers. Today, a new blue-collar worker is called a golden egg, and to recruit him a year in advance of his graduation is called *aota-gai,* or buying rice when it is still green in the paddies.

It remains to be seen how much this growing manpower shortage will force changes in Japan's economic structure. As labor costs go up, Japan will certainly lose its comparative advantage in labor-intensive industries, such as textiles. Some prices in the service sector, where productivity increase is hard to achieve, are rising fast, and a haircut will soon cost as much in Japan as in the United States. Whether rising labor costs will bring inflationary pressure or not depends on how smoothly the Japanese economy can be transformed to meet the new situation and on how fast productivity increases can be achieved in manufacturing. In spite of its fast growth, Japan's labor productivity is still one-third that of the United States, and there is plenty of room for further rationalization of industries. Already today, it is reported that labor-saving investment is growing faster than that for expansion of production.

Together with rationalization within industries, labor mobility will have to be encouraged so as to facilitate the movement of workers from less productive sectors of the economy to more productive ones. Though the agricultural labor force dropped sharply in the last decade, 18 per cent of the total labor force still work on farms, their employment made possible by an expensive rice price-support program. Department stores have too many receptionists who do nothing but bow to customers. Offices have too many secretaries who do nothing but clean desks and bring cups of tea to guests. There are more girls in the entertainment industry than in the textile industry. This contributes to the Japanese consumption of beer and also to the inflationary trend of the economy. Utilization of older workers (traditionally the compulsory retirement age in business firms has been fifty-five years) and of part-time women workers (married women usually have not worked) will also have to be expanded.

Nevertheless, there is a possibility that gains in productivity and redistribution may not be sufficient to keep prices down, and if that happens the growth rate will have to be checked and the transformation process slowed down. Since any adjustment necessarily brings some pain to some people, the expansion of the social security system will become a necessity.

Energy or power may become another significant bottleneck to Japanese growth. Availability of relatively cheap sources of power is essential to economic growth. Japan has depended heavily on foreign countries for its fuel supply, especially for oil. Heavy fuel oil consumption in Japan, most of it coming from the Middle East, increased thirteen times from 1955 to 1968, while the GNP increased only six times. If something happened to the fuel supply line, the Japanese economy would immediately collapse. In this sense, Japanese prosperity has depended on world peace, hence the economic basis for Japan's advocacy of pacifism.

There is another side to the problem—air pollution. If the current rate of increase in oil consumption continues, the day is not too far distant when a 300,000-ton tanker will have to leave a Japanese port for the Middle East every three minutes to accommodate it. The thought scares many Japanese. Among Japan's sources of energy, the percentage of liquid fuel is 58.4 and that of natural gas, which creates less pollution, is only 1.4. (In the United States the former percentage is 39.9, the latter 36.1.) Japan is now hunting seriously for oil with a smaller sulphur content. In addition, it is trying to import more natural gas and is discussing the possibility of building refiner ships that can process oil in transit. Yet these measures are not likely fully to alleviate the problem, which is further complicated by the fact that few potential hydroelectric power sites remain.

All this seems to suggest that Japan will have to depend increasingly on atomic energy in the future, though atomic energy is still expensive at present and its use will not completely solve the problem of pollution. Yet the Japanese, who still suffer from the wartime shock of the atomic bomb are, as some people say, in a state of atomic *arerugi* (allergy), and anything atomic scares them. Whether Japan will be able to adjust successfully to the atomic age will be a significant factor in the future economy of Japan.

As already stated, Japan has relied on the intensive use of its stock of social overhead capital to achieve rapid economic growth. Prices are kept low artificially in most services, and this discourages new investment. As a result, transportation and public utilities are in seriously short supply today and, except for a few scattered cases, the modernization of their facilities is lagging behind economic growth. Practically all modes of transportation and public utilities are crowded, creating high distribution costs. Unless we increase the investment in these areas, they can constitute serious bottlenecks to further growth.

Japanese National Railways has been known abroad as one of the most efficient systems in the world. However, a glance at its balance sheet will reveal its pathetic financial condition. Costs are rising faster than revenues, and debts are accumulating. The system makes ends meet on only five lines; all others run in the red. Instead of abandoning expensive local lines, the government, under pressure from local politicians, is still building new ones, the management of which will be left to National Railways. One small ray of hope lies in the commercial success of the New Tokaido Line. National Railways is now planning to build 3,100 miles of wide-gauge track on which to run super expresses.

Road-building may be more important in the future than today, because trucks carry far more goods than railroads, and trucks' share in the total freight carried is increasing very fast. However, road conditions in Japan today are, again, pathetic. Only 15 per cent of the roads have hard surfaces and only a little more than 1 per cent are paved with concrete. A large-scale road construction program is now under way, and within fifteen years Japan is expected to have thirty-two express highways with a total length of more than 4,700 miles. Problems here are the mountainous terrain, high land prices, and the lack of the concept of eminent domain, all of which contribute to high construction costs.

The creation of adequate port facilities is another area in which Japan has lagged behind. Most of Japan's ports cannot handle increasing freight volume efficiently today, further contributing to high distribution costs. Expansion and modernization of facilities and the construction of new integrated terminals on land and sea are urgently needed. The two main international airports, Haneda and Osaka, are simply overcrowded. The construction of a new international airport in the Tokyo area has been delayed, mostly because of the opposition of residents near the site, but is due to open in 1973.

Water consumption in Japan jumped from 32,580,000 tons a day in 1960 to 78,640,000 tons a day in 1967, and the problem of keeping an adequate water supply for households and industries is fast becoming a headache for local governments. A scientist has even suggested covering all the lakes and reservoirs with inflated vinyl sheets to prevent evaporation.

The high demand for telephones is causing a huge backlog of orders. To meet unfilled orders, the Telephone and Telegraph Public Corporation launched a five-year plan to install an additional 9 million phones by 1972, but the backlog of orders will remain even after its completion.

Whether Japan will succeed in ameliorating the pressing conditions in these areas by securing enough funds—and without sacrificing its famed growth rate—remains to be seen. However, it seems rather essential at this stage for Japan to review the whole pricing structure of these services and to put future investment in these areas on an economically sound basis.

Less than ten years ago, Japanese economists argued that the economic base of Japan was shallow and that chronic difficulty in the balance-of-payments situation would continue to haunt the Japanese economy. Few, if any, predicted that Japan would soon be in the position where people would not know what to do with the accumulating foreign currency surplus. Today the foreign currency reserve exceeds $4 billion and is still increasing. Government officials are still plagued by a miser's psychology and do not know how to use these funds. They fear being forced to revalue the yen again under the pressure of world public opinion (it was revalued more than 15 per cent in December, 1971). Here a major shift in policies is needed, and the people should be prepared for the consequences.

Current accumulation of foreign currencies is due to the rapid expansion of exports and the relatively slow rate of increase in imports. There are several reasons for this development. First, Japanese exports have increased on the average at a rate 1.8 times the rate of increase of total world imports. World imports have been expanding fast in the past years, and correspondingly, so are Japanese exports. Second, the Japanese industrial structure has adjusted successfully to the production of heavy industrial and chemical products and has thus been able to take advantage of the demand in the world market, a demand that has been growing faster than that for other products. Third, although consumer prices have risen considerably in Japan, wholesale prices have been relatively stable, and thus the country has been able to keep a comparative price advantage for many goods despite worldwide inflationary trends. Fourth, the prices of goods Japan imports have not risen as fast as those of the goods it exports, with the result that terms of trade have continued to be favorable to Japan. Finally, contrary to the experiences of other advanced countries, Japan's imports have not increased proportionally with the per capita rise in income. In other words, the Japanese economy is becoming more self-sufficient with the rise in income.

This last reason is puzzling to most economists, since it is generally assumed that the propensity to import goods should rise along with a rise in personal income. High marginal propensity to save in Japan may be one explanation for this analogy, but formal and informal control of some imports and tariffs may be another significant explanation. If so, the direction in which the Japanese economy should move is very clear—import liberalization. After all, the Japanese are eating the world's highest-priced rice and meat. Consumer prices are rising generally, and an import increase will help in fighting inflation. It is also likely that some foreign markets will be virtually closed unless Japan quickly liberalizes its imports. Already one can hear complaints from many corners of the world that the Japanese are self-centered and are interested only in selling, not buying. One cannot blame other Asians who denounce the new imperialism of Japan, for in most Asian eyes the Japanese look as if they were conquering Asia again, with yen and briefcases this time. If one asks a Filipino about the possibility of developing light industries in the Philippines, he will invariably ask: "How do you think we can compete with Japan in those products?"

Import liberalization cannot be attained without pain to some people. The bureaucrats who have wielded the power over exchange control will lose their power and with it the possibility of advancement in the bureaucracy. Politicians from the farm areas may not be re-elected. The Liberal Democratic Party may lose the solid support of the farm bloc. Businessmen and farmers who receive the direct competition of expanded imports will be the hardest hit. In spite of all these hardships, import liberalization must be carried out if the Japanese economy is to improve its efficiency and grow further.

With import liberalization, the Japanese industrial structure will be forced to change to some extent. Agriculture will be the first to be affected. Imports of agricultural products per person in Japan amount to only one-fourth of those of Great Britain and West Germany. If we increase imports, some farmers, a group that constitutes 18 per cent of the labor force but creates only 7.3 per cent of GNP, will be forced off their farms. The manufacture of products of labor-intensive industries, such as textiles, textile products, sewing machines, binoculars, and transistor radios, may well be shifted to developing countries, thus giving these nations hope. Naturally, some unemployment will be created at home, at least temporarily. Yet productivity in Japan will rise by concentrating on the production of capital-intensive and technically sophisticated products.

Admittedly, this is easier said than done. A few years ago there was a debate on the importation of grapefruit. The Agriculture Ministry had previously encouraged farmers to grow *natsumikan* (sour summer oranges) in an attempt to diversify farm products. The ministry could not afford to permit liberalization in the importation of grapefruit, which was expected to be directly competitive with the summer orange, because this would make the government's mistake in farm policy clear to everyone. What Japan needs today is a concentrated effort to persuade various interests not to block the way to further growth.

Liberalization of foreign investment should also be on the agenda. A Toyota man will invariably say, with great pride, that Toyota cars are the best in the world, at least in a certain range of horsepower. Yet, if one asks him about the liberalization of foreign investment, he will argue that, if Japan did this, the big three U.S. auto makers would build assembly plants in Japan and would instantly destroy the domestic automobile manufacturers.*

This seemingly contradictory statement, which one often gets from the Japanese, reflects the psychology of businessmen and government officials. What they fear is domination of the domestic market by foreign capital. This fear may be difficult to understand for Americans, who have much more land area and much larger markets. Yet, unless reciprocal treatment is given to foreign firms in Japan, Japanese goods will not have access to foreign markets, especially when foreigners hear the Japanese boast of the size of their GNP and the amount of their foreign currency reserves.

This suggests that Japan is entering a new stage in its international relations, whether it likes it or not. Advanced countries will increasingly look at Japan as a fierce competitor and insist that it compete on an equal basis. Developing countries will regard Japan as an economic giant that should take on more of the responsibility of being rich. Also, the world community will feel that it cannot neglect Japan politically. The new situation may satisfy the Japanese ego, yet whether Japan can face competition with a responsible attitude is hard to predict, especially because it tends to regard a competitor as an enemy rather than as a friend, and because it can often be a bad loser. In any event, a narrowly nationalistic point of view will not help the future of Japan.

Conclusion

So far, some of the significant factors that are expected to influence the future course of the Japanese economy have been dis-

---

* Although the big three American auto makers have negotiated affiliations in Japan, liberalization is not yet complete.—ED.

cussed. All these factors seem to suggest that to keep the current growth rate high will become increasingly difficult in the future. It may even be better for the growth rate to fall in order to provide more decent living conditions for the Japanese. "A wise man does not hurry history," Adlai Stevenson once said, but the Japanese have been hurrying it by aiming at maximum GNP growth. Probably a more balanced growth is in order at this stage. Yet a political problem still remains. How smoothly can Japan adjust to the changing economic structure demanded for further growth, creating a minimum amount of dissatisfaction among its populace? Can the average Japanese, who is accustomed to having a sizable income increase every year, be satisfied with a smaller income increase? How can national pride in the fastest economic growth in the world be redirected by the Japanese leadership? In this sense, if the 1960's and early 1970's can be categorized as a period in Japanese history when economic matters were paramount, the later 1970's and 1980's may become a period dominated by politics and diplomacy.

In the world community, Japan is gradually becoming a proponent, within limits, of idealism, as is apparent in its interest in a nuclear test ban, free trade, world peace, and equality among races. However, mere emphasis on idealism can hardly be a good substitute for the fastest economic growth. Leadership will be necessary. Among many others, maybe that is one reason why Japan recently collected enough courage to resist strongly voluntary textile export quotas. Japan is still timid, cautious, and basically inner-oriented. Yet this may be the beginning of Japan's realization that a "hands-off" attitude does not work to its advantage.

Most of the problems the Japanese economy faces today are new to the Japanese, but to try to avoid them will be useless. The people's energy should be given a new and constructive direction. If we can do this, later historians may then characterize the early 1970's as an important turning point in Japanese history.

PART THREE

Youth—Ideals—Education

10

Changing Images Among Youth in Modern Japan

Hidetoshi Katō

The Meiji Period: Ambition

Starting in the autumn of 1902, a novel by Kenjirō Tokūtomi, *Roka* or *Notes of Reminiscence,* appeared serially in a daily paper, *Kokumin Shimbun.* Soon it became popular among the youth of Japan and among a wide range of readers. There was an even greater response when the novel was published in book form in 1903. Readers felt an empathy with the sentiments of the book, sensing that, with fortitude and resolution, one could overcome hardships and discouragement. The novel gave expression to a certain vitalizing spirit that appealed to the youth of the Meiji Period (1868–1912).

Notes of Reminiscence portrays an idealized image of youth that was prevalent in the latter half of the Meiji Period. Shintarō Kikuchi, the hero of the novel, was born in Kumamoto in northern Kyushu on the eve of the Meiji Restoration in 1868. He comes from a family of wealthy winemakers that enjoys high prestige in the village. However, Shintarō's father goes bankrupt during a period of serious inflation and then has bad luck in his new business enterprise. His house and all his belongings are taken away, and he dies from the great shock of his misfortune. Shintarō and his mother then move into an uncle's house not too far away. *Notes of Reminiscence* describes how a youth with no property and no rights grew up in late nineteenth-century Japan. How is he to live, and what goals should he choose?

As Shintarō is leaving his village after his father's death to move to his uncle's house, Shingo, a former servant and now a charcoal-maker, says farewell and urges him, "Please come back as a person of great renown. It is not worthwhile to stay in a village like this." On several later occasions, Shingo again says, "Strive for renown." In another scene, Shintarō's mother admonishes him to be ambitious and successful.

Some years later Shintarō goes to Tokyo, and the first letter he receives from his mother contains the following passage:

> You have the great task of rebuilding the house of Kikuchi. Please think well upon it and be careful not to disgrace the name of Kikuchi. It is my hope that you will always strive for renown.

Her phrase, "strive for renown," echoes in his mind, but how can Shintarō be successful? He decides that there is one sure way —by studying hard and diligently. First of all, he enters Nishiyama Private School near his uncle's house and learns classical Chinese. But when he is fifteen the school closes because classical Chinese is no longer in demand for the future of Japan. Teachers at the school now encourage all the students to study other foreign languages instead.

Meanwhile, a school called Ikuei Gakusha has just been established. To it comes a teacher of foreign studies named Tetsujirō Komai. He provides Shintarō's first contact with foreign studies. Komai leaves the school after a short while, but Shintarō now hopes fervently to study foreign ways in Tokyo. He decides to go there and, after some difficulty, studies first at Kwansei Gakuin University and then at Tokyo Imperial University.

In this period away from home, Shintarō confronts many hardships and troubles. On one occasion, he has to surrender his coat because he does not have the money for a bowl of noodles at a restaurant. He works delivering newspapers, but he never gives up his ambition.

Studies form a significant part of Shintarō's life. At night he quietly lights a small lamp in a closet and studies mathematics. He never misses his English classes, which meet twice a week. He often finds a quiet refuge in a corner of a library when the dormitory is too noisy. Once in a while, Shintarō sits under a tree by a pond and indulges in meditation. At Tokyo University, he tries his best to economize on school supplies. This is Shintarō's college life, and he graduates with the highest grades from Kwansei Gakuin University and is then second in his class at Tokyo University.

Shintarō's prime purpose in studying is to attain fame and success. Yet he tries not to be dependent on anyone. He makes his decisions without regard to what other people think, basing them solely on his own judgment of what is just and right. When he becomes discouraged, he recalls his determination to succeed on his own.

At Tokyo University, the other students are superficial in their commitment. All are interested in renown and success after graduation, but many hope to find a short cut to social success by seeking favors from men with prestige and influence. Shintarō objects to this, and he expresses himself as follows just before his graduation:

> When the time comes and there is a chance, I will sit on a golden chair. But for unexpected success, I cannot beg and make silly faces at the door of somebody influential. . . . Thus, my principle is that if I become successful through my own efforts, I shall gratefully give thanks to heaven. Success and social fame attained justly I shall gladly accept. However, if I have to give up my own integrity as the price of success, I shall maintain my principles and carry my head high until it is cut off.

For Shintarō, life is a battlefield. The entrance examinations for the university are his first battle. As he says, "This battle must be fought with all my might, so that my disgrace can be washed away, my hardships rewarded, my honor maintained, and my mother comforted."

For Shintarō, friends are rivals. Matsumura, his grade school friend, is the son of the president of a large company. He goes to Tokyo before Shintarō does. Most of his friends at Kwansei Gakuin University come from wealthy families, but Shintarō must first earn his tuition and his living, and then excel over his friends in studies.

In the end, Shintarō wins his battle and attains fame and success. Among his friends, Matsumura has also had a successful career, and friendship is reaffirmed among those who have succeeded. For those who have failed there is sympathy, but not much attention is paid to them.

The Taishō Period: Human Feelings

The young people of the Taishō Period (1912–25) found it difficult to project and plan their future clearly on a straight, single track as Shintarō had. No clear pattern of means and ends existed in the process of attaining goals. Perhaps for this reason, the relationships that young people established in the course of attaining their goals became more important than the goals themselves.

The novel *Friendship (Yūjō)* by Saneatsu Mushakōji gives the flavor of youthful attitudes in the Taishō Period. Nojima, the protagonist, falls in love with Sugiko, the sister of a friend. Ōmiya, another friend of Nojima's, tries his best to help the couple, but, ironically, Sugiko falls in love with Ōmiya. The novel is largely an exploration of the feelings existing between Nojima and Ōmiya.

For Shintarō Kikuchi in *Notes of Reminiscence*, there are almost infinite possibilities to choose from in planning his future. Nojima, on the other hand, is shy and takes fewer chances. He often spends time reflecting on people whom he admires. At twenty-three, Nojima is not at all self-confident; he thinks he has little ability and regards himself as worthless. His perceptions are directed inward. He often thinks about how other people think of him. As a result of this extreme introspection, he becomes bored with life and then desperate. He analyzes his longing for Sugiko:

> Some think marriage provides a good chance for promotion in one's jobs or brings primarily a dowry. Some look on marriage as a trifling thing, or something sweet, but I cannot stand such ideas. Sugiko looks as if she does not know about such things, but I should feel kind of lost if, after all, she really did have such hopes.

Nojima is wrapped up in contemplation about himself, the delicate feelings of other people, and his changing relationships with them. Then, in reaction, he sinks into despair and tries to forget it all. For example, when Nojima, who is not a very good table tennis player, plays the game at a friend's house, he tries to think that being a poor player is nothing to be ashamed of.

That is a good excuse, but if I were good, I wouldn't feel such inferiority. Oh, I would feel great if I were really good. Since I am so poor a player, I think there is no need to show off, but if I were skillful, I would never have to bother with such petty thoughts; I would feel much better.

Note that the word "feel" is used several times. It expresses the various thoughts about certain incidents that appear and disappear in Nojima's mind. He is upset when he sees Sugiko with her friend at the beach, but he thinks that it is stupid to be jealous, feels a little ashamed, and then tries not to think about it. He is not certain of his identity and worries about it. Always uppermost in his mind is a concern about a small social circle consisting of a few friends and their families.

Youth of the Meiji Period found the world to be a place of vast, almost infinite opportunities for the future. In contrast, Nojima's world is merely the small society in which he lived. He is happy in this well-protected and comfortable world. In one of his frequent chats with Ōmiya, there is this exchange.

NOJIMA: I've started to write a novel.

ŌMIYA: Yes, I feel like doing something. I should study, too.

NOJIMA: Let's help each other to do well.

In Shintarō's case, success is a matter of personal effort, but for Nojima it is a joint effort. Nojima's ideal is to maintain a good relationship with his friends; his friends provide the context within which security and peace can be found.

When Nojima falls in love with Sugiko, Ōmiya acts as a sincere adviser. Because Nojima is too bashful and modest, Ōmiya counsels him to meet more often with Sugiko so that she will have a chance to get to know him better. He tells Nojima not to be shy and pretends to act coldly toward Sugiko himself. Unfortunately, Sugiko is drawn to Ōmiya, who decides to go to Europe so as to be away from Sugiko and to encourage Nojima and Sugiko to get together after all. Ōmiya writes to Sugiko from Europe:

I am not trying to praise Nojima simply because he is my friend, but because he is actually one of the few persons I admire. It is a great delight that he likes you. I hope you will spend time with him.

Nevertheless, Sugiko feels drawn more to Ōmiya, but Ōmiya is puzzled and does not know what to do. After a long period of uneasiness, Ōmiya finally accepts Sugiko's love. He tries his best to reassure his friend, but in the end he marries Sugiko. At this point, the friendship between Nojima and Ōmiya ends. It is a great blow to Nojima. The secure and well-protected microcosm that had been his life has finally crumbled, and he envisions the future as dark and desperate. The novel ends with Nojima facing constant loneliness. He writes his last letter to Ōmiya and then scribbles in his diary: "I have withstood my loneliness up to now. Do I have to endure it any further by myself? God, help me!"

The Shōwa Period: Action

The generation born in the early years of the Shōwa Period 1925–) differs somewhat from that of Shintarō or Nojima. An example of Shōwa youth may be found in *Season of Violence (Taiyō no Kisetsu)* by Shintarō Ishihara, a well-known contemporary writer.

If Shintarō Kikuchi devoted most of his time to his studies and to competition and if Nojima anxiously contemplated his and others' feelings, youths in *Season of Violence* find excitement in action. They try to pick up the first girl who comes along; they go out to dance and enjoy themselves—plunging ahead from one act to the next. It is in action that they find their identity.

Tatsuya, the central character in *Season of Violence,* is fascinated with boxing. Boxing is a direct method of reassuring oneself of one's physical existence. Beaten down in the ring, with blood streaming from cuts, Tatsuya revels in physical sensation and enjoys the fact that he is really alive.

For youths in *Season of Violence,* sex is linked with action. Youth of the Taishō Period had a somewhat restrained idea of love; their attitudes were more or less platonic. For Tatsuya's generation, love is a temporal satisfaction and not at all grand or holy. The characters in *Season of Violence* almost regard the word love as something laughable; for them, it has a mawkish and silly connotation. Indecent remarks are made to those who have not yet had sexual relations with girls.

One day, Tatsuya becomes acquainted with a girl named Eiko in the downtown area of Tokyo. For Eiko, sex is its own purpose. Tatsuya thinks of boxing and action as being their own purpose and as providing a means of finding himself. Thus, Tatsuya's attitude toward boxing and Eiko's toward sex are parallel. After a sexual encounter on a yacht on a quiet evening, they fall in love. As Tatsuya says, "For human beings, love and affection are emotions that cannot be kept burning forever. Does love not seem to burn most brightly when flesh and flesh are one? Men and women only find themselves physically one at this moment." The incident on the yacht deepens Eiko's feelings for Tatsuya, but it makes him feel shy and anxious. Her love frightens him, and he begins to be cruel to her. Tatsuya is frightened because his generation regards human relations as something dry. They scorn friendships like Nojima's and Ōmiya's and those of their fathers' generation and consider them soft and uncalculating. Although the Shōwa generation acts courteously in a group, there is no touch of that good-natured friendship that had been the norm for high school students in earlier decades. Friendship for the Shōwa generation has little of the element of personal sacrifice. A careful debit and credit balance sheet is recorded, and those who cannot repay debts are automatically erased from the list.

Nojima experiences loneliness for the first time as a result of the terrible breakup in his friendship with Ōmiya, but for Tatsuya man is a lonely creature from the beginning. One lonely creature becomes friends with another merely by chance, and it is by chance that one finds a girl to play with. In this sense, there is no place for love in Tatsuya's world, but once a feeling of love does appear, it is likely to threaten the concept of a relationship as a balance of debits and credits. Although Tatsuya is afraid of Eiko, he helplessly feels a growing attraction to her.

For Meiji and Taishō youth, love as an end in itself had been hidden behind a romantic veil. In contrast, Tatsuya's generation thinks of sex as a purpose and method by which to find oneself. But once love has slipped in, the concept of sex as an end in itself starts to crumble.

Eiko becomes pregnant, but peritonitis sets in after a Caesarean operation and she dies. As the author comments: "Her death was her supreme challenge. Tatsuya has lost his favorite toy, the toy he could never break no matter how much he battered it."

After Eiko's funeral, Tatsuya goes straight to a college gymnasium to hit punching bags. Eiko's words come back to him: "Why can't you love me in a more straightforward manner?" For a moment, he sees Eiko's smiling face in the punching bag, and he strikes at it madly. Tatsuya's world rejects love as if it were water that must be kept away from a dry object. Each individual lives with a fence around him, and it is through these fences that each must find ways to socialize. If the fences are cleared away, it is unbearable, because "good fences make good neighbors."

The Trend Toward "Micronization" in the Images of Youth

Although it is doubtful that these three characters represent the only characteristic images of the youth of their respective periods, each novel was widely read and accepted in its own period. Each belonged to its time and might not have appeared or been accepted in other periods. By comparing the values expressed in the three novels, it is possible to draw several conclusions about changing attitudes of youth in the three periods of Japan's modern experience.

First, it becomes clear that the frame of reference for individual lives has tended to become smaller over the years. Shintarō Kikuchi's frame of reference is Japan as a nation. He is like a rocket shooting out from a small Kyushu village. His concern is nationalistic, and he always refers to and relates his interests to national concerns.

The youths of Taishō, Nojima's generation, find their frame of reference in a small social circle composed of friends and their families. Nojima and his friends have created a world with a salon-like atmosphere; the image of an entire society or a nation lies somewhere in the hazy background. What, then, is the frame of reference for Tatsuya? Actually, he does not have any group to relate to, but perhaps he may be said to be his own frame of reference. As the frame of reference has shifted from the nation to a group of friends and finally to the individual, its scope has become incredibly small.

Second, within society the role of the individual has changed. For Shintarō, the independent individual is the ultimate principle. Life is a course set on a straight track, and he dashes toward a fixed goal without worrying about what other people think. He is stern and single-minded. But the Meiji Period was a time when single-minded persons could get ahead. Nojima's life is not characterized by individualism but is tinged with isolation and loneliness. When he loses his friends, he is alone and helpless. Tatsuya has a sense of loneliness, but he places positive value on solitude. He regards aloneness as something good and enjoyable and feels threatened when "love" becomes a part of his world.

The youth of Meiji was single-minded, the young man of Taishō wore himself out nervously worrying about his relationships with the people around him, and the youth born during the early Shōwa Period was neither simply single-minded nor much concerned about his neighbors. He just did not care too much about conforming to his surroundings. In general, the youth of Shōwa has been filled with a sense of anomie.

These different concepts of life naturally led to changes in ideals and goals. Shintarō's goal is to go to Tokyo and be successful. The members of Nojima's generation encourage each other to succeed, but success as a goal does not have real significance. Tatsuya's generation judges the word "success" to be outdated jargon. Had there been youths like Shintarō and Nojima in Tatsuya's group, they would have been laughed at and perhaps beaten up. An individual's goal is something distant; "success" sounds too optimistic; the Shōwa youth wants to experience immediate satisfaction. The future is not important to him; rather, the present is his ultimate concern.

We may call these changing characteristics of youth "micronization," for we can see that the frame of reference narrows from nation to a group of friends and finally to an individual.

There was a time many decades ago when the phrase "Boys, be ambitious" thrilled the youth of Japan. However, the presumed infinite possibilities in Japanese society have now been filled by such people as Shintarō. In the crowded society of today's Japan, there are fewer possibilities. The stories of Shintarō, Nojima, and Tatsuya, therefore, can be seen as the history of shrinking physical space, declining opportunity, and narrowing concepts of the individual and his life.

11

Student Protest in Japan:
What It Means to Society

Tsutomu Ōno

Activists in the Student Movement

Rabble-rousers or students? The mass media have concocted a number of labels for activists in the student movement. Obviously such labels have been designed to create the impression that activists consist of a handful of politically oriented professional organizers who drag average students into campaigns. But though we can distinguish active from nonactive students, and the "activists" are a minority, these facts do not justify derogatory labels for two reasons. First, "rabble-rousers" alone could never sustain a dynamic protest movement without considerable support from the rest of the students at a university. Second, even if the leaders were only an isolated, contentious "political element," there would be no reason either to deny that they were students or to treat them as a special group apart from the student body as a whole. It seems to me, therefore, that the mass media's claim that activists are rabble-rousers rather than *genuine* students is not just a slip of the tongue. It is an intentional effort to ease the media's guilt feelings and to repress the sense of responsibility for what students are doing.

We can see the same psychological mechanism at work in the way we think of criminals. We unconsciously betray a self-righteous attitude when we regard them as less than men. We must not allow ourselves to think of student activists in that way. When we do, we reveal our inner feelings of hostility and guilt. It is difficult to understand the student's viewpoint, but we might attempt to understand by seeing the relationship between activists and the student body in terms of a simile. Just as the athlete in his vigor and robustness embodies man's youthful aggressiveness, so the activist may be said to embody the youthful, aggressive aspect of the student mentality. This analogy may help explain why the "rabble-rousers" have won such a wide following—so wide, in fact, that even graduating seniors have become sufficiently infected with dissent to prevent well-known universities from conducting annual commencement exercises.

Outcroppings of student protest have been as unpredictable as a temperamental volcano. The postwar student movement hit a peak of activity in the late 1940's during the first two or three years after formation of the Zengakuren (National Federation of Students' Self-Government Associations). Another outburst, an especially energetic explosion, occurred during the 1960 furor over the United States–Japan Mutual Security Treaty. The movement seems alternately to fizzle and fume. Citizens are aware of student protest only when it explodes in violence.

What is the source of this explosive power? What generates the violent eruptions? Answers to these questions are likely to reveal that the activist personifies the dynamic idealism of contemporary students. Dynamic idealism means a combination of unselfish devotion to ideals and a genuine passion to alter reality. More specifically, the history of the postwar student movement reveals a high correlation between quickened student activity and commitment to ideas. Conversely, periods of relative inactivity most frequently correlate with periods of schisms in theory and rivalries in ideology. Of course, we cannot stress conceptual or ideological factors to the exclusion of the external situation, which provides the context for student reaction.

The postwar student movement has consistently aimed at the realization of two ideals: peace and democracy. We must remember, of course, that most Japanese people once subscribed to these ideals too; peace and democracy were the cornerstones, the guiding principles, for our fresh start as a nation after 1945. But as the standard of living improved, many lost sight of the need for a wholesome tension between reality and progressive ideals. It may well be that student groups alone in Japan have consistently upheld these basic ideals and have been absolutely uncompromising in their attempts to realize them. While it is true that leaders of the student movement have frequently gone to extremes, the energies of student activists arise from a commitment to values held in common by most Japanese in the postwar period.

There is accordingly little justification for the current tendency to single out these activists as pariahs, to claim they are not part of the bona fide student population. True, they have appointed themselves as paladins of peace and democracy. True, to uphold these values they often resort to reckless, unconventional, and violent acts. But we should respect, not condemn, their attempts to champion values the entire society ought to honor. Once we take a sympathetic attitude, we will begin to see that students resort to violence in order to preserve what we intuitively know *we* should be preserving. By alienating them, we in fact betray the principles for which they stand. Those who do not even try to understand the meaning of the student movement and yet claim they are for peace and democracy are hypocrites.

From the "age of ideology" to the "age of technology." Student activists play a unique and valuable role in the age of technology. Let me elaborate on this point by reviewing shifts in Japan's mental climate since 1945. Spiritually, we Japanese were completely disoriented during the immediate post-surrender years. At that time we dissociated ourselves entirely from the wartime slogan, "the universe under one roof (*hakkō ichiu*)," one of the ideals militarists propounded to support Japanese ultranationalism. We started out to create a new Japan using an entirely new set of ideals: peace and democracy. In those moments after the war when we had only potatoes and squash to hold off starvation, when life was filled with trials and suffering, we accepted the dream of peace and democracy. In its extreme adversity, the whole nation shared these ideals and eagerly looked forward to their ultimate materialization.

We can describe those days as the "age of ideology"—not because we applied the concepts of peace and democracy to our environment, but because a powerful sense of revolutionary values and a strong desire to change the environment rather than passively adapt to it dominated our psychology. The reigning concept was "democratic revolution." But times change and fevers cool. Gradually the turmoil subsided, society stabilized, people settled into the featherbed of normality. As is so often the case in normal times, however, men readily turned from an interest in principle to concern for more concrete issues: Where can we make a study corner for junior in a tiny three-and-one-half-room apartment?

With stabilization, social change automatically becomes patterned and directed by the orderly functioning of the system. People begin to regard their affluence as an inevitable trend of history and believe that their personal comfort and security are more important than abstract values and ideals. The intensive search to find junior a study corner is but one example of the urge for comfort and security. In short, we no longer live in an age of ideals or ideology. We live in a technological era in which everyone is most concerned with "getting by." "Getting by," the slogan of the age of technology, signifies the onset of an era concerned with skills. In this era, people calculate their self-interest: They are motivated by whatever seems advantageous and avoid whatever seems disadvantageous.

What has happened to the student movement in this transitional age? Leaders of the movement have adamantly, perhaps even obstinately, insisted on preserving ideals, values, and concepts, all of which transcend the calculation of self-interest alone. Indeed, commitment to principle stimulates activity that may clearly be disadvantageous to the participant. Thus, a devil-may-care dedication to ideals is a thread running through the entire student movement in postwar Japan. The student orientation to ideals contrasts sharply with popular orientation to consumer comforts. Thus, a lack of material orientation is a primary characteristic of the student movement. This very fact makes the student movement the most conspicuous form of heresy in our time, but heresy has no meaning unless there is an orthodoxy with which it can be contrasted, nor can we define orthodoxy in the absence of heresy. Therefore, rather than designate a few students "heretics" because they challenge society to stand up for ideals that the average citizen has apparently consigned to oblivion, we should attempt to gain a full understanding of why these students have taken radical action and of how the concepts supporting their action were formed. The 1966 student strike at Waseda University affords us a convenient means of gaining such an understanding, because it represents a new stage in the postwar student movement. From that vantage point, let us look back over the entire movement and investigate the morphology of its ideology.

The Ideology of Student Activists

Prototypes of student experience. Cold logic alone cannot move people to take violent action for the sake of an ideal. And if we look closely, we shall find that the raw emotions that produce student violence swell from actual experience. Thus, we must ask what models or prototypes of theory and experience motivate students to act. If we can discern these motivating forces, perhaps we can discover an experiential bridge between the average citizen and the student activists who appear, at first glance, to be irrevocably isolated.

In trying to discover such a bridge, I went to Waseda University several days before the scheduled graduation ceremonies and talked with five students who had been involved in the protest movement. At the very outset of the interview, these five made it clear that the student movement had changed.

> As you know, the postwar student movement in Japan started as a struggle for the reconstruction of war-devastated campuses. It was a movement of hope because its aim was to *win* peace and *build* democracy. By contrast, ours is a movement of desperation because it is, in fact, a last-ditch defense of ideals the Japanese people once shared. As we see it today, both peace and democracy are on the verge of total collapse.

This statement is not a propagandistic plea for the modesty of student demands. Prompted by an extraordinary sense of imminent crisis, it is rather a poignant and sincere plea for the two principles students feel most compelled to preserve: peace and democracy.

What are students really worried about? Are peace and democracy just slogans for their campaign? How do they personally describe their efforts to preserve these ideals? Students who survived the Pacific war had been made aware of the value of peace. They had lost many friends and acquaintances, undergone many trials, and suffered many hardships. Therefore, I asked these students whether they felt they possessed some common experience comparable to that shared by the immediate postwar generation. Their reply is revealing if not quite to the point: "We think the war experience had little effect on the Japanese. As a matter of fact, the people didn't really learn a thing from it." Thus, students did not respond by offering any common experience. Instead, they criticized the peace movement. Can we conclude from this that their basic experience consists of dissatisfaction with the peace movement and negative reactions to the ways in which that movement has been conducted? Judging from student evaluations of their high school days, I suspect the answer to this question is yes. Regarding his precollege experience, one student said:

> The struggle over the Mutual Security Treaty in 1960 truly stimulated all of us, including those attending country schools far removed from the hubbub. Even the split in the movement against nuclear bombs pulled at our heartstrings. We had many doubts about the movement and wondered how schisms could arise. Anyhow, as we prepared for college entrance exams during our three years at senior high, our doubts and concerns could only smoulder. They lay dormant. Then, when we got into college, all our suppressed uncertainties about the *status quo* flamed up. In high school, we were engrossed in ourselves and had no time to devote to what we sensed were serious problems. But once we got into college, we were free to explore them. Since then our thoughts have rapidly taken shape.

Today, there is an interesting theory abroad about contemporary college students. People say they lack such personal experiences as war, mobilization, bombing, and evacuation, which students of the previous generation shared. Thus, the argument contends, college students nowadays have no backbone; their thought is "spongy." I cannot tell whether this theory is right or wrong, nor at this moment do I know of a study that either proves or disproves these contentions, but I prefer to approach the question from another angle. It seems to me that people may have valid experiences that do not conform to stereotyped notions of what constitutes an experience. The basic event in the student's

consciousness may actually be a nonexperience, a lack of participation in the postwar movements that occurred before the present
generation of college students came of age. Criticism of events in
which a person has not directly participated may be vacuous and
imprecise, but today's students are struggling to begin from the
point at which the immediate postwar student generation arrived
after much personal suffering.

Attitudes toward theory. Some say that student activists mature
rapidly after entering college in their ability to handle theoretical
problems. Presumably, the concerns and questions suppressed
during years of preparation for entrance exams blossom forth
shortly after students become freshmen. How does it happen that
they suddenly provide their activities with a theoretical foundation? If we examine the books they read, and if we ask not *what*
they read but *how* they approach their reading, we might find a
clue to the answer.

They regard it as their existential right to choose which authors
to read and what theories to exploit for their movement. This
means the only works that students read by their own choice are
those regarded as profitable to their cause. Any outsider may think
this only natural, but a review of the postwar student movement
reveals that past student activists did not exercise the same degree
of freedom.

Immediately after the war ended, students avidly devoured
newly available works on Marxism, a taboo subject during mili-
tarist days. Formation of the Zengakuren followed. By the early
1950's, however, their interest had turned to more practical problems. Thus, they read Lenin's works for hints on how to apply
Marxist theory. When that period passed, and when the Japan
Communist Party (JCP) began using Molotov cocktails and similar unlawful tactics to stimulate an armed revolution, students
looked for theoretical guidance in the writings of Mao Tse-tung
and Liu Shao-ch'i, men with many years of experience in anti-
colonialist guerrilla warfare. They also read widely in Stalin's
works. It was not until after the JCP officially altered its attitude
toward armed revolution at its Sixth National Congress in July,
1955, and after Nikita Khrushchev launched his criticism of
Stalin in 1956, that student activists began to read such unortho-
dox Marxists as Leon Trotsky. By 1960, what had previously

been regarded as heresy became among many Japanese students
an object of intensive study and discussion. It was, of course, these
"Trotskyite" students who led the 1960 Mutual Security Treaty
struggle to an unprecedented climax, moving far beyond the
point where the "orthodox" (that is, the JCP, the Japan Socialist
Party, and others) were prepared to go.

In this thumbnail sketch of reading habits, the obvious point
is that the literature student activists read is closely related to the
particular conditions of their movement at any given time. They
do not read simply for enlightenment. They read to discover information that will guide and help them solve the practical problems of student protest. They regard no revolutionary thinker—
whether Marx or Lenin or Mao—as infallible. Their attitude
toward theory is highly pragmatic and independent. In the past,
when the JCP controlled the Zengakuren, Party leaders always
foisted a "required reading list" on student activists. Present student activists, by contrast, do not tolerate the authoritative impo-
sition of reading materials. Moreover, apparently no student
leader takes the initiative in synthesizing diverse ideas to formulate a theoretical system for the movement. Judging from the
statement of one of the interviewees, students apparently recognize that this represents a change:

> A long time back, leaders of the movement were leaders in theory,
> too. That was the case with Teruo Takei, the first chairman of Zenga-
> kuren's Central Committee. But nowadays the roles of theoretician
> and practical leader are completely divorced.

The reason for the separation derives at least in part from the fact
that the student movement is no longer unified. There is no single
Zengakuren organization, nor does the JCP have monolithic
control.

As a result, student activists now assume surprisingly flexible
attitudes toward theory and practice. They no longer expect, for
example, that practical leaders offer doctrinal or theoretical
guidance. Similarly, individual writers have had little to do with
the practical aspects of the movement. Perhaps it is not altogether
unfair to explain student flexibility toward theory and practice in
terms of current activist thinking on revolution. Most believe a
revolution can occur only in the distant future. They are accord-

ingly more "relaxed," so to speak, than students of the immediate
postwar generation, who seriously believed they stood on the
threshold of a major upheaval. While this is an interesting and
helpful explanation, I attribute present student attitudes toward
theory to two factors: the collapse of the once-powerful myth that
the JCP is the true vanguard, and the schisms that now rend the
entire revolutionary movement in this country. And these factors
may in turn involve a third. As one student put it:

> If you read Masao Maruyama's work, you'll find he points out certain
> predetermined conditions that forced Marxism to be introduced into
> prewar Japan as an ethic, as a science, as a philosophy. In a word,
> Marxism was considered a kind of cure-all, something to satisfy every
> demand. But the real problem with Marxism is that it was not
> adapted to our tradition. No matter what kind of ideas one intro-
> duces, they must contend with Japanese conditions. No matter what
> the thought, if it does not adapt to the situation in Japan, it will flop.
> Since before the war, dogmatic application of foreign theory has been
> a conspicuous characteristic of Japanese Marxism. But if you think
> about the problem a bit, you get to feeling we must analyze the in-
> digenous situation a good deal more deeply before we apply theories
> —that's why I think we must study more about the Emperor system,
> Japanese romanticism, and so forth.

Today's students most certainly stand at an important point in
their country's history, the moment at which Japan's democratic
movement has come of age. They are trying seriously to assume
the responsibilities which that moment requires of them. For example, intense dedication to adapting theory to Japan's specific
conditions has involved students in more than 200 study groups on
the Waseda campus alone. Their concern also crops out in class-
room discussions. This probing, analytical atmosphere both tem-
pers and nurtures the many questions and concerns that had been
substantially "fettered" by high school study schedules, for the university permits tremendous freedom and allows students to absorb
theory in any way they wish.

Given this liberty, it is possible to emerge as a student leader
without having one's theoretical views examined too deeply.
Moreover, once schisms divided the movement, there was no
longer any monolithic theoretical armor with which to clothe the
leaders.

Experiential foundations. A large number of seniors and freshmen became activists as a result of the 1966 Waseda strike. In fact, by early 1966 activists had swelled to roughly twice the number of those who struggled against the normalization treaty with South Korea in the autumn of 1965. Freshmen provided most of the sudden increase. Then, on the eve of graduation at Waseda, a large number of seniors faced the decision: Shall we join or oppose the movement? Like it or not, each senior had to decide whether he would take action with his classmates.

But on what would they base a resolution to act? First, let us turn our attention to the seniors. At the time I visited Waseda, I attended a teach-in sponsored by the seniors. Their theme was: "What does the Waseda struggle mean to us?" This is a very poignant question, especially if we keep in mind that these seniors were not only leaving Waseda and facing their futures, they were in jeopardy of losing their diplomas as well. One after another, teachers and students paraded to the rostrum. It soon became obvious that many seniors had been active in an organization outside the student councils set up in departments throughout the university. This organization, a senior student league, cut across academic departments. General dissatisfaction with the type of education they were getting, not similarity of academic interest, bound the members together.

A girl in the College of Education said:

> We have been dissatisfied all along. Even in our major subject, classrooms are sometimes so packed we can't find a seat. But if we shuffle our feet a little as we stand up listening to the lecture, the professor is put out at us for disturbing everybody. Looking back on it now, I'd gladly have failed the entrance exam if they would have accepted many fewer freshmen and reduced the size of each class.

She went on to speak candidly:

> After that, I actually halfway resigned myself to the fact that all colleges are as miserable as Waseda. I never thought we could do anything about the situation until after I took part in the strike against a tuition raise. When I began to fight to improve the school, I realized we should do whatever we can to reform the place. To tell you the truth, I had never thought seriously about society, politics, or anything until after I participated in the protest movement.

Others have reported on the absence of humanity in the mammoth universities and on the lack of genuine education in schools that mass-produce graduates, so I refrain from covering that ground again. At this point, I shall rather try to clarify the experiential basis of a student's decision to act. Had the inertia of university life forced students to resign themselves to the *status quo,* or had this inertia forced them into an awareness of their plight? The difference is important, for once a person becomes aware that he is in trouble, awareness itself becomes the source of remedial activity.

The girl just quoted was not committed to a particular ideology. Nevertheless, she did become an activist. And she helped sponsor a teach-in, passed out handbills, and had the pluck to speak her mind and assert candidly that "the graduation ceremony is a mere formality." Girls like her took an active part in the student movement. But they were motivated by despair, not by ideology. Their road to action was a natural one based on firsthand experience. Thus, the seniors' response was to break through the shell of complacency. Freshmen, on the other hand, reacted to their great disappointment in college life.

The experiential background of the freshmen is especially interesting. After their three-year preparation for college entrance exams, a process that tremendously constricted their thought, they were suddenly exhilarated by a feeling of relief and liberation. But the university life to which they had aspired betrayed them. The college was not really interested in them. It failed to satisfy their long-cherished hopes and expectations of intellectual stimulation and human concern. Just then, Waseda became embroiled in the debate on student autonomy. This provided the spark. Those who sought meaning in student life debated with fresh sensitivity, hoping not only to realize their great expectations for college education but to overcome their sense of alienation.

And what do students mean by "alienation"? The term has many facets. When students use it, however, they are not thinking of specialized philosophical, economic, or sociological definitions. *Alienation* is student slang to describe a condition in which human beings are not treated as humans. And since there is no way to overcome it except by struggle, this becomes the experiential basis for students' decision to stop being passive observers. Further, the struggle is rewarding:

> Our struggle has involved us in a countless number of memorable experiences. For the first time, we have been able to know each other as human beings. There are quite a few seniors who figure that, if there had been no student protest, they would have graduated from college without having had this taste of comradeship, without having shared this common experience.

These students had experienced alienation. But there is more to it than that. Once having decided to act, once having begun the struggle, it is only natural that students should feel the need to equip themselves with theory. Thus, they are particularly attracted to ideas that justify their struggle.

The early postwar struggles of the Zengakuren were rooted in the euphoria of emancipation, the sense of having been liberated from militaristic and absolutist controls. Zengakuren students were accordingly attracted to ideas that justified their vigorous antiwar campaign in protest against the growing international tensions that enveloped Japan in the wake of the cold war and the Korean conflict. A later generation needed a different theoretical base. These youngsters, absolutely disenchanted with the Japan Communist Party and its leadership, hoped avidly that a true vanguard party would appear. They wanted a leadership with an attitude as forward-looking as theirs; but though they sought, they did not discover this attitude in the "established" anti-establishment forces. Hence, student disillusionment with the JCP continued after 1960. Then, in 1966, student protest flared in reaction to university authorities. Students seethed with fresh vitality, not in search of a theory to justify their struggle but in an attempt to overcome their alienation.

The immediate postwar peak of the student movement reflected an intense feeling of liberation, and the 1960 peak showed an equally strong desire for independence, this time from the degenerating Old Left. The third peak, the 1966 student protest at Waseda and elsewhere, differs from the first two, for alienation is its experiential and psychological foundation.

Characteristics of student thought. One of the activists describes the nature of the Waseda struggle as follows:

On the surface, our protest resembles what happened last year at Keiō. It appears to be a simple case of student resistance to a proposed tuition raise. In our case, more is at stake than money. We know that, if the issue is a tuition raise, the ruling class will make certain concessions. But aside from money, there are definite limits to what they will concede. They will not, for instance, give in to any demand that might jeopardize the established structure of class relations in this country. Our aim is to get them to make concessions beyond financial matters. We want to break through the social framework established by and for the ruling class. By contrast, last year's student strike at Keiō was conducted *within* that framework. This is how the Waseda struggle is decidedly different from the one at Keiō.

The struggle at Waseda was anti-establishment. It was part of the broader student movement, a struggle against alienation.

Absence of true educational concern for the student, alienation of student from teacher and student from student on our campuses—these are inevitable results of the mechanical mass production of graduates. Waseda students representing the anti-JCP faction, however, believe that multiversities and all their distortions result basically from the class relations of an industrialized society. They argue that colleges in a capitalistic society become centers that produce "commodities" for monopoly capital. These "commodities" are the men who will eventually occupy middle and top management positions or become staff technicians in big business corporations. Student protest is a frontal attack on the "academic-industrial cooperation" that is rapidly converting Japanese colleges into assembly lines for "organization men." Students hold that they must combat this cooperation. There is no other way to overcome their alienation. Attacking a tuition hike is therefore only a tactic, a means for coming to grips with more fundamental problems. One activist in the Zengakukyōtō Conference made this point clear in a statement that criticized the pro-JCP faction:

> Minsei people were ignoring the most fundamental problem of all: alienation. They imagine they can dispose of their problems by externalizing them, by divorcing them from the broader social and human contexts within which they have taken shape.

Students from different factions thus approach their task and perceive their mission in conspicuously different ways. Some analyze the source of their problems subjectively; they see themselves personally immersed in a college environment that literally bristles with alienation and alienated individuals. Others approach their problems more objectively; they tend to stress economic factors and to apply to Japan's concrete social conditions the view urged by their faction. One anti-JCP student said, "We are seeking a new quality of solidarity among students, one that transcends established norms of 'social relations and conduct.' We hope to realize the 'restoration of man' within the context of that solidarity." The struggle of the anti-JCP activists with whom I spoke is founded not on economic aims but on student desires to achieve human and cultural objectives.

> Thanks to our strike and classroom discussions, we felt truly united. For the first time, we engaged in a genuine human exchange of ideas with fellow students. That unity was later strengthened when the student body participated in the strike, when the seniors boycotted their comprehensive exams, when we occupied the administration building. Throughout, our objective was increased solidarity. We wanted to give students a sense of purpose. Occupying the administration building was not necessarily the objective. We elected that course of action with the aim of unity in mind.

We can break down anti-JCP student thought into three separate characteristics. *First,* the activists are not seeking material ends. Their objectives lie outside the economic dimension, even though their slogans call for opposing the administration's tuition raise. As they put it: "We want to establish new human values by rejecting the materialistic values that dominate our society."

Second, these students refuse to acknowledge the authority of the Japan Communist Party, the Japan Socialist Party, or any other revolutionary movement. They say, "We should believe in ourselves and in our own action to combat alienation. If we have faith in ourselves and in what we do," they reason, "we can ignore and transcend the present progressive parties and their tendency to seek solutions to alienation outside of the conditions that cause it."

Third, students think they can best deal with the social conditions that have produced their alienation by selecting the proper target to attack. Thus, one activist told me, "It is important for students to make people aware of our problems. We are not concerned about the inconvenience we cause government or school authorities."

Those supporting the JCP stand represent a contrasting pattern of activity. The Minsei faction looks to the JCP for advice, and students are supposed to play out their roles completely within the Party program. The general approach taken by the Minsei faction is to deal with student demands and dissatisfactions so as to gain greater sympathy among students. The anti-JCP activists censure their pro-Communist colleagues for "competing [for popular support] in the same dimension as the bourgeoisie."

The relationship between the pro- and anti-JCP factions is revealing. One broad generalization applicable to the postwar student movement is the alternate acceptance and rejection of Communist leadership. Even control of the Zengakuren has shifted back and forth between factions for and against the JCP. It is interesting to note, however, that the student movement has generally been most explosive and most ideologically dynamic when anti-JCP activists assume leadership. In a word, Japan's student movement is most characteristically a *student* movement when the Party is not in control.

The future outlook of the movement. Student activists are quite young. Presumably, they have an arduous task and many years of life ahead of them. How do they appraise their prospects and what are their hopes for the future? As one student said:

> The struggle we are currently engaged in is peculiarly Japanese. No other student movement in the world has an aim like ours. After setbacks following opposition to the 1960 Mutual Security Treaty, students themselves rebuilt the movement. We have complete confidence in the results. But, at the same time, you'll recall that ever since 1960 students have not organized any spectacular activity. The reason is a defeatist attitude. We always seemed to end up on the losing side because we took off without letting the movement build up its own head of steam. It's hard, though, to describe our mixed-up feelings in a few words.

This candid confession reveals that students have taken a firm and positive attitude toward their mission in spite of their realistic admission that the fight will be a long one. They seem to have realized that it is impossible to make a profession out of student protest. I had the notion when I tried to interview activists on this issue that some of them might discover in the student movement an opportunity for their life work, and that this discovery would give them a feeling of intellectual accomplishment. I was unable to get explicit answers to this question.

A few responded to my queries by saying they were too involved in the maelstrom of struggle to think of the distant future. This made me wonder about their intellectual maturity. If they cannot project themselves beyond the moment, I suspect they have some growing up to do. Note, for example, the attitude of one senior: "It isn't possible that our thinking will change just because we get a job and have to conform to the company. In our new positions, though, we will have to face up to the problem of how we can continue to develop our thought." In a word, he converted the problem from the abstract to the concrete dimension. If one considers students as budding intellectuals, however, it seems fair to expect them to transcend their immediate private situations.

But one group of student activists allegedy attempts to cultivate a "new quality of awareness" that will make all its members professional revolutionaries. However, this group involves only a small, atypical sample of activists. In contrast to the philosophy of such a group, the students I interviewed believe that after graduation each individual must choose his own path. I was unable to find a single student with a clear idea as to how Japan's revolutionary forces might come together to form a united front in order to bring about a successful revolution. Nor did I meet any who regarded the revolutionary activities of student life as anything but one phase in their lifetime. Instead, students see their plight in terms of coming to grips with alienation:

One thesis, dating from around 1960, defined students as "forerunners." This thesis assumed that if the student movement made a big splash, the workers would be stimulated to rise up, too. The 1960 campaign against the Mutual Security Treaty was launched with this hope. But of course, it wasn't quite that easy to get workers to respond. Thus, the "students as forerunners" thesis was soon replaced by one that defined them as allies of the proletariat. But now we have something different in mind. We're thinking that there will be no solidarity at all if students as students and workers as workers fail to contend with their concrete situations and overcome their own alienation.

Students who perceive the problem in these terms are not likely to think that their activity must necessarily lead them to a revolutionary career. It is simply that they object to considering future goals before attaining immediate objectives. They seem to feel that the process is more important than the goal. As one senior girl told me, "I didn't face up to 'problems' till I was on the verge of graduating. Now I'm leaving school without having solved them. But at least I know what they are and I also know how serious they are."

The Meaning of Student Protest

A search for the realization of principles. School management and the university system are primary causes of the strife that has so frequently disrupted campuses across Japan. To prevent future outbreaks we must obviously attack the sources of the strife. Although I recognize the necessity of attacking the outbreaks at their source, my rough sketch of student ideology has emphasized a different aspect of the problem, that is, the inner consciousness of protest. To explore this problem, we might ask, "What lessons can society learn from the behavior of student activists?" From the viewpoint of the average citizen, we might ask, "What does society have to say to the militant student?"

People have leveled many criticisms against the student movement. They claim it illustrates the wrong-headed heroism young people often admire. Or they say it demonstrates the results of a sudden emancipation from comfortable dependence on one's parents, of a radicalism drunk on new concepts, of an insolence bereft of common sense and opposed to mediation, of a subversiveness barren of constructive plans. And they say students are irresponsibly heedless of the rights of others, that they surrender intellect to activity, and so on, *ad infinitum.* Each of these criticisms is based on an appropriately valid complaint. I admit that. On the other hand, I feel each rebuke undermines our ability to make a sober evaluation of students and the student movement.

I stated at the outset that I cannot approve of criticisms which assume the activist student is generically different from other members of his society. Nor do I intend to support the purely emotional position which holds that we should appreciate the youthful enthusiasm and purity of heart displayed by these activists. On the contrary, I think student thought and action have special significance for our society. Perhaps I might discuss this special significance by summarizing what I take to be five common characteristics of the formation of student ideology.

1. Students feel a strong sense of alienation. They are dissatisfied with the current situation and accuse society of responding inadequately to human desires.

2. They regard their own dissatisfaction with the present situation as only one aspect of the problem. Their directional antennae locate the cause of their estrangement in the total society, not just on the campus.

3. Student thought is restricted. Naturally, students are young and have had very little social experience, either in breadth or in depth. One natural consequence is that they are bound by the limitations of their immediate backgrounds.

4. Paradoxically, the lack of broad social experience can also be a strength. Students are wholly confident in their own power because their thinking has been restricted to the current situation. They see value only in what they consider meaningful and worthwhile *now*. As a result, they reject all authority—organizational or theoretical—not validated by their own senses. Unfortunately, however, limited experience fails to make students aware of their unconscious predilection for dogmatism.

5. They oppose the *status quo*. One conclusion implicit in the four points above is that student behavior tends toward a violent rejection and negation of the current situation. They are convinced that only by taking a negative stance will they produce anything positive. They direct their protests and denials to university authorities and the government as well as to the progressive forces, the Communists and the socialists.

Granting differences in nuance and emphasis, the thinking of contemporary students has a good deal in common with that of

participants in earlier protest movements. Though views expressed by activists appear to trace a meandering, zig-zag path,
students are definitely making a fresh contribution to the intellectual history of the postwar period. They promote a commitment to independence that strives to outshine even the revolutionary spirit of Japan's progressive forces.

Students' challenge to society. Earlier in my discussion, I asked
about the significance of the student movement for Japanese society as a whole. What does the movement tell us about the
growth of concepts among Japanese youth, and what do these
concepts suggest about social change? To approach the student
movement with such questions means we must decide how to interpret it and at what level we shall deal with it. For instance, we
must examine the implications both of the selfless, uncalculating
way students expend themselves to realize the postwar ideals of
peace and democracy, and of youth's radical demands for the universal, thorough, and complete realization of these ideals.

The intensity of student commitment, as it has cropped out at
the peaks of the student movement, proves that the ideals of democracy and peace have neither vanished nor been entirely modified in postwar Japan. Moreover, the weaker the general public's
commitment to ideals like peace and democracy, the more radical
the student protest becomes. If the student movement is an accurate barometer of the nation's adherence to these ideals, perhaps our first reaction to youth's extreme behavior should not be
to lecture them on the need for common sense. We should rather
ask ourselves, what has happened to our ideals? Has our commitment to them really faded? Such reflection is the responsibility of
all who claim to support peace and democracy. It may be the only
way to attain solidarity with students. The radicalism of the student movement seems no more than a painfully frank expression
of the fact that in Japan there is too much indifference to ideals
and principles, to peace and democracy.

PART FOUR

The World Scene

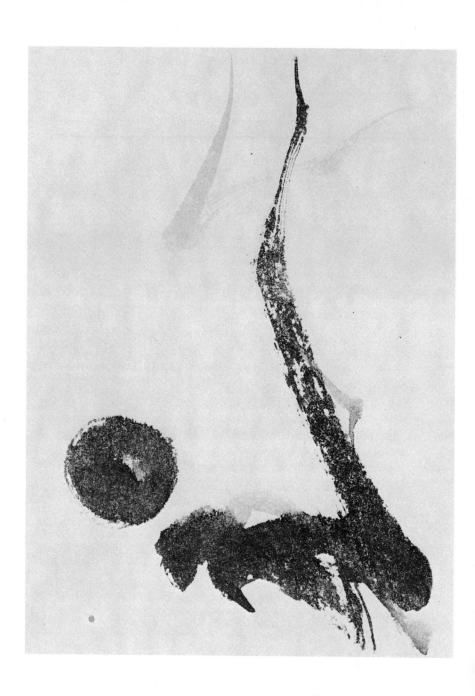

12

The 1970's: Japan Enters the "Losers' Return Match"

Sōichi Ōya

It is my understanding that in boat racing, unlike other sports, there is a provision for a losers' comeback race. Japan in the 1970's presents the appearance of a former loser who, to everyone's surprise, is threatening to walk off with the trophy.

A review of the century since Japan joined the family of nations shows that, at intervals of ten to twenty years, Japan has found itself in a major war. The first was the Sino-Japanese War, the next was the Russo-Japanese War, and then World War I.

But World War I was a very special war for Japan. Since it was fought almost entirely in Europe, the great powers temporarily retired from the Asian arena. The opportunity was not lost on Japan. Like a thief in the night, Japan declared war on Germany and, without waging anything resembling war, found itself included among the winners and even managed to be considered one of the "Five Powers." World War I was a good season for Japan. The scoreboard read: games played—none; games won—one.

Encouraged by this profitable adventure, Japan set out on a plan to conquer all of Asia. Seeing that Japan's schemes seemed to be proceeding smoothly, Nazi Germany decided to play the same game. The result was World War II, which, viewed from a global point of view, might be considered the semifinals of the world tournament.

Germany and Japan were the clear losers, but virtually all the other countries involved emerged exhausted from the fray. The only two countries able to field a team for the finals were the United States and the Soviet Union.

Those two countries soon far outdistanced all competition. In preparation for the trophy play, the two superpowers developed a frightening arsenal of nuclear weapons and other efficient means of mass destruction. Clearly, any new war between them would mean mutual suicide and probable reduction of all the achievements of mankind on this planet to smouldering, radio-active rubble.

Thus, there seems to have been a slight delay in the scheduled main event, while the two giant competitors stand toe to toe and sullenly glare at each other. This improvised game is called "cold war."

In the meantime, Japan's rapid economic expansion has brought it to third place in GNP. America, on the other hand, with its defeat in Vietnam, the race problem, and the weakening dollar, has had its hands full at home and abroad. At the same time, the Soviet Union's increasingly tense confrontation with China, its loosening hold on the East European satellites, and the domestic pressures for liberalization have led to the crumbling of the one-time "monolithic structure" of the Communist movement. The plight of Great Britain, once proud ruler of the seven seas, is even more pathetic. It has been reduced from a vast empire to a mini-power.

In this framework of shifting power relationships, the Satō administration decided to take the plunge and demand the return of Okinawa. "Until Okinawa is returned to Japan," said Mr. Satō, "the postwar period will not be over." Turn this ringing pronouncement around a bit, and you have a defeated nation's declaration of intent to enter the "losers' return match," a new challenge to the winners of the semifinals.

There is little doubt, then, that the decade of the 1970's will see Japan's attempted comeback. The question is in what area of endeavor the match will proceed: cultural, economic, military, diplomatic, or some other field. We must also ask whether Japan has any chance of victory.

But first, I think there is a need to review, from a new angle, Japan's game up to the semifinals and its trouncing on that field of play.

As I see it, what prompted Japan to embark upon a course leading to a war that it had not the slightest chance of winning was the "unearned win" gained in World War I. Having once tweaked the nose of European power in Asia, Japan was in a mood to carry the game further. This mood was expressed in the slogan, "Down with the *status quo*" (*genjō daha*), which of course referred to dislodging the Western powers from the position of dominance built up in Asia since the eighteenth century. This slogan supplied the impetus for Japan's string of military actions in Manchuria and China leading to the Pacific war. The man who coined the slogan had a close connection with Japan's subsequent fortunes.

The slogan first appeared in a Shanghai newspaper article in 1919. Its author, Fumimarō Konoe, was at the time on his way to the Paris Peace Conference as aide to the Japanese Chief Delegate, Kimmochi Saionji. It was meant as a strong expression of Japan's determination to oppose Western imperialism, and as such it had wide repercussions at home and abroad. It soon became a catch phrase all over Japan. When Konoe was Prime Minister during Japan's time of troubles in China, he again played the phrasemaker with his famous "No talks with Chiang Kai-shek." This "gem of wisdom" threw the Japan of those days into new ecstasies. But in the end Japan was defeated. Konoe was charged with war crimes and committed suicide by taking poison.

When I consider Prime Minister Satō's pronouncement about Okinawa along with Konoe's efforts at slogan-making, it is difficult to avoid the feeling that history is repeating itself. Present-day Japan is displaying dazzling economic growth and creative vitality. World War I and the years following also saw a great increase in Japan's prosperity and standard of living. Those were rosy days, when Japanese could travel through Europe in royal fashion for pennies, the days of a fresh concern for "culture," the era of "Taishō Democracy."

They didn't last long. Panic hit Japan, the economic sector slumped into the depths of depression, the ranks of the unemployed swelled, and degradation of every kind appeared on all sides. "Culture" degenerated into the erotic, the grotesque, and the meaningless. Democracy was supplanted by socialism, Communism, anarchy, and Dadaism. National pride, too, took a downward turn when America and England pressured Japan into armament reductions. The resulting fierce resentment among the military, coupled with the impoverished condition of the countryside, made a fertile seedbed for fascism. The drift to the right gradually grew into an all-embracing, top-to-bottom, hot-eyed militarism.

Since then, several decades have passed. The Western powers, which were so insistent in the 1930's that Japan reduce its military power, are now, lo and behold, pressing Japan to build up its military capability and take over its share of responsibility for defending Asia and the Pacific area!

In this, we have what is tantamount to recognition of Japan's bid for a losers' return match. And America, favored to take the championship, has the disadvantage of being on the defensive, while Japan is moving into a strong offensive position. With this in mind, we must consider in what area, and what form, this new game is likely to be played.

The postwar struggle for supremacy between the United States and the Soviet Union has been carried out for the most part in the military, economic, and cultural fields. The three are closely intertwined, but if we consider the cultural field to include activities such as space exploration, it is clear that Japan can by no stretch of the imagination be considered among the competition. When we come to military power, the gap opens to a gulf. The only field remaining is economics.

Here Japan shines. If its economy continues to grow at the present pace, it will catch up to and outstrip the United States. The opinion has even been voiced in American academic circles that the twenty-first century will be the century of Japan. And here we find what lies behind the Prime Minister's rather circumspect statements: "An independent Japan intends to play a major role in increasing prosperity in Asia by economic aid and other nonmilitary means." But that "major role" sounds very suspicious indeed. Under the cloak called economics, I catch a glimpse of that old vision of an Asia united in a "Greater East Asia Co-Prosperity Sphere."

The alliances forming a chain from the Aleutian Islands to

Indonesia, including the United States–Japan Mutual Security Treaty, SEATO, ANJUS, ASPAC, and so forth, were for the most part formed at the initiative of the United States. The aim was to contain Communism in Asia. With the American military defeat in Vietnam, however, the structure began to crumble. And now Okinawa, the keystone of the structure, has been returned to Japanese control, and Tokyo and Peking have agreed to establish diplomatic relations.

The fact that America agreed to return Okinawa is of great significance, but the factor that might well have the most influence on Japan's course in the 1970's is not the conditions under which Okinawa was returned, but Okinawa's condition after return. There is a surprising absence of concrete plans for Okinawa's incorporation into the Japanese economy.

While it is no doubt true that the Satō regime's push for early reversion was partly motivated by the desire to maintain the party and Mr. Satō himself in power, my opinion is that the administration considered Okinawa's reversion only in relation to Japan's "return match" and either underestimated or chose to ignore all the difficulties inherent in a precipitate return.*

The principal reason for Japan's defeat in World War II was the weakness of its economic base. It is a tribute to the clarity of hindsight that this opinion has become commonplace in Japan. If, in the 1970's, Japan should decide to challenge the United States militarily as well as economically, it would be because Japan had procured a new pair of rose-colored glasses through which it can be clearly seen that Japan is in an unassailable position as an economic power.

Leadership is also a factor to consider. Both Mr. Satō and his brother, former Prime Minister Kishi, are from Yamaguchi, which boasts more war criminals than any other prefecture in Japan. After the Pacific war, Yamaguchi City was the very first to erect a "monument to the patriots" in the local shrine of the war dead. Among the war criminals honored at this shrine is Yōsuke Matsuoka, who led Japan out of the League of Nations and along the road to fascism and war. There is little doubt that the militaristic

---

* Although Prime Minister Satō stepped down in July, 1972, and was replaced by the more colorful and dynamic Kakuei Tanaka, the questions discussed here remain relevant.—ED.

atmosphere of their birthplace has had a shaping influence on the psychological makeup of Kishi and Satō, whether or not they themselves realize it.

Added to this consideration of the "exciting" nature of the nation's leadership is the inescapable fact that Japan's present prosperity rests squarely on an economy based on a cycle of import-process-export. One absolutely indispensable condition for this cycle is unrestricted use of sea lanes. If Japan's lines of trade are threatened at some point, we cannot rule out the possibility of a resort to military force in a knee-jerk impulse to protect what are, literally, lifelines of the nation's economy. We have, after all, only to consider the kind of armed interference in the internal affairs of its smaller neighbors that a superpower such as the Soviet Union is capable of. And not over a direct threat to economic life, but in the name of peace and protection of ideological purity.

It is in this context that the developing "economic superpower" consciousness in Japan is potentially dangerous. And there is no refuge to be found in the belief that the business community serves as some sort of check on reckless military leaders and their politician puppets: It is by no means rare for economically motivated civilians, especially arms makers, to pull the switch for war. It is certainly an unsettling thought, but who can say with any assurance that in the 1970's Japan won't walk down the road it has walked before?

"Charisma" is an elusive quality but one that deserves careful consideration because of the part it continues to play in the affairs of men. Most great periods of innovation and progress have been under the leadership of a charismatic personality. Lenin, Mao Tse-tung, Gandhi, Nehru, Sukarno, Nasser, Castro, Guevara, Tito, Nkrumah—all have shown what charisma can do. In Japan, high-voltage charismatic leaders such as Shōin Yoshida and Takamori Saigō appeared and brought about the Meiji Restoration, which in turn led to Japan's century of modernization.

But Japan's progress, its success in creating the only nonwhite modern nation-state, has depended less on individual charismatic leadership than on the charisma of the Japanese people themselves. And the nucleus of this national charisma, the power source for Japan's modernization, was the Emperor system. In having "national charisma," Japan resembles Germany. But the reason that a super-charismatic leader such as Hitler did not appear in Japan is that the unique super-charisma of the Emperor institution was so all-encompassing and powerful that there was neither room nor need for a Hitler.

National charisma and great charismatic leaders serve to mobilize national or ethnic energies, and they often raise voltage levels so high that the nation is led into a reckless gamble resulting in ultimate ruin. This is why Germany has suffered the same fate time after time.

If Japan should find itself wedged among America, Russia, and China and should decide to resort to military force in its "return match," the cause could no doubt be found in either a resurgence of Japanese national charisma or the emergence of a high-charisma leader. A search of the horizon of the 1970's does not reveal any great probability of such an emergence, but there are a few figures, still no more than shadows, that seem to have some potential.

Three personalities come to mind: Shintarō Ishihara, Daisaku Ikeda, and the anti-establishment leader Makoto Oda. All seem to be at least possible charismatic leaders. Among the present crop of political and industrial figures, search as we will, there are no such potential leaders. If one looks long and hard, there is a certain amount of charisma perceptible in Kōnosuke Matsushita, the electronics magnate, and Sōichirō Honda of motorcycle fame. But they are first, last, and always businessmen, and their charisma, such as it is, is considerably diluted by an overweening concern with balance sheets.

Shintarō Ishihara, the writer and brother of a popular actor, gained his seat in the Diet by an impressive vote of 3 million and has subsequently been quite active, ambitious, and shockingly reform-minded and liberal for a Liberal Democratic Party Diet member. Ishihara appears to be completely serious about his position, but he is still classed with other entertainers who got into the Diet on the strength of a kind of novelty vote. Ishihara must think about his position in regard to this "novelty" phenomenon. He must also realize that, as a liberal, he runs the risk of being used by his own conservative party as a kind of sandwich man, and when his usefulness is outlived, he might very well be discarded or be forced out by his own principles. And of course, there is the possibility that the reformer just might end up being reformed himself—into a full-fledged conservative. Politics is a rough game, and Ishihara will no doubt find that it rarely goes as smoothly as the plot of one of his novels.

And then there is Daisaku Ikeda. As the commander-in-chief of Sōka Gakkai, the fastest-growing religious group in the postwar era, he has displayed a full measure of charisma and generalship.

Close scrutiny shows that the secret of Sōka Gakkai's phenomenal growth lies in its compatibility across a broad spectrum with the informationalized society. As a first step, Sōka Gakkai was able to organize a large following from the lower social strata by skillful use of paramilitary methods and by playing on a "good-old-days" (in this case, predefeat) nostalgia. Next, it poured its considerable funds into publishing, so successfully that at present Sōka Gakkai is more a publishing house than a religion. In mass dissemination of publications of every variety—dailies, weeklies, monthlies, paperbacks—Sōka Gakkai is right up in the top bracket of the industry. And the extraordinary strength of the enterprise lies not so much in sales volume as in the profit it makes: The cost of publishing and distributing, on the one hand, is wonderfully reduced by the donated labor of church members, and the zeal of the general membership, on the other hand, guarantees a reliable mass market.

The Kōmeitō (Clean Government Party) is the political department and mouthpiece of this religious business organization. In this important respect, Kōmeitō office holders are a completely separate breed from the other Diet members. The only other political party resembling the Kōmeitō is the Japan Communist Party, which also depends on publishing profits for Party support.

More than ten years ago, I met Jōsei Toda, the true founder of Sōka Gakkai and the man who taught Daisaku Ikeda and started him on his way. At that time, Toda was a third-rate publisher in Kanda. After Toda's death, when leadership passed to young Ikeda, Sōka Gakkai experienced explosive growth, and today it is influential enough to cause headaches for both the conservative and liberal camps. That this remarkable performance was based on Ikeda's personal charisma goes without saying, and the growth itself, in my opinion, was brought about by skillful coordination of the organization's character and mode of operation with the growth of the informationalized society.

The question now is whether the religion and the party can continue to grow at the same high rate, or whether indeed they have already reached their peak. It is a question that ranks with that of Japan's economic outlook for the future as one of the weightiest questions of the 1970's. One thing we can say: If the Kōmeitō expects to have a political future, it must divest itself of the image of religious fanaticism that has been all too evident up to the present.* It must, in short, change from the Sōka Gakkai party to a people's party. But if it does, it faces a new problem: The factors that have been the strength of the organization will become minus factors and create a braking effect. The Kōmeitō faces a period of transition that promises to be difficult indeed.

Makoto Oda, organizer and leader of the Beheiren (League for Peace in Vietnam) and currently the object of international attention, is one of the most unusual personalities of the postwar generation.

Oda is, in certain ways, representative of a new breed of anti-establishment leaders. Typically, men like Oda have a finely tuned sense of the times, a tough-minded activism, and an aura of intense individuality, creativity, and appeal as human beings. Unmistakably anti-establishment elements are prominent in their philosophies, but these elements are not based on any systematized ideology. For this reason, they enjoy freedom of action, and it is easy for them to take activists of many hues under their wings. However, this very lack of dogma largely negates what might well be called a genius for organizing, for the organizations themselves tend to be extremely loose, and the larger the organization the more fragile it becomes.

These new leaders seem to combine in themselves substantial elements of religion, philosophy, science, literature, and journalism, but the dominant element appears to be a penchant for agitation. Their keen sense of the times and their ability to mobilize

---

* In early 1970, the Kōmeitō was rocked by strong public criticism of an attempt by the Sōka Gakkai to suppress publication of a book critical of the church and the party. In the general election of December, 1972, the party suffered a stunning defeat: Its Diet representation was reduced by half.—Ed.

the masses come from this remarkable combination of talents. However, if they should overplay their role of agitator, there is the possibility that they will degenerate into demagogues and speculators.

In an attempt to make some sort of forecast for Japan in the decade ahead, I have dwelt at some length on three men, Shintarō Ishihara, Daisaku Ikeda, and Makoto Oda, since I consider them the most interesting and the most likely to engage in noteworthy activities during the 1970's. In the next ten years, how they develop, emerge, change, and grow will very likely have a bearing on the course and nature of Japan during this period. Of course, there is always the possibility that some other, more charismatic leader will emerge and pull Japan in a wholly unexpected direction. Nor can we rule out acts of God, catastrophes, and entirely new developments in technology, in the social system, and in the economy of the nation. But even so, by keeping a close eye on these three men, I believe we can make predictions concerning Japan and its "return match" in the 1970's that are at least as reliable as those of a racetrack tipster.

13

Japan's Foreign Policy Objectives
in a Nuclear Milieu

Yōnosuke Nagai

Aims and Strategies

The foreign policy of any contemporary nation-state is circumscribed by the constantly shifting interests of all other nations
and influenced by pressures and public opinion at home. For a
foreign policy to be democratic, it must embrace both a long-
term vision representative of the values of all the people and
middle-range plans capable of bridging the gap between the
ideals of the vision and the constraints of reality. Japanese foreign policy must envision creating a world order of pluralistic
values where Japan can participate in a workable and secure international order able to assure a lasting peace. Until such a
world order is realized, I think we would be well advised to direct our efforts to the following problems: First of all, in order to
promote lasting peaceful coexistence, we must try to achieve a
balance of power among the Soviet Union, the United States, and
China; second, we must provide for Japan's security on the basis
of the power balance; third, we must pare down our national defense expenditures to the lowest possible limit and use the funds
thereby saved to build a democratic socialist society.

I mean by a democratic socialist society one in which, as Marx
pictured it, people can truly be human, where they can probe the

furthest limits of their potential as men. I mean the sort of democratic community that makes economic, social, and political institutions into means instead of ends by subordinating them to man's ultimate task of creating cultural values. Contemporary postindustrial society has set the stage for such a community by liberating human beings from drudgery. The release of man from slavery to his work is a revolutionary development that explains, in part, why many modern governments, especially the superpowers, attempt to convince their people of life's meaning by emphasizing common national goals. The emphasis on common national goals is designed to stimulate nationalistic feelings against the enemy on the basis of competition between vying social and political systems, races into space, and rivalry in armed might. Japan must not rely on such a facile solution to the problem of discovering man's meaning in the meaninglessness of postindustrial society. It must instead explore untried possibilities by continuing its peaceful, noncompetitive values. We must be proud of the fact that Japan alone is attempting to do this and confident that we can succeed. But if we are to generate pride and confidence, we must marshal all our ingenuity, political acumen, and ability to apply scientific ideas and techniques and must penetrate the unlimited dimensions of human creativity.

In contradistinction to this long-range vision, the United States tends to view Japan from the short range. It demands, for instance, that we rearm and join the camp of "freedom-loving nations." If the United States continues to press such demands on us, there will be dire results at home and abroad. At home, Japanese right-wing elements will gain ground and anti-Communist ideology will be amplified; abroad, these demands will cause us trouble with China. Lest the United States commit the foolish error of getting us involved in a spiraling arms race with China, it ought to recall the historical fact that the rearmament of West Germany after the Korean war—an act sired by the illusion that military power solves all problems—succeeded only in providing a major barrier to the relaxation of East-West tensions. In Asia, Japan's most effective role is not as a military power but as a model to which the developing nations of the world might look. For Japan can teach these nations that it is possible for an Asian country to develop, on the basis of freedom, a stable, affluent, culturally advanced, democratic socialist society. As a model and an inspiration, Japan could become a most powerful political deterrent to Chinese influence.

Japan's progressive forces, also unable to take the proper long-range view, commit several fundamental errors. With regard to the areas of diplomacy and international politics (in which any government, no matter how progressive, is limited in its scope of action), progressives give constant lip service to a course so radical as to impede the creation of a national consensus. In spite of their radicalism with regard to foreign problems, however, they are remarkably passive when it comes to contributing to domestic social reform. Their mission should be to develop a truly forward-looking vision and concrete plans to realize it. Instead they are wrapped up in a conservative, nineteenth-century outlook, and—to put the most favorable interpretation on their inertia—they seem to have become skeptical about what they can do to change Japan's social realities. The progressive camp will have to reverse these trends if it is to live up to its responsibilities and promise. With respect to international politics and foreign diplomacy, progressives must become more thoroughly realistic; they might begin by studying the dynamic sensitivity to power politics exhibited by our leaders in the Meiji Period.

Once the progressives assume a more realistic stand on foreign policy, it will be possible for the Japanese people to arrive at a consensus on certain medium-range objectives. The most vital of these is the establishment of normal relations with China. The best way to attain this objective is to adopt a roundabout, indirect strategy. By this I mean we should use a "multiple-option" diplomacy—to adapt a phrase from McNamara's strategy—that would provide us with a consistently wide choice of action. A nation with such a strategy must coordinate all its political, economic, diplomatic, and military policies and concentrate them on the single objective of minimizing the number of hostile nations and maximizing the number of friendly nations.

To accomplish the single objective of an indirect strategy, Japan will have to pursue both an "active policy" and a "passive policy." Our "passive policy" would be to avoid situations where we have no diplomatic options; our "active policy" would be to increase the number of our friends and allies by means of a dynamic diplomacy. If our "active policy" is to be successful, we must be especially careful in distinguishing friend and foe, especially the latter, because we cannot maximize our allies until we know who our potential enemies are, and we can neither make allies nor minimize our enemies if we imagine that international politics is a kindergarten playground where we can hold hands and make friends with everybody. And we dare not make the mistake of trying to distinguish friend and foe on the basis of ideology, that is, free versus Communist, capitalist versus socialist, imperialist versus anti-imperialist, have versus have-not, white versus colored, West European versus Asian, and so forth. We must make our choice on the basis of economic, political, and geopolitical national interests, and in doing so we must assume that Japan is (1) fundamentally a *status quo* power, (2) situated in the Asian cultural bloc, (3) an advanced nation whose high technical capabilities have brought it to the stage of mass consumption, and (4) a maritime state that, as long as the U.S. Seventh Fleet controls the Western Pacific, is destined to remain under the American nuclear umbrella.

Having made these four assumptions, Japan will find it necessary, first, to maintain friendly relations with various Western nations and, second, to normalize relations with the Soviet Union and those countries of Eastern Europe that have come to support the economic and political *status quo*. Strong ties with the *status quo* nations will be to our mutual advantage because of the community of interests we share; strong ties with the Soviet Union open the possibility of establishing a Moscow-Tokyo-Washington axis. Japan must therefore make indirect overtures to the Soviet Union and seek to conclude a peace treaty with it, even if this means temporarily shelving certain territorial issues. Normal relations with Moscow might make it possible for us to work through the Kremlin toward instituting friendly relations with Pyongyang. Although the North Koreans, given the realities of geopolitics, cannot be expected to alter appreciably their fence-sitting policy, they do seem predisposed to lean more toward Moscow than Peking.

A long-range plan of diplomatic action grounded on the four assumptions presented above could, as I have suggested, conceivably lead to the formation of a Moscow-Tokyo-Washington axis.

In the process of forming an axis of this sort, Japan would not only have to help overcome the economic and ideological disparities that exist between North and South Korea but also have to help initiate talks on the removal of military forces from the 38th parallel. From an even longer-range view, Japan must extend every possible assistance to the Korean people's attempts at political unification because of the profound influence the peninsula's unity and stability would have on Japan's national defense. Furthermore, within the context of a Moscow-Tokyo-Washington alliance, we must give serious consideration to participating in cooperative peaceful enterprises—such as the development of Siberia—which could lead to establishment of a demilitarized northern zone from Hokkaido through the Kuriles to the Aleutians.

Policies Toward China

Solution of the China problem is the medium-range aim of Japanese diplomacy. We cannot hope to convince China of our friendly intentions if all we do is display our bad conscience and apologize for past crimes of aggression on the continent. A foreign policy directed to Peking must be based on present realities.

One of the surest of these realities is the ultimate objective of China's policy vis-à-vis Japan: It would like to see our country withdraw from its military alliance with the United States and become neutral. In fact, Peking is so intent on accomplishing this objective that it has set aside its scruples regarding nuclear blackmail. China's frequent attacks on the Soviet Union for having stooped to such blackmail have consistently been grounded on the moralistic stand that a socialist nation ought not to coerce others with nuclear threats. It is a matter of record that, even after its atomic tests, China refrained from pursuing an open policy of nuclear blackmail, albeit partly to avoid irritating the United States. If China's ultimate objective is a neutral Japan, its immediate aims are, first, to prevent Tokyo from revising the Mutual Security Treaty to allow American nuclear weapons on Japanese soil and, second, to encourage an anti-American mood in Japan and lend support to domestic trends toward neutrality by emphasizing that a military alliance with the United States makes Japan less, rather than more, secure.

Japan's most effective answers to the potential threat posed by Chinese nuclear weapons are domestic political stability, maximization of friends and allies, and an increase in international bargaining power. The answer is certainly not to enlarge our military capabilities and get involved in a spiraling arms race. We must avoid such myopic "solutions" and instead establish a long-range view with respect to our China policy. To begin with, any general policy must recognize certain facts, the most obvious of which is that the People's Republic of China is not likely to fade away in the foreseeable future. It is also vital to realize that, even if Sino-Soviet tensions multiply, we cannot afford to indulge in the wishful thinking that Moscow and Peking will completely sever relations with each other. Our future is linked with coexistence, and our basic policy should be to encourage China's political and economic structure to move toward acceptance of the peaceful coexistence ideal.

If we are to create a favorable Sino-Japanese environment, we must pursue three specific policies. First, we must expand the number of exchanges of private citizens. A start has been made, but if we have learned the lesson of the Soviet thaw we will vastly increase the number of journalists, scholars, businessmen, union representatives, authors, and artists exchanged between China and Japan. Let us remember that in the Soviet Union it was the intellectuals—the nuclear scientists, technicians, and managers of atomic plants—who, because they were incontestably necessary to Kremlin leaders, came to hold enormous power and to challenge the architects of a rigid policy. Sino-Japanese exchange could very well create a similar group of men in China whose commitment to peace and truth would open a path toward internationalism.

Second, as a long-range objective we should work toward expansion of Sino-Japanese trade. Trading so-called strategic materials with the Chinese is, of course, a sensitive point, especially for Washington. And there is no reason to believe that a market would exist for Japanese television sets, nylon stockings, and other consumer goods in a country that gives the development of nuclear weapons precedence over the production of trousers. Expansion of our China trade would not, therefore, involve primarily consumer goods, so it could not weaken the Chinese masses' revolutionary morale, which, because the people are involved in a perpetual struggle for justice, obviates the need for comforts. Consequently, we should not optimistically imagine that trade alone might promote a thaw in China's internal and external behavior. When we talk of expanding trade, we also need to consider the question of timing, especially if we get involved in trading on a deferred-payment basis. Should that occur, we would be wise to prepare ourselves for the possibility that China might use deferred payments as a weapon to disturb Japan's internal political conditions.

Third, Japan should make a long-range effort to get China accepted into the United Nations. Whether or not China wishes to be a member, and irrespective of the current barriers to its admission, our government must pursue a one-Taiwan/one-China policy.* At the moment, America's wisest policy would be to work toward the eventual relaxation of Sino-American tension by casting Japan in the role of mediator between Peking and Washington.

For Japan to make such a contribution, however, it must jealously preserve its moral eligibility. Japan's main qualification as a mediator is its powerful progressive forces, the existence of which gives Japan lines of communication that are closed to Western nations. Unlike most countries in the free world, Japan's progressives have political "hot lines" to Peking and Moscow. If the Japanese Government takes advantage of these connections with Communist capitals, it could conceivably establish an outstanding multiple-option foreign policy.† We cannot, however, expend all our energies in trying to realize the diplomatic goals we have been discussing here. We must exert at least a minimum effort to guarantee our national defense and security.

Japan's National Security

Many commentators have a blind spot with respect to the problem of Japan's security. They miss a possible source of

---

* Although Tokyo did not play a role in gaining Peking's representation in the United Nations in 1971, it has agreed to establish diplomatic relations with Peking and has reduced its ties with Taiwan to economic ones only.—ED.

† It is interesting to note that the Japanese Government did just this in the summer of 1972, using not only Socialist Party representatives but the head of the Kōmeitō as message bearers in the contacts that led to Premier Kakuei Tanaka's visit to China.—ED.

trouble because they are so intent on looking elsewhere for a potential enemy that they completely overlook the eventuality of
defense against the United States. Most countries have deferred
to a classical, iron-clad maxim when planning national defense:
the rule that defense plans are prepared on the assumption that
every nation is a potential aggressor. Prewar Japan was, in fact,
nothing more than a garrison state organized on the basis of this
classical military rule.

The English, however, have not laid their defense plans on the
basis of that maxim. There is probably not a single Englishman
who worries in the least about the United States in spite of the
fact that Great Britain is practically defenseless against the
United States. At the present moment, though we imagine that
an analogous feeling exists between Tokyo and Washington, we
must admit that our sentiments are not grounded on the same
deep historical ties of race, religion, and economics that bind the
United States and Great Britain.

Differences in Japan's historical relations with the United
States can be illustrated most dramatically by the fact that until the postwar era we were calling the British and the Yankees
"Anglo-Saxon devils." We would be wise to keep this in mind
lest we get too romantic about our relations with the United
States. To achieve any kind of relationship at all, Tokyo and
Washington must make concentrated attempts at mutual understanding. Like all international involvements, Japanese-American
relationships are a matter of give-and-take based ultimately on
cold calculations of self-interest. Those who have forgotten this
fact tend to sit back and relax, confident and secure in their illusion that no matter how unreasonable our demands might be,
Uncle Sam cannot afford to discard us.

To assume a more realistic view of the United States, we must
realize that the historical significance of the "Greater East Asia
War" has nothing to do with the *ex post facto* interpretation that
Japan was attempting to liberate Asians from colonialism. The
war was rather a power struggle between two great naval powers
straddling the Pacific Ocean who had to pay a horrendous price
to win their present hand-holding friendship. We must seek the
significance of the Pacific war in the cost of this amity, and we
must etch on our minds this basic principle of diplomacy and

self-defense: We should never again make the United States our enemy. To forget this principle would be to negate the price paid by those who fell in the Pacific war and make their deaths meaningless.

As long as the Sino-American confrontation exists, any Japanese act that fundamentally alters the *status quo* will only exacerbate East-West tensions; it will not lead to stability in Asia. Those who insist that the most helpful contribution to peace in the Far East would be, for some vague reason or another, to make Japan neutral and nonaligned, completely ignore the geopolitics of the Japanese islands and overlook the political influence such an act would have on Washington.

The unconditional dream of a neutral, unaligned Japan overlooks the fact that, if cold war tensions continue in the Far East, it will be extraordinarily difficult to maintain Japan's domestic political stability. One of the reasons for the difficulty is that Japan's left-wing political forces are divided into various factions, some of which support Chinese policies and others of which support the policies of the Soviet Union. The resulting competition for hegemony over the progressive movement could very easily generate so much domestic strife that a foreign power would be tempted to intervene on the pretense of lending economic and military assistance. To complicate matters, the right wing in Japan would doubtless respond to the left's offensive by becoming more reactionary and radically opposed to the progressives, a development that could easily precipitate a military *coup d'état*. In view of the remnants of fanatical nationalism in postwar Japan, a coup is far from improbable; although Japanese reactionary fanaticism may have assumed slightly different ideological coloration, it is not dead. Domestic strife would obviously prevent Japan from contributing to the alleviation of tensions in the Far East.

Aside from the question of whether any nation might plan aggression against Japan, from the viewpoint of capability we have to admit that the United States presents the first, the Soviet Union the second, and the People's Republic of China the third most serious threat to Japan's security. It thus behooves us to deal with each of these nations in turn, giving the United States top priority. And, if we can maintain friendly relations through diplomatic channels and establish some sort of security system that will diminish the potential threat from each of these countries, we should be able to economize on national defense expenditures. Such a policy would permit Japan the widest possible latitude and freedom of action.

Some might rebut this suggestion by saying that, as long as Japan is an integral part of the U.S. security system, it will be exposed as a potential target of Soviet or Chinese nuclear attack. This argument stems from an ignorance of nuclear deterrent strategy. While it is true that the danger of an attack from these two nearby powers will never be nil, Japan has no choice but to acknowledge its geopolitical situation. It stands in a valley overshadowed by three great powers, China, the United States, and the Soviet Union; as long as tension exists among them, the Japanese people cannot think that neutrality will make their country any safer than it is now under the American security blanket. Because the three giants who tower over us have completely different views of our strategic importance and of what they expect from a neutral Japan in terms of their national interests, they can never be exactly certain, and hence can only uneasily surmise, what each of the others has in mind. Some Japanese believe that Japan could solve its problems by becoming an independent military power. However, the United States obviously considers the security of the Japanese islands crucial to its interests; it would demand of such an independent Japan defenses sufficient to discourage intimidation or military intervention by either the Soviet Union or China. The Russians would not make such a strong demand. On the other hand, neither the Soviet Union nor the United States would be very happy were Japan suddenly to become an unarmed neutral.

Unarmed neutrality is an anomaly in contemporary world politics. Perhaps our passion for unarmed neutrality relates to the fact that Japanese sensibilities are not disturbed by the idea of suicide. Sensibilities are quite different in the West, where suicide means the self-abandonment of a responsible personality. If the Japanese notion of "unarmed pacifism" is indeed a reflection of our traditional moral approval of self-destruction, it is doubly inapplicable in the realm of international relations, where no country is free to commit national suicide.

Whenever a potential aggressor's gains (economic, political, and military) from the military and political control of a given country exceed the price (political, military, and moral) of achieving control, it is axiomatic that neighbors with peaceful intentions will be uneasy about the fate of the country in question. If one applies this axiom to the problem of Japan's national defense, one finds there are only three ways to realize security by means of nonaligned neutrality. The first is to decrease Japan's economic and strategic importance by reducing its desirability as an object of conquest. Even if Japan became a "hibernating, pacifistic" country, however, it could never become truly isolated, because it cannot escape its geopolitical position. The second is to arm every citizen, like the Swiss, or to maintain an independent nuclear arsenal. The third way is to stay under the U.S. nuclear umbrella, perhaps in a quasi-independent form of neutrality, where we could buy time to provide ourselves with a stock of conventional arms, develop a scheme of independent defense, and at the same time try to switch to a security system wherein American troops could enter Japan only to meet a national emergency, and then only at the request of the Japanese Government.

The first choice is too unattractive even to consider. That leaves the second and the third, either of which would mean that, should we decide to divorce ourselves from the current Japan–United States mutual security system and take the path of independent neutrality, we must be prepared to pay the price of our decision. Just as a revolutionary theory that fails to require the people to make the necessary sacrifices is nothing but propaganda, so theories of pacifism and neutrality that call for no sacrifice are nothing more than attempts to pull the wool over the eyes of the people. Here we discern the basic dilemma of Japan's contemporary progressive camp. The left has yet to resolve the contradictions inherent in their concept of a secure but unarmed and neutral Japan. The progressives' route to "security" leads to defense by defenselessness—hardly a defense at all. Progressives seem to be perfectly satisfied with the isolationistic mood that urges that "we never again become involved in war" or alliances, and the antiarms mood that opposes the Self-Defense Forces and Japanese rearmament. They appear completely oblivious to the fact that both these moods flatly contradict the nation's need for security. Perhaps the very popularity of the peace mood in Japan, so long the prop of the progressive movement, will in the end turn out to be the millstone that drags Japan's progressives down onto the horns of this dilemma.

Can Nuclear Arms Preserve Peace?

We face a serious decision: Does the road to independent neutrality inevitably require nuclear armaments? To provide background for this decision, let us begin by examining the ideas of the retired French General Pierre Gallois, which, following their publication in the *Mainichi Shimbun* on January 3, 1964, caused immediate and widespread reaction in Japan. We can summarize Gallois's theory of nuclear strategy as follows:

1. It is no longer possible to wage unlimited war without destroying the very objects for which war is usually fought, that is, the enemy's cities, resources, and wealth.
2. Neither the United States nor the Soviet Union would consider using atomic weapons unless they came under nuclear attack.
3. To guarantee its security in the nuclear age, a country has no alternative to possessing its own nuclear weapons. The fear of retaliation prevents nuclear arms from becoming offensive weapons.

In short, Gallois holds that the country that possesses nuclear weapons is an independent sanctuary impervious to threat.

With its simplicity and clarity, Gallois's plan readily appeals to a naïve, nationalistic mood. The fundamental snag in his theory is that he has mistaken the strategy of nuclear deterrence for the strategy of an actual nuclear war. There is, in fact, reason to believe that Gallois has deliberately confused the two. Though his theory may accomplish its political objectives, it will not stand up under the scrutiny of a specialist in military strategy.

If Gallois is wrong and autonomous diplomacy does not require nuclear arms, we are still faced with the problem of how to guarantee our security as an independent state. There are at least six things we can do to provide ourselves with the versatility necessary to maintain our diplomatic freedom of action.

First, we must recognize that the basis of an autonomous diplomacy lies not in possessing our own nuclear weapons, but rather in impressing the United States with the fact that Japan is politically trustworthy and steadfast. Indeed, one purpose of our Self-Defense Forces is to win America's trust by indicating our seriousness of purpose in matters of national defense. In order to make the SDF a more adequate indication of our resolve, we have no choice but to invest at least 2 per cent of our total national income in direct defense expenditures.

Second, in the face of the increased nuclear threat from China, Japan must remain under the protection of America's nuclear umbrella. However, our government must absolutely oppose any American proposal to build hardened nuclear installations on Okinawa or the Japanese main islands. We will have to live with Polaris submarines if we expect America to be able to guarantee our security, but this is a matter of fate, not of choice.

Third, we must attempt to get rid of American bases on Japanese soil. Diplomatic endeavors to establish a Moscow-Tokyo-Washington axis assume our efforts to reduce Sino-American tensions. As these tensions are eased, the United States–Japan Mutual Security Treaty could be gradually converted into an instrument allowing U.S. troops to be stationed on Japanese soil only in the event of a national emergency. Reduction of American military strength in Japan will take place, however, only if we are willing and able to fill the resultant power vacuum with indigenous conventional military forces.

We must also be prepared to resist "indirect aggression" from ideological and political quarters. We should buttress external relationships by improving diplomatic strategies and internal ties. The need for internal cohesion underscores the urgency of alleviating areas of antagonism in our own "domestic cold war." One area that demands immediate attention relates to the attitude of the faction within the conservative camp that favors a showdown with the left. Men from this faction are irrationally terrified of China's nuclear threat from without and the progressives' challenge from within. Their fears are likely to prompt them to intensify domestic tensions and spur the left to form a broad and unified front against them. Socialists, on the other hand, must not abandon their commitment to peaceful coexistence, as have, for example, the Communists, who subscribe to revolution as a clear-cut political objective.

Fourth, we must realize that nuclear arms have become psychological means to political ends; they are utterly unusable as weapons in the normal sense of the term. We must therefore stick firmly to our position that the side that first uses nuclear weapons has to bear the onus of being branded the enemy of mankind. Though Japan has the ability to produce nuclear weapons, it must continue to maintain its moral superiority by resisting the temptation to do so. Japan must make a worldwide appeal for a series of large-scale peace campaigns aimed at checking the proliferation of nuclear devices. In order to realize positive results, however, Japan will have to take vigorous joint action with both the Soviet Union and the United States.

Fifth, we must discover peaceful uses of atomic energy in order to maintain our level of nuclear technology. Rather than maintain nuclear technology through weaponry, Japan should exert its main efforts on nuclear research for peaceful ends. By so doing, it would be serving peaceful ends while at the same time maintaining the over-all level of its national power.

Sixth, we must also establish large centers for collecting information and studying strategy and arms control. Our goal here would be to provide basic data on the specific diplomatic behavior of nations. Such centers are absolutely necessary if we hope to remain sensitive and receptive to the extraordinarily complex changes that constantly take place in international conditions.

Even after doing these things, however, we will be no closer to peace unless we also affirm the coexistence of the United States and the Soviet Union, the two major *status quo* powers. It is incumbent on those who talk of peace these days to help sustain the Soviet-American "cold alliance" and thereby help mankind move beyond the present grave turning point in human history.

It is not easy to talk of peace unless we have a clear notion of its relation to justice. However, many liberal Japanese intellectuals still naïvely imagine that achieving peace is tantamount to achieving justice. The truth is that neither Japan's revolutionaries nor its intellectuals have clearly perceived the profound significance of the advent of the atomic age: Nuclear weapons have so radically altered revolutionary justice that it can no longer be considered a meaningful or viable concept. Pacifists who grant peace a higher value than justice, and visionary revolutionaries who worship justice as a value transcending peace, are not really men of the twentieth century.

14

Systems of Power Balance and the Preservation of Peace

Hiroharu Seki

Realists and the Balance of Power

Emergence of the new realists. The term realism, as used by contemporary Japanese analysts of international politics, merely represents a kind of political conservatism. Paradoxically, we might even call the "realistic" approach to global problems a form of idealism, because it so optimistically "idealizes" political situations. When realists analyze the problems of international politics, they tend to focus all their attention on strategies that the major world powers, including China, have formulated on the basis of national aims. As they fix their concern on the policy goals and national interests of the powers, they narrow the scope of their concern and tend to lose the capacity to sympathize with the sufferings, aspirations, and struggles of the peoples of Asia, Africa, and Latin America. Because the realists assume that the policies and interests of the major powers alone determine the entire structure of international relations, they naturally fail to see the extent to which the peoples of Asia, Africa, and Latin America have the potential energy to change the world. The realists' analyses are consequently limited to a search for methods by which their own country might best adjust its external behavior to the national interests and goals of its ally, the United States.

They have constricted reality rather drastically by taking this "realistic" approach.

The restricted optimistic idealism of the realists is especially apparent in their use of "balance of power," a concept they employ as a weapon to criticize the progressives. Analysis of international politics based on the assumption that a balance of power will preserve peace is unscientific because it abandons even the pretense of making a systematic investigation of the facts. Nor have progressive scholars conducted any strictly scientific analyses of the power balance concept. Their approach to world problems is characterized by active sympathy for the suffering, less affluent peoples of the world. Rather than analyzing power relations, they try to understand what is in the minds of the hundreds of millions of barefoot people who populate the vast underdeveloped parts of the world. The progressives suspect that in the aspirations of these people lie the hidden seeds that, in a decade or two, will sprout into a new force to challenge *status quo* political leadership and reform the world. They believe, furthermore, that social and behavioral scientists must deal adequately with these potential agents of world change if for no other reason than to develop their own disciplines. Thus, it is not at all surprising that progressive social scientists disparage the conservatives' balance-of-power theory as "idealistic optimism" because it fastens on a momentary equilibrium among the haves and completely disregards the enduring reality of the have-nots.

Conservatives are concerned with power holders rather than with the masses, because their principal value is preservation of the *status quo*. It is quite natural, therefore, that Professor Yōnosuke Nagai, who regards himself as a conservative in the best sense of the term, would base his discussion and analysis of the international situation on this value. His article "Restraints and Options in Japanese Foreign Policy" shows that, although he is a member of the neorealist school, he has fallen heir to the traditional realists' optimistic faith that power balance is the key to maintaining the peace. The ideas developed in his essay deal with a power balance that takes the form of a Northern, Moscow-Tokyo-Washington axis; they literally brim over with the rosy realism I have just described. Nagai asserts that mankind will neither survive the present crisis nor enjoy peace in our time unless the nations of the world affirm Soviet-American coexistence and support the "cold alliance" between these two *status quo* powers.

But surely we cannot believe that our only alternative is peace based on a *rapprochement* between Moscow and Washington, a kind of *Pax Russo-Americana* predicated on hostility toward Peking.

In view of the way political conservatives have become captives of their restricted aims, the real task of the progressive student of international politics is to offer an entirely new aim, or an end value different from the "preservation of the *status quo*." Only then will a "progressive" alternative be meaningful. As long as progressives are content merely to criticize or disparage the conservatives' "realistic" alternative, they will get nowhere. They must move one step further and formulate a scientifically valid alternative within a new framework, a new dimension, different from that in which conservatives operate.

Those who talk of peace based on a balance of power say we must acknowledge power politics as a reality of international relations and choose diplomatic policies and methods accordingly. This is precisely the neorealist view taken by Nagai and Masataka Kōsaka,* both of whom imagine that if Japan is sufficiently clever at manipulating power politics it will be able not only to preserve the peace but to enhance its national strength as well. If we are to deal scientifically with the concept of power balance, however, we must understand it objectively in terms of its functions and internal mechanisms and not reduce it to a mere ideological myth, that is, we must not base our analysis on the *a priori* assumption that a balance of power is essential to maintain the peace.

The function of balance-of-power systems. The most effective way to criticize the neorealists and their approach to world politics is to lay open the weaknesses of their pet theory: power balance. An essay that has effectively attacked this core of realist thought, "The Fiction of 'Power Balance,'" by Yoshikazu Sakamoto,† begins by pointing out the ambiguities of the term itself.

* Professor Kōsaka is a prominent conservative scholar at the University of Kyoto and a member of the Diet.—ED.

† Sakamoto is a respected and widely read political scientist who writes frequently on matters of foreign policy.—ED.

According to Sakamoto, the term balance of power is employed in several different ways. First, it is used to designate a policy aimed at maintaining the national interests and power relations of contemporary nations. Second, it denotes the state of equilibrium among themselves that major powers regard as the objective of their foreign policies. Third, it is on occasion consciously utilized, or perhaps it would be more accurate to say manipulated, by the ruling elite—first, on the domestic scene as an ideological symbol to prevent the people from attaining an accurate insight into the problems of self-defense, and also on the diplomatic scene to justify national policies. These varied usages invite ambiguities to slip into our understanding of the concept.

Sakamoto accurately diagnoses how difficult it is to gain a proper understanding of "balance of power." Although he deals with an important aspect of the concept, I believe it is also necessary to come to grips with balance of power in terms of its function as a system. We must see how the concept operates as a rule or basic principle to fashion the pattern of interaction among the several nations in a state system where the nations are not subordinate to the higher authority of an international body. Analysis of balance of power as a system will help clarify the manner in which it sometimes operates to provoke armed conflicts and thus will help discredit the exceptionally tenacious myth that such systems can insure the peace. At the very least, dealing with the concept as a system will enable us to expose the fuzzy thinking that imagines that power balance contributes to international harmony.

How can balance of power be achieved and maintained? There are three theories of adjustment. The first assumes a natural or automatic equilibrium, the second a semiautomatic, and the third a system in which balance is consciously manipulated. From the first theory to the third, we can see a process of historical evolution, a transition that begins with the idea of implicit, and ends with the idea of explicit, control. This process might also be described in terms of the gradations between an involuntary muscular activity (a heartbeat) and a voluntary action (a finger movement). Jean Jacques Rousseau (1712–78) supported the theory of automatic, involuntary balance. Of course, he lived in an era that had romantically idealized the notion, expressed by

Adam Smith (1723–90) in his *An Inquiry into the Nature and Causes of the Wealth of Nations* (1776), that capitalistic development was guided by "the invisible hand of God." More than a generation later, the Prussian historian Leopold von Ranke (1795–1886) stated that each state's "guardian deities" would preserve the international (that is, the European) power-balance system. No doubt these views reflected the Arcadian nature of international affairs in those days. Nevertheless, the model of an automatically adjusted equilibrium is worth noting because—in presupposing a divine balancing authority, an unseen, transcendent power—it becomes set over against reality.

The second theory assumes a semiautomatic process of equilibrium maintenance. Proponents of this theory go a step beyond the first by contending that adjustment of balance should be in closer conformity with reality. They designate a specific country as the force that carries out the function performed by God in the first theory, a seen rather than an unseen hand. England is their model. Great Britain acted as the "balancer," they say, and maintained equilibrium among the members in the European state system. The other states behaved naturally with regard to their external affairs and did not consciously strive to achieve equilibrium. Thus, the theory assumes the existence of a single member in the system who is consistently concerned. As a result of its concern, the role of the watchdog member is to maintain or redress the balance by shifting its weight to the momentarily weaker side.

The third theory assumes a completely volitional process of maintaining power balance. Those who advocate this process say that one must consciously manipulate equilibrium, and so they refuse to credit either of the other theories. In fact, they ridicule the idea that any one state has a "divine mission" to calculate the need for adjustment and then effect it. They are also contemptuous of the notion that some automatic mechanism mystically regulates the balance in a state system. Proponents of the third theory ask rather whether the states constituting the system can produce responsible statesmen to manage their foreign policies, and whether these men have the ability to choose the wisest policies to maintain a balance of power. The third model makes the following tacit assumptions: First, if a crisis occurs in a system that has achieved a measure of equilibrium, most member states will begin acting in concert to retain or regain the balance; second, statesmen are not concerned with their own states so much as with stabilizing the system, that is, they aim at peace and choose the most rational and effective policies to achieve it.

These three theories are, needless to say, no more than analytical paradigms. It is quite another matter to inquire into the concrete machinations exhibited by any specific power-balance system. That task would require an empirical historical study. In any event, if we were to analyze contemporary international politics within the framework of these three theories of power balance, our first chore would be to investigate whether or not the members of the system have, in fact, the ability to achieve an equilibrium—an ability expressed in terms of responsible statesmen or a nation's "mission" as a balancer. Although many studies have been made, I have yet to find one scientific investigation that in any way verifies the contention that the "peace will be threatened if one disturbs the balance of power." If no verification exists, it is clear that this contention, far from being an objective proposition bearing on international security, is nothing more than a myth fabricated by, and shot through with the characteristics of, political conservatism.

The function of war in balance-of-power systems. Irrespective of the ideals implicit in the myth that power-balance systems help maintain the peace, it is obvious that history has yet to produce a system that has been successful either in eliminating war or preventing the outbreak of war. According to Frederick L. Schuman, the dean of international political scientists, "war is obviously the ultimate means of coercion in interstate relations," even in redressing the imbalance of a power system. Hans J. Morgenthau goes a step beyond Schuman when he says that "most of the wars that have been fought since the beginning of the modern state system have their origin in the balance of power." Any unbiased look at the facts makes it difficult to conclude that power-balance systems can effectively deter wars. Their poor peace-keeping record calls for a theoretical investigation of the reasons why they have been so ineffective.

One important cause of the ineffectiveness of power-balance

systems lies in certain psychological factors related to the possibility of surprise attack. When two nations with virtually identical
strength face each other, the side that makes a surprise attack
effectively deprives the other side of its parity and gains a tremendous advantage. In the case of a weaker nation facing a more
powerful one, there is an even greater temptation to gain an advantage, or at least to achieve parity, by a surprise attack. The
raid on Pearl Harbor is a perfect example illustrating how a
weaker nation succumbed to that temptation. Thus, a given
country that is "subjectively" on the defensive is readily captivated by the logic that it must always try to be more powerful
than a potential aggressor and thus prevent an attack. Thus the
nation on the defensive, caught up in the process of trying to
meet power with power, quite naturally becomes a potential aggressor in the eyes of its opponent. It is difficult to imagine, however, that such a nation would be consciously aware of the way
tooling up its defenses against attack might make it a potential
attacker, ironically lured into aggression because of its defense
policy. The security of one nation consequently becomes a source
of anxiety for another. As this seesaw psychological mechanism
of security and anxiety begins to operate on both sides, a great
chain reaction occurs that eventually drives each protagonist into
an arms race intended to overcome anxiety and achieve security. One aspect of U.S. nuclear strategy, for example, is containment of China; China's reaction has been to develop nuclear
armaments. Both sides have been motivated by the desire to gain
security. As a result of the interaction of policies intent on security, each side has expanded its power and become caught up in
an anxiety-ridden situation over which it has no control.

Arms races can occur, therefore, even when a power-balance
system has achieved its stated aim of equilibrium. John H. Herz
states in *International Politics in the Atomic Age* that "the most
dangerous stage of all [is] a slight imbalance." There can be no
doubt that uncertainty breeds uncertainty. The end result can
only be rupture of the equilibrium, not the maintenance of
peace. From another angle, one might say that a condition of
equilibrium encourages some nations to imagine that, if it came
to a showdown, they might be able to win. This prize fighter's
pre-bout psychology increases the danger of war in such systems.

Whenever it is clear to all that one nation is vastly superior to another, the inferior of the two is not likely to start a war with its peerless neighbor.

Consequently, it seems unlikely that any diplomat or statesman in history has ever pursued a power-balance policy merely to create a true equilibrium. Statesmen who have tried to establish a balance of power have done so to further national interests and not to preserve the peace. This is why it is nearly impossible to create an equilibrium that will satisfy every member of the system, and this is why the very attempt to do so has consistently produced the opposite effect. At the same time, a state of disequilibrium may characterize a period in which there are no open hostilities, but it also spawns the conditions that eventually cause war. This is the idiosyncrasy of a balance-of-power system: When one nation feels an intense antagonism toward a potential enemy, the closer the two approach an equilibrium of power, the greater the probability that war will break out between them.

Chinese and American Miscalculations

U.S. errors: intimidating actions. In this section I would like to analyze the kinds of miscalculations both China and the United States have made, with particular reference to the confrontation between the two in Vietnam. My analysis, meant as a case study in the impossibility of maintaining either the peace or the *status quo* by a power-balance system, will try to show that deterioration of the situation in Vietnam provides a superb example of the absolute invalidity of power-balance theory. Moreover, we shall take careful note of the fact that there is a noticeable heterogeneity in the pattern of miscalculations made in Peking and Washington owing to the fact that these powers commit their errors on the basis of utterly incompatible assumptions and standards. Neither nation is able to "get through" to the other side. Each finds the other's standards unintelligible. The lack of communication attests to the imminent danger that, in the absence of commonly accepted standards, either side may make further miscalculations.

American miscalculations began with the ill-conceived Staley-Taylor plan, which in 1962 attempted to establish strategic hamlets in Vietnam as a means of suppressing the Vietcong. The failure of the plan to accomplish its political objectives resulted in military escalation. During the process of escalation, Secretary of Defense Robert S. McNamara made continual miscalculations in estimating the number of American troops necessary to pacify Communist guerrillas in Vietnam. At first, he said 12,000 men were necessary to suppress the Vietcong. That figure later grew to 24,000. Then the number jumped to 40,000, and then to 75,-000. In April, 1966, McNamara talked in terms of 350,000 men.

Even Secretary of State Dean Rusk's testimony before the Far Eastern Subcommittee of the House Foreign Affairs Committee revealed his concern over tensions with China and the possibility of nuclear war. He testified that Washington ought to assure Peking that America had no intention of making an attack. Immediately after Rusk's statement was made public, American bombers struck at the outskirts of Hanoi and Haiphong. The coincidence of these events made one wonder whether Rusk's declaration to the Foreign Affairs Committee was not the signal to commence a new phase of escalation. It is as though Rusk intended to "mortgage" the success of American escalation in Vietnam to Washington's ability to communicate and China's ability to comprehend American signals.

If this is what the Secretary of State had in mind, we can say he was implementing on the chessboard of reality a strategy of intimidation, a strategy that seems to follow the outlines of the "revised game theory" contrived by Thomas C. Schelling. Schelling explains his theory in terms of a traffic problem. When a big car meets a small car at a crossroad and neither recognizes the other's right of way, Schelling says, the driver of the large automobile can safely negotiate the intersection merely by sounding his horn and accelerating. No matter how you look at it, this is a self-willed, aggressive way to drive. Schelling recognizes that size and power are decisive factors in getting through an intersection when there is doubt about the right of way; he intimates that sheer bulk is quite effective in intimidating a smaller car. I wonder, however, if momentum *per se* gives a person the right to blast his way through an intersection. Is it not a good deal more rational to approach a cross street with concern for pedestrians and to stop momentarily to consider the welfare of the other fellow?

Schelling's logic adds an important new factor to the third model of a power-balance system, the model in which one assumes that member states must consciously manipulate equilibrium. If we apply Schelling's traffic problem to the third model, the aggressive driver of the large car becomes the cognate of the nation determined to become the "invisible hand of God," the regulator of the components of the power-balance system. Applied to the Sino-American confrontation in Southeast Asia, the United States becomes analogous to the regulator nation. By what authority does it acquire the right to act as a policeman? What if China claims to be the duly constituted authority at that crossroad? Remember that Peking by no means promises to abide by the rules of the game Washington has elected to play. The United States could acquire the right to be the "balancer" of power on only one condition, that the peoples of the world, particularly those living in Asia, Africa, and Latin America, unequivocally recognize the functioning of an organized power-balance system. Only then would the United States's self-appointed role as "policeman" be sanctioned. If, on the other hand, this condition is not met, the U.S. "revised game theory" approach to international tensions only increases the risk of a serious accident. After America has dashed unscathed through the intersection several times, it is likely to feel it is not playing "Russian roulette" and that the odds will always be on its side.

The fact that Washington's *procedure* in pushing escalation to a higher stage has been faultless in no way guarantees that miscalculations have been avoided in the *substance* of escalation. What is at issue here resembles the problem of a mathematician who, satisfied merely that his formula works smoothly, pays no attention to whether or not he is using the right figures; oblivious to the mistakes that can be multiplied in such a situation, he proceeds to commit ever more serious errors. That is what has happened in Vietnam, where the concept of escalation is itself the miscalculation resulting in further stages of escalation. Given this situation, utilization of the "revised game theory" becomes tantamount to the philosophy of living dangerously in a fool's paradise where people believe that an accident-free record is proof of a safe driver.

In Vietnam, America the mammoth has had its heels nipped

by a country as small as a mouse because its policy objectives in
international politics have somehow caused it totally to run
amok. U.S. goals abound in confusion and error. Somewhere
along the line, the United States took the wrong turn, and in order to reach its destination it is inclined to push the accelerator
to the floor. That only hurries it farther and farther from its
goal.

   Mistakes in America's Asian strategy. Since World War II, the
United States has had the opportunity to make a number of
choices with regard to its policy in Asia. Its current embroilment
in Vietnam can be considered the result of having chosen neither
the wisest nor the best course.

   Perhaps the greatest single blunder the United States made
was to assume that the new masters of China were mere puppets
manipulated from Moscow. The Americans seem to have a passion for making that particular error as they project an identical
misconception on the Vietcong, believing that they are Hanoi's
and Peking's cat's-paws. The pattern of American analysis is
clear. Every time a revolutionary government appears, Washington's standard reaction is to apply the puppet cliché and consider
the radical regime a front for some other power that operates
the strings by remote control. Washington's ingenuous application of the puppet stereotype to every revolutionary situation
suggests that U.S. leaders have fallen into the trap of ignoring the
specific internal psychological causes that, like spontaneous com-
bustion, produce national revolutions in Asia.

   Another blunder concerns America's evaluation of China's intervention in the Korean War. Recent research indicates that the
Chinese bear absolutely no responsibility for the outbreak of
hostilities on the peninsula. Rather, it is fair to say that the
United States forced the Chinese to intervene. At any rate, Washington had the opportunity to rectify some of its errors and set
the record straight during the truce negotiations but failed to do
so. In fact, the Truman Administration reduced the possibility
of settling accounts by having the United Nations brand China
the aggressor in Korea. By agreeing to the truce, the United
States partially balanced the account.

   The Eisenhower Administration also missed an opportunity
to change the direction of American foreign policy when, at the

April, 1954, Geneva Conference, it elected to inhibit the growth
of neutralism in Asia by splitting Vietnam, and when it forced
the formation of the Southeast Asia Treaty Organization
(SEATO). The United States let another excellent opportunity
for reconciliation with China slip through its fingers when it
took a negative attitude toward the April, 1955, Bandung Conference, held during a time of rising Asian neutralism. To snarl
further the wires of possible communication with Peking, in the
late 1950's the United States gradually began to shift the orientation of its nuclear strategy by designating China rather than
the Soviet Union as its most likely enemy. As a result, the United
States sharpened the antagonism between Taiwan and the mainland, stiffened its stance against Peking, and thus made itself a
strong potential threat to China.

How has American nuclear strategy evolved during the postwar years? The most important point to note is that European
nations have constantly monitored the Pentagon's nuclear strategy, and on several occasions they have effectively checked its
application, much to the good fortune of the United States. For
example, the United States's European allies restrained MacAr-
thur's desire to bomb Manchuria during the Korean War and
derailed Dulles's plan to use nuclear weapons in Indochina during the mid-1950's. Nevertheless, in spite of these pressures from
its allies, the United States continued to expand its global construction of military bases on the supposition that it might one
day resort to its massive retaliation strategy.

The orbiting of the first Sputnik in 1957 and the successful
tests of the first Russian ICBM signaled the advent of a new
reality, however. After 1957, domestic military bases and American cities were no longer inviolable, and Washington's massive
retaliation strategy became meaningless.

What could take the place of this strategy? On the one hand,
General Maxwell Taylor suggested, and Henry A. Kissinger provided theoretical underpinning for, the idea of limited war. On
the other, the Pentagon probed the possibilities of fashioning a
new system of deterrent strategy based on the accumulation of so-
called second-strike forces. After the Soviet Union had also developed the ability to strike back in a secondary attack, however,
an attack on Soviet strategic nuclear installations was out of the

question, and the way was open to allow armed intervention in peripheral areas where there was no real danger of a life-and-death nuclear struggle. Later on, however, even that approach was rendered meaningless and inapplicable. It is terribly ironic that McNamara's strategy of multiple options, having become bottled up on various levels, has given rise to renewed advocacy of massive retaliation. The nub of the problem is this: Irrespective of changes in international power relations, Washington seems intent on giving the impression that a preventive attack is a possible option of American nuclear strategy, even though the reliability of nuclear weapons for deterring aggression has considerably diminished. Unless the United States commits itself to a principle that rules out the possibility of a preventive attack, it will be unable to improve its position or to negotiate an arms control agreement with other nuclear powers, including China.

Chinese errors: adhering to a revolutionary image of the world. America's miscalculations have arisen from its use of intimidation and military power. By contrast, China's have arisen from its expectation that the various countries and peoples in Asia, Africa, and Latin America would give the People's Republic their wholehearted moral support. A number of examples will illustrate my point. The Second Afro-Asian Conference, planned for June, 1963, had to be postponed because of a military *coup d'état* in Algeria, the host country. The postponement was naturally a bitter pill for China to swallow, considering its great expectations. China also miscalculated the potential of the Indonesian Communist Party (PKI). The failure of the premature coup on September 30, 1965, meant the demise of the PKI—the largest Communist Party in the non-Communist world—and its destruction resulted in the utter collapse of the Peking-Djakarta axis.

Nor did Peking's errors stop there. China supported Pakistan against India in the dispute over Kashmir but gained no political advantage for its trouble. The dispute was resolved through the mediation of the Soviet Union, resulting in the January 10, 1966, Tashkent Declaration, which revealed that Pakistan had capitulated and accepted many Indian demands. Meanwhile, following the 1965 Algerian *coup d'état,* Africa witnessed successful coups in the Congo, the Republic of Dahomey, Upper Volta, Nigeria, and Ghana. Almost all the new regimes came out in favor of establishing friendly relations with Western Europe rather than with China. Even Cuba, which Peking had regarded as the base of the Latin American revolution, published an anti-Chinese statement on February 6, 1966.

China was nevertheless undaunted. Peking felt that none of the momentary changes in the objective situation in any way altered its subjective analysis of reality. For China, the transient victory of reactionary elements only substantiates the belief that there is a worldwide tendency toward a reorganization and differentiation of political forces.

Dynamics of action and image. At the outset I said that, although they are grave on both sides, Chinese and American miscalculations exist in different dimensions. China continually exhibits an uncompromising attitude, but its errors occur primarily in the dimension of the revolutionary image it is attempting to communicate to the underdeveloped nations. The United States is equally uncompromising, but its errors occur primarily in the dimension of its military action. Given the structural differences between the two orders of miscalculation, it is hardly surprising that an asymmetry differentiates the errors made by Peking and Washington. The American strategy can be characterized as military deterrence designed to obstruct the kind of political changes China anticipates and attempts to foster in the contemporary world. Meanwhile, China exports its revolutionary strategy as an ideology of violence in order to facilitate a transformation of the world order and subvert the American international position. The Chinese are trying to export a world image that is a perfect inverse image of the rigidity that U.S. nuclear intimidation seeks to preserve. In other words, the asymmetry of the miscalculations made by China and America is a product of the global structure of world politics.

In the case of China, Peking has thus far made a careful distinction between its image and its actual behavior. Its military actions, especially, have been decided on the basis of a sober appraisal of its strength and strategic position rather than on the basis of its violent image of the world situation. Whether China can always make such a distinction, however, is quite an-

other question, because a short circuit between image and action
could one day occur under abnormal circumstances.

Conflict Resolution and National Aims

From intimidation to consent. Even from within the structures
of political power, it is possible to shed light on the complex
dynamics of how man's images relate to his deeds in the over-all
mechanism of human behavior. One of the political philosopher's
basic propositions, as old as the discipline itself, is that political
power rests on two primary factors: coercion by power and consent of the governed. Modern political scientists, considering
one of their main tasks to be the analysis of the functional dynamics between a system of intimidation by coercion and a system of integration by consent, have broadly accepted this basic
proposition. At one pole is coercion by police and military power;
at the other, a community with many characteristics of familial
organization. A system of intimidation is characterized by the
ability of those holding political power to deprive citizens of
what they most value: life, property, respect, loved ones. The
system of integration is characterized by an exchange in which
concern for the people's welfare is reciprocated in terms of respect for the holders of power. It is the system of consent that
legitimizes political power. To the degree that political power
relies on intimidation to solve conflicts of interest, it is less able
to obtain the consent of the governed.

On the level of international politics, intimidation by coercion will, in the long run, prove tremendously costly to the co-
ercer. For example, even though a nation has capitulated to the
threat of violent military action, its surrender is not a free act
of the will, and there is no guarantee that suppressed resentment
might not crop out one day to cause the victor a great deal of
difficulty. The history of colonialism accurately demonstrates
such a probability. In a word, cheap intimidation does not really
solve the conflict; it only drives it "underground" and postpones
the actual solution. In the end, that kind of conflict resolution is
very dear, because forcible solutions demand an exorbitant price.

The history of human progress might be described as a process
of giving more and more precedence to the long-term, as opposed

to the short-term, costs of conflict resolution. During this historical evolution, as the relation between man's image and his action
has become more and more indirect, men with political power
have found it more and more necessary to exercise self-restraint
in the use of intimidation by coercion. The same evolution has
also resulted in the increased ability to forecast trends and in the
improved capacity to perceive with accuracy the state of affairs as
it exists at any given moment. These developments have given
rise to the possibility that those who hold political power might
freely alter their objectives in order to avoid using intimidation.
The essential nature of power balance as a system prevents political power from actually acquiring that ability.

Rigidities in the system of power balance. Both domestic and
international politics thus are composed of a synthesis of two ingredients: coercion and consent. The reason the balance-of-power
system in our time has become so complex is that these two
ingredients can now be combined to produce an infinite number
of patterns.

In spite of the increased complexity of the contemporary situation, power-balance analysts now tend to focus concern on a
single fragmentary aspect of the whole. Those concerned with
only partial measurements omit from their consideration the
factor of how freely a nation is able to control its power and actions. As a result, the whole problem of power is treated in terms
of isolated, quantitative indexes such as national income, military strength, foreign-trade volume, industrial output, agricultural yields, and the like. True national strength, however, is the
capacity to alter national objectives and maneuver national
policies autonomously and freely. If, for example, the United
States had the ability to withdraw from South Vietnam, its withdrawal would indicate a tremendous ability for self-discipline and
self-control. Contrariwise, if the United States really wants to
withdraw but is helpless to do so, this indicates—stupendous nuclear power notwithstanding—that its true level of national
strength is no higher than Vietnam's.

In any event, the new relationship between intimidation and
persuasion in the power-balance system reflects a worldwide expansion of the system. Previously, both coercion and consent
were aspects of a state's behavior toward other states, and the

dimensions of coercion and consent in domestic politics were relatively differentiated. When international communications became perfected, however, and when nuclear weapons and missile systems capable of delivering them anywhere on the face of the earth became realities, all peoples were united in a single community of common destiny in which every rigid boundary and line of demarcation between domestic and foreign behavior suddenly became meaningless—at least on the level of nuclear intimidation.

At the moment, the two superpowers enjoy a virtual monopoly of nuclear power and missile systems. But no monopoly of weapons is destined to last forever. Those who talk in terms of power-balance systems ought to remember that fact. The "realists" should also realize that even the most insignificant miscalculation, if repeated indefinitely, can become a mighty glacier, gouging history with scars that are difficult to heal. And when faced with a glacier of accumulated errors, men tend to feel impotent, and in their assumed impotence they confront a rationally solvable problem with the attitude that it cannot be solved.

One element in the no-choice myth, a notion that realists would have us believe, is that one has no freedom in the selection of one's enemies, that some countries are *inevitably* one's enemies. Such a conclusion arises from the ideological rigidity of a power-balance system. The idea of no choice betrays a lack of pliability in the system of deterrent strategy.

An equilibrium achieved at any specific moment in time leaves room for a considerably broad variation in the way one combines the two elements of consent and coercion. If a nation recognized that these are indeed the vital ingredients of a power-balance system, it would enjoy a greater number of policy options. For example, if the United States withdrew from Vietnam and subsequently established friendly relations with the new Saigon government, it would prove that it had given greater priority to the element of consent. This act would definitely expand available options and increase U.S. national power and ability to regulate the use of coercion.

As I have already indicated, the application of America's nuclear strategy at any given point in time has consistently been held in check by its desire to gain the consent of its European allies. I think it is possible to claim that the element of consent has played an increasingly important role since the end of World War II. Even the bewildering fluctuations of nuclear strategy have, for the most part, occurred as a result of shifts in the patterns of consent in international politics. The current nuclear stalemate can only intensify the tendency to lay more stress on this element. The United States, China, and the Soviet Union cannot alter, they can only hope to influence developments. This fact is evident from the way Indonesia opposed Chinese intentions in Asia and from the way Peruvians waged guerrilla war against their government contrary to the wishes of the United States. These examples transcend state-to-state relations. As I have pointed out, however, the radical expansion of communication and transportation has ushered in a situation that forces us to think in terms that transcend purely national boundaries. We no longer live in an age where a state can draw sharp differences between domestic and diplomatic behavior.

The attitude that works against the conversion of nationalism to internationalism looks not to the future so much as to the past, to ancient traditions and the specific history of a specific people. Irrespective of the energy of this countertendency, the move toward internationalism will survive. We have patently arrived at a new juncture in time when we must study the disparity between different images held by men in the modern world and probe into the dimension beyond mere state-to-state confrontations.

Ability to alter national objectives. Analyzing the miscalculations made by China and the United States in terms of a single, if asymmetrical, system has enabled us to discover serious pitfalls in the theory of power balance.

Changes in world politics continue apace. We cannot prevent conditions from changing, but we can recognize that changes occur. To the extent that the national objectives and policies of states involved on the international scene respond creatively to new conditions, we can be sure that the classical concept of what constitutes a balance-of-power situation will also change. Changes in the political context in which any nation implements its policies are attributable to shifts in the relative importance of the factor of consent in world politics, over which no single nation has control. Intimidation by power alone does not determine the patterns of power balance, for the factor of consent plays a significant role, perhaps with greater effect than raw power has ever had.

If leaders in the Japanese Government were capable of fixing the present international patterns of consent just as they are, they would very likely lend their support to the contemporary power-balance situation in which the United States largely intimidates others by its might. Their "realistic" decision to ignore the new element of consent would betray their ignorance of the fact that there are alternate ways to preserve a system of power balance. For example, to follow the line of argument presented here, rather than resign itself to the "realities" of power, Japan could try to discover the precise patterns of consent that have evolved in the interplay of world politics and, having recognized them, attempt to persuade others, especially its ally, that national objectives should be modified so as to conform to shifts in reality. If perchance our ally is not powerful enough to change its national objectives, we would have to conclude that, despite its great size and wealth, the United States absolutely lacks the ability to steer a consciously determined course. Such a nation may be destined to disintegrate like the Roman Empire.

Should Japanese statesmen fail to adopt a firm stance with regard to the amelioration of tensions in Asia—that is to say, should they refuse to discern new international patterns of consent and to adjust their objectives accordingly—their diplomacy is not likely to influence China's national objectives, even if it successfully cultivates a friendship with the Soviet Union and develops the Moscow-Washington-Tokyo axis which Yōnosuke Nagai has recommended. Tensions in Asia manage to prevent Peking from fostering flexible national objectives. Few will deny that these tensions have been aggravated both by the adamant American nuclear strategy of containment and by its fixed aims in prosecuting the war in Vietnam. China's nuclear development has, in fact, been expedited with great vigor so as to alleviate as quickly as possible the threat of American nuclear encirclement. Now that China has nuclear arms, some argue that the United States and its allies must make greater efforts to contain China by military means, and they attempt to justify escalation of the war in Vietnam as one of those means. I think it is exceedingly risky to argue in these terms.

Wherever world politics are charged with a perilously high voltage, such as in Vietnam, any system of deterrent strategy is likely to develop increasingly grave functional disorders and contradictions. Japanese leaders will therefore find it more, rather than less, difficult to follow Nagai's suggestion to make Tokyo the diplomatic center of peaceful coexistence, even if they follow his suggestion to pursue a roundabout foreign policy and establish a Northern axis. Tokyo is not likely to be such a center unless it has first become the site of various functional meetings attended also by representatives from Peking. Only when conferences of this sort are practicable in Tokyo will it be possible to draw Japan's ideological militants into the new era of the scientific revolution or, in Nagai's words, to make them "men of the twentieth century."

Biographical Sketches

Editor

JACKSON H. BAILEY is Professor of History and Director of the Center for East Asian (Japanese) Language and Area Studies at Earlham College in Richmond, Indiana. His interest in Japan dates to his service there in the U.S. Army of Occupation in 1945–46. He received his Ph.D. degree from Harvard University in 1959. From 1951 to 1954, he directed the program of International Student Seminars and Work Camps in Japan and Hong Kong for the American Friends Service Committee, and he returned to Japan most recently in the autumn of 1972. He has written a number of articles on Japan, China, and Asian studies and has played an active role in the development of Asian studies at the college level. He is a member of the U.S. Advisory Committee to the Japan Foundation.

Contributors

KIYOSHI AKIYAMA is a pacifist poet. During World War II, he dared not publish his antiwar poems and kept them in a drawer for twenty years. He was fifty when his first collection of poems, *Shiroi Hana (White Blossom)*, was published in 1960.

TSUTOMU FUKUDA, a bilingual poet in Japanese and English and a master of the *haiku* and *tanka* forms, is a member of an international group that publishes and promotes poetry in the English language. He is Professor of English Literature at the Kyoto University of Foreign Languages.

SHINTARŌ ISHIHARA is a distinguished writer and a successful politician. He is the author of *Taiyō no Kisetsu (Season of Violence,* 1966). A bestseller, it was later made into a movie. In the 1969 elections for the Upper House of the Japanese Diet, he was among the top two or three vote-getters in the country, and in the 1972 general election for the Lower House, he was elected as an independent. As another essay in this book suggests, he is a new star in the political firmament, one that bears watching in the 1970's.

TEIJI ITOH, a well-known critic and student of architecture, has written and lectured widely on various aspects of Japanese art. He is the author of the text for *The Roots of Japanese Architecture* (1963), photographed by Yukio Futagawa, and *The Japanese Garden* (1972), photographed by Takeji Iwamiya. Born in 1922, Mr. Itoh graduated from the University of Tokyo and later taught there. In 1964–65, he was a member of the faculty of the Institute of Asian Arts at the University of Washington in Seattle.

HIDETOSHI KATŌ is a member of the staff of the Communications Institute at the East-West Center of the University of Hawaii. He was a member of the Institute for Research in the Humanistic Sciences of Kyoto University until his resignation in 1970 to protest the lack of real reform within the university system. Born in 1930, he is a graduate of Hitotsubashi University in Tokyo. A prolific commentator on contemporary affairs, he has also co-authored a series of research papers on Japanese culture, which were published under the title *Nihonjin no Chie (The Wisdom of the Japanese)* in 1962. In 1964–65, he was Visiting Professor of Sociology at Grinnell College and the State University of Iowa at Cedar Falls.

JŌJI MORI, a grandson of Ōgai Mori, one of Japan's distinguished modern authors, is also a writer and a literary critic of British, American, and Japanese literature. Born in 1931, he completed his undergraduate and graduate work at Waseda University, earning his Ph.D. degree there in 1961. In 1970–71, he was Visiting Professor of Literature at Earlham College, and he is currently collaborating with Professor Richard Wood of Earlham on a critical study of social values in postwar Japan as seen through literature.

SHIRŌ MURANO, who was born in 1901, emerged in the 1920's as a writer of the terse and expressive *haiku* form of Japanese poetry. He then moved on to freer, more colloquial verse and is praised by Japanese critics for boldly exploring widely different poetic styles. Although he is in his seventies, he still rises early in the morning to give himself time for chin-ups on parallel bars in a nearby park before the rush-hour traffic pollutes the Tokyo air.

YŌNOSUKE NAGAI is Professor of Political Science at the Tokyo Institute of Technology. Born in 1924, he graduated from Tokyo University in 1950. A student of Masao Maruyama, a pioneer political scientist of postwar Japan, Nagai has written extensively on pressure groups and power politics. His series of essays, later published as a book, *Heiwa no Daishō (The Price of Peace*, 1967) caused a sensation in the mid-1960's and continues to stimulate discussion of Japan's place in the world.

MAKOTO ODA is the intellectual leader of and strategist for Beheiren (The Committee for Peace in Vietnam). In his work for this peace group, he has attempted to mobilize ordinary citizens rather than ideologically committed ones or political organizations. Born in 1932, he is a graduate of Tokyo University and also spent a year at Harvard University as a Fulbright research scholar. His articles on current topics are widely discussed in Japan and abroad.

TSUTOMU ŌNO was born in 1928, graduated from Gumma Prefectural University, and then entered teaching, becoming active in the All-Japan Teachers Union. For a brief period thereafter, he was a member of the Japanese Communist Party but withdrew out of disillusionment with its doctrinaire approach to Japanese and world problems. Since 1955, he has been associated with a group of intellectuals called "The Science of Thought Study Group," which publishes a significant monthly Shisō no Kagaku (The Science of Thought). Ōno is especially well known for his critiques of the labor movement and his analyses of Japanese economic life as reflected in current social conditions.

SŌICHI ŌYA was a popular writer until his death in 1970 at the age of seventy. A broad-gauge and provocative critic, he was nicknamed the "poisonous tongue." He was interested in international politics and Japan's role in the world but often wrote about the needs and concerns of ordinary people. His essays are celebrated for their style as well as their content. He was self-educated, having dropped out of the University of Tokyo without graduating to join the proletarian movement of the 1920's.

YASUO SAKAKIBARA is Professor of Economics at Dōshisha University in Kyoto. His special interest is the economics of transportation, but he has also been concerned with cross-cultural exchanges. Born in 1929, the son of a Buddhist priest, he has written perceptive essays on the assimilation of Buddhism into Japanese culture. He has studied and taught abroad as well as in Japan, most recently in 1970–71 as Visiting Professor of Economics at Carleton College in Northfield, Minnesota.

HIROHARU SEKI is Associate Professor at the Institute for Oriental Culture at the University of Tokyo, from which he graduated in 1953, but he has also served on the faculty of several other Tokyo universities. Born in 1927, he has traveled and studied in Southeast Asia and in the United States. He has published widely on various aspects of Japan's international relations.

REIKO SUNAMI is a distinguished young weaver whose work has been well received in one-woman shows in Kyoto and Tokyo. A graduate of the Kyoto University of Fine Arts, she was Artist-in-Residence at Earlham College from 1968 to 1970, where she taught both weaving and brush painting.

Kyōzō Takagi, born in 1882, is one of the greatest Japanese poets of the common language. A dentist, he lives in the Tohoku region of Japan's main island, Honshu. He has published *Shijin de nai Shijin no Shi de nai Shi (Poems That Are Not Poems by a Poet Who Is Not a Poet)*.

Shinkichi Takahashi is Japan's foremost Zen poet, but he first won literary attention in the 1920's with the landmark book of poems, *Dadaisto Shinkichi No Shi (Poems of the "Dadaist" Shinkichi)*, and a novel entitled *Dada*. He later became interested in Zen Buddhism and studied under a Rinzai master. A second volume of his poems was published in 1934. His third, which was published in 1938, brought censure from the increasingly powerful military government. Takahashi has also written other works of fiction, essays, and critiques of the religious art that impressed him on his travels.

Shuntarō Tanikawa was born in 1931, the son of a philosopher. He was fourteen when the U.S. air raids over Tokyo intensified and he moved to Kyoto with his mother. He published his first book of poems at the age of twenty-one and now has at least a dozen volumes of poetry, some with photographs, to his credit. He has also been a prolific writer of radio plays, short stories, film scripts, and essays.

Mitsuru Uchida is Assistant Professor of Political Science at Waseda University in Tokyo, from which he graduated. Born in 1930, he is a student of comparative legislative process and political attitudes and behavior. In 1958–59, he was a Congressional Fellow in Washington, D.C., working for a time in the office of then Senator Lyndon B. Johnson, and in 1968–69, he was Visiting Professor of Political Science at Earlham College.

Toshinao Yoneyama, born in 1930, is Professor of Sociology at the University of Kyoto, from which he graduated, and a member of the research staff of its Institute for Research in the Humanistic Sciences. In that capacity, he has participated in field research projects in East and West Africa. In 1959–60 he did graduate work at the University of Illinois, and in 1969–70 he was Visiting Professor of Sociology at Earlham College. His research on rural topics in Africa, the United States, and Japan has established his scholarly reputation at home and abroad. Active in civic affairs, he appears frequently on the radio and writes often for the mass media.

Translators

Noah S. Brannen is Associate Professor of Linguistics at International Christian University in Tokyo. He is the author of *Soka Gakkai: Japan's Militant Buddhists* (1968) and co-translator, with William I. Elliott, of *Festive Wine: Ancient Japanese Poems from the Kinkafu* (1969).

WILLIAM I. ELLIOTT is Associate Professor of English at Linfield College in McMinville, Oregon, and the co-translator, with Noah S. Brannen, of *Festive Wine: Ancient Japanese Poems from the Kinkafu* (1969).

JAMES KIRKUP has lived for many years in Japan. He has translated works from several languages into English and is the author of *Filipinescas: Travels in the Philippines Today* (1968) and *One Man's Russia* (1969).

MICHIO NAKANO is a graduate of Kobe City University of Foreign Studies. He has for some time collaborated with James Kirkup in translations of Japanese poetry.

SHŌICHI OGURO is on the faculty of Waseda University in Tokyo, where he teaches English and linguistics. He has translated other works by Teiji Itoh.

ATSUHIRO SAWAI published several novels before he finished college. He recently turned to poetry, and his first collection, *Seishun no Ma (Devil of Adolescence)*, was published in 1969.

SHŌZŌ TOKUNAGA has often collaborated with James Kirkup in translations of Japanese poetry.

HAROLD P. WRIGHT is known for his translations of modern Japanese poetry, which have appeared in a number of journals and anthologies.